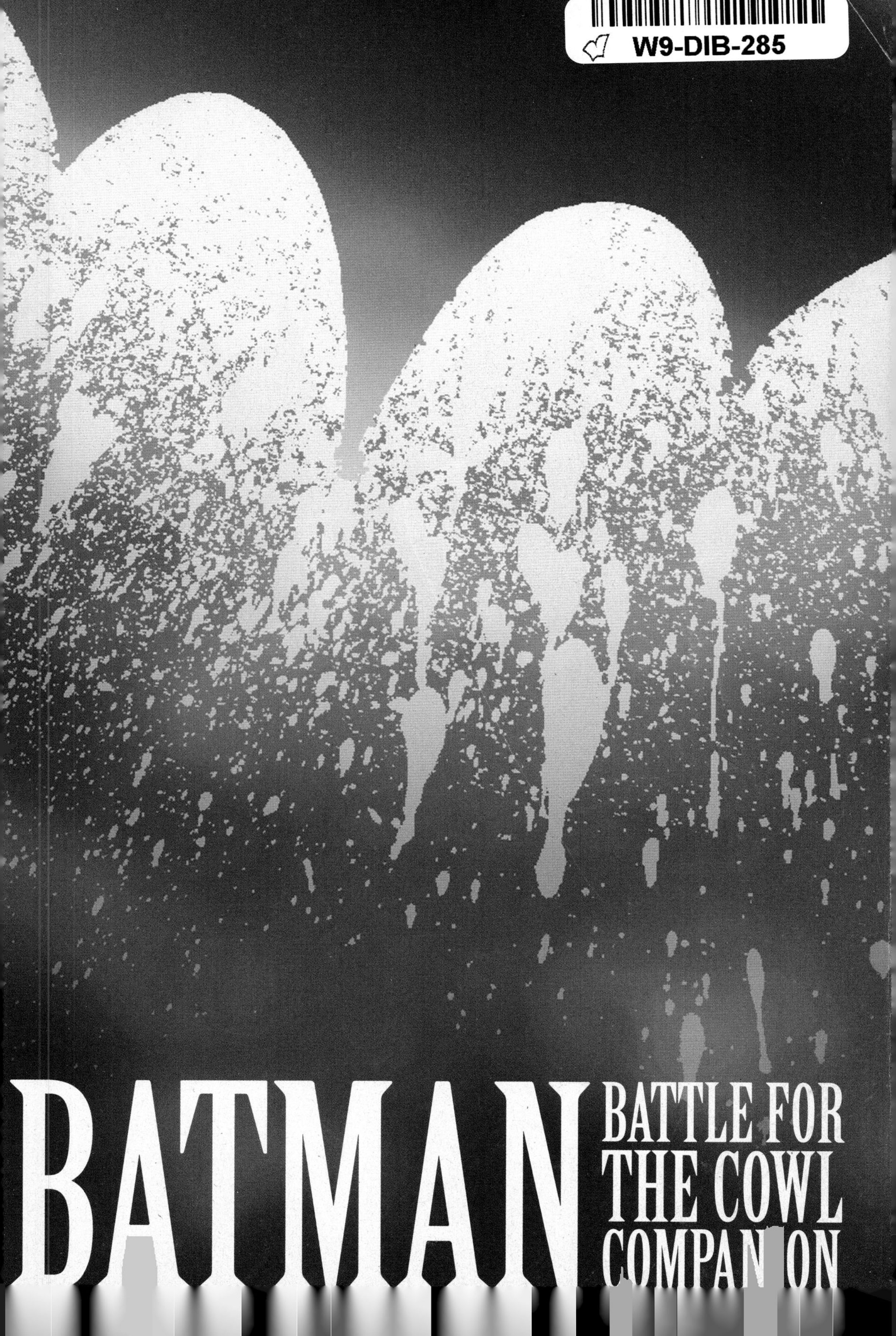

BATMAN BATTLE FOR THE COWL COMPANION

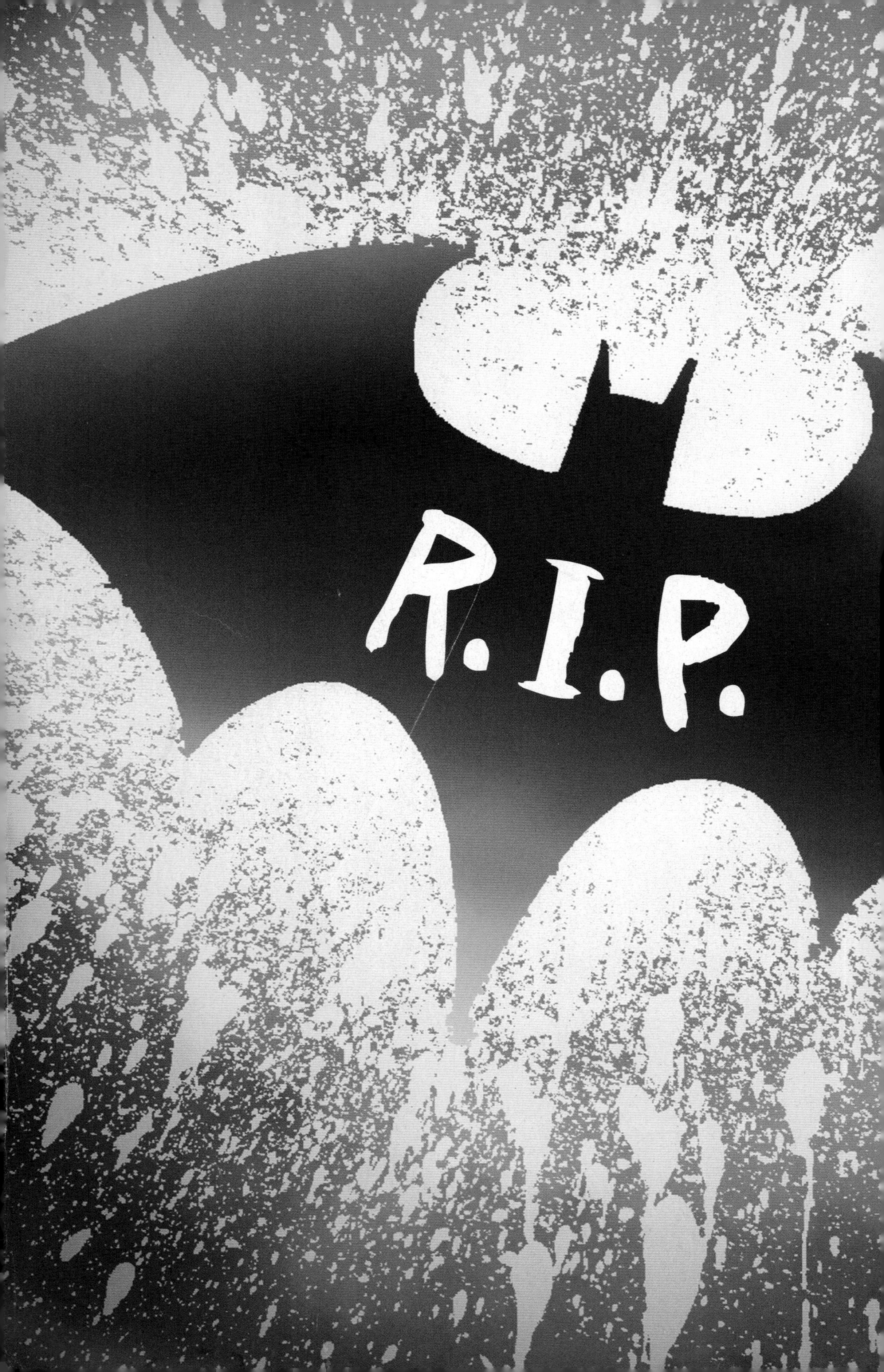
R.I.P.

BATMAN

BATTLE FOR THE COWL COMPANION

Royal McGraw
Joe Harris
David Hine
Chris Yost
Fabian Nicieza
Writers

Tom Mandrake
Jim Calafiore
Jeremy Haun
Pablo Raimondi
Don Kramer
Mark McKenna
Artists

Guy Major
Richard & Tanya Horie
Brian Reber
JD Smith
Colorists

Sal Cipriano
Swands
Pat Brosseau
Letterers

Ladrönn
Original series cover artist

BATMAN created by Bob Kane

Dan DiDio   SVP-Executive Editor
Mike Marts, Michael Siglain   Editors-original series
Janelle Siegel, Harvey Richards   Assistant Editors-original series
Georg Brewer   VP-Design & DC Direct Creative
Bob Harras   Group Editor-Collected Editions
Anton Kawasaki   Editor
Robbin Brosterman   Design Director-Books

DC COMICS
Paul Levitz   President & Publisher
Richard Bruning   SVP-Creative Director
Patrick Caldon   EVP-Finance & Operations
Amy Genkins   SVP-Business & Legal Affairs
Jim Lee   Editorial Director-WildStorm
Gregory Noveck   SVP-Creative Affairs
Steve Rotterdam   SVP-Sales & Marketing
Cheryl Rubin   SVP-Brand Management

Cover illustration by Ladrönn

BATMAN: BATTLE FOR THE COWL COMPANION Published by DC Comics. Cover, text and compilation Copyright © 2009 DC Comics. All Rights Reserved. Originally published in single magazine form in BATMAN: BATTLE FOR THE COWL: COMMISSIONER GORDON 1, BATMAN: BATTLE FOR THE COWL: MAN-BAT 1, BATMAN: BATTLE FOR THE COWL: ARKHAM ASYLUM 1, BATMAN: BATTLE FOR THE COWL: THE UNDERGROUND 1, BATMAN: BATTLE FOR THE COWL: THE NETWORK 1. Copyright © 2009 DC Comics. All Rights Reserved. All characters, their distinctive likenesses and related elements featured in this publication are trademarks of DC Comics. The stories, characters and incidents featured in this publication are entirely fictional. DC Comics does not read or accept unsolicited submissions of ideas, stories or artwork.

DC Comics, 1700 Broadway, New York, NY 10019, A Warner Bros. Entertainment Company   Printed by World Color Press, Inc., St-Romuald, QC, Canada 10/07/09. First Printing. ISBN: 1-4012-2495-0

SUSTAINABLE FORESTRY INITIATIVE   Certified Fiber Sourcing
www.sfiprogram.org
Fiber used in this product line meets the sourcing requirements of the SFI program. www.sfiprogram.org PWC-SFICOC-260

BATMAN: BATTLE FOR THE COWL: COMMISSIONER GORDON

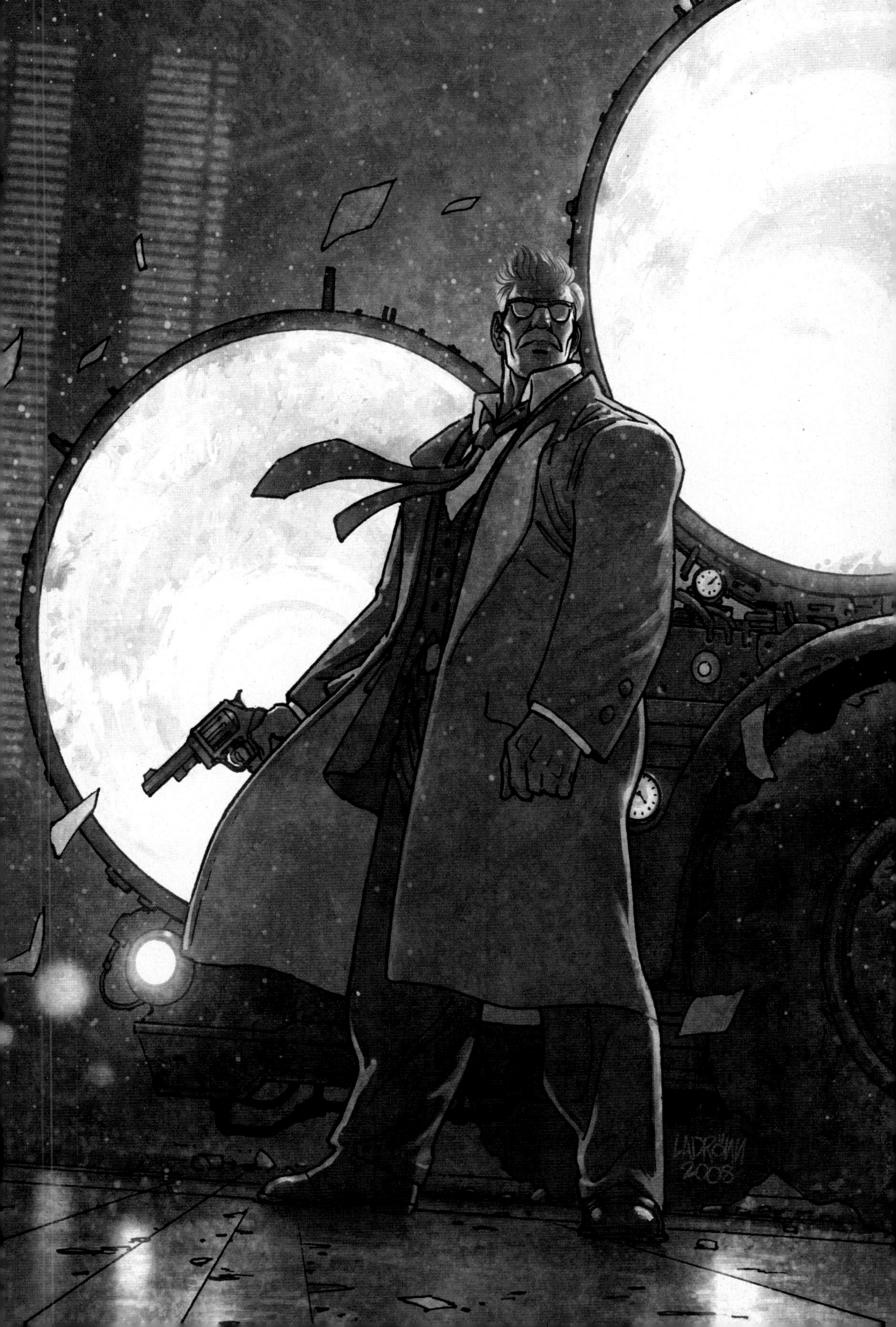

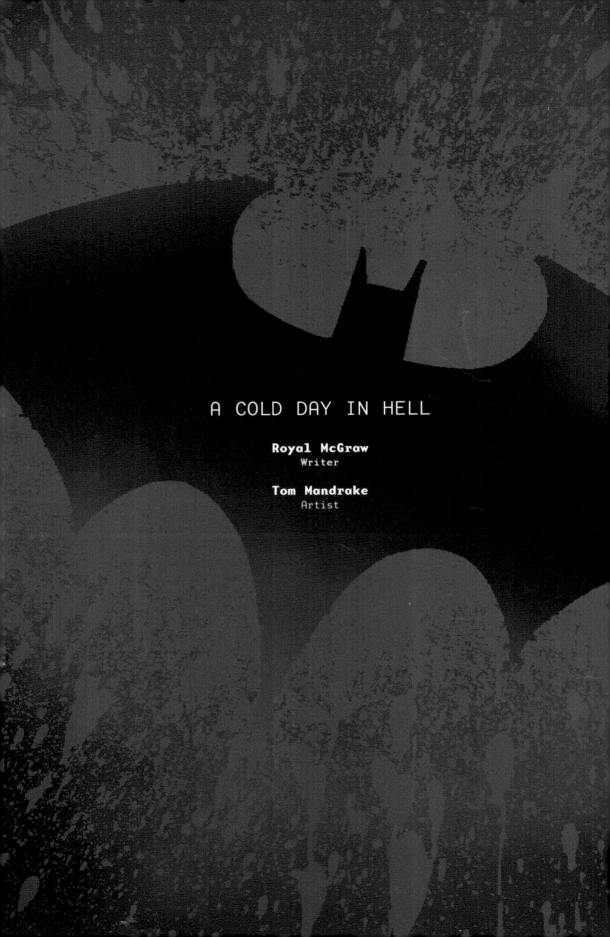

A COLD DAY IN HELL

Royal McGraw
Writer

Tom Mandrake
Artist

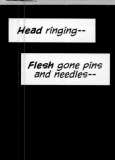

Head ringing--

Flesh gone pins and needles--

Barely even feel my *fingers*.

Concussion?

No--

Breath gives it away.

Wherever I am...it's *colder* than sin.

NNH.

AH, THE *CAPTIVE* STIRS.

That *voice*--

I *know* it. Deep but *tinny*. Electronic. A voice from a speakerbox.

DO YOU KNOW WHAT *PART* THIS IS, COMMISSIONER?

YOU AND I HAVE BEEN HERE *MANY TIMES* BEFORE.

Somehow he must've *taken* me--

But *how?*

It happened so fast.

THIS IS THE PART WHERE *BATMAN* LEAPS DOWN FROM THE RAFTERS AND SAVES YOUR LIFE.

ONLY THAT *ISN'T* GOING TO HAPPEN THIS TIME, IS IT, COMMISSIONER?

WE BOTH KNOW THE *TRUTH*.

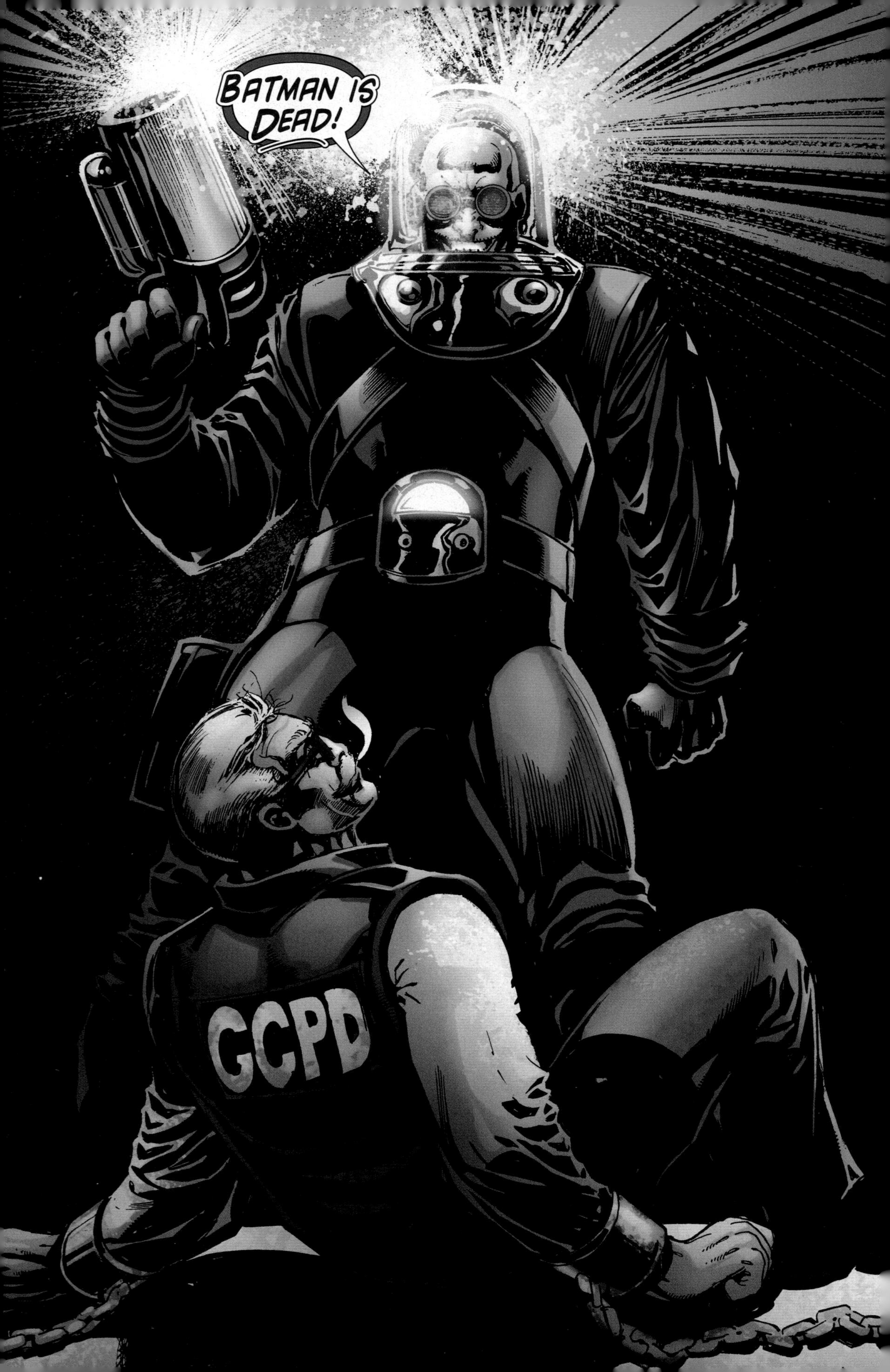
BATMAN IS DEAD!
GCPD

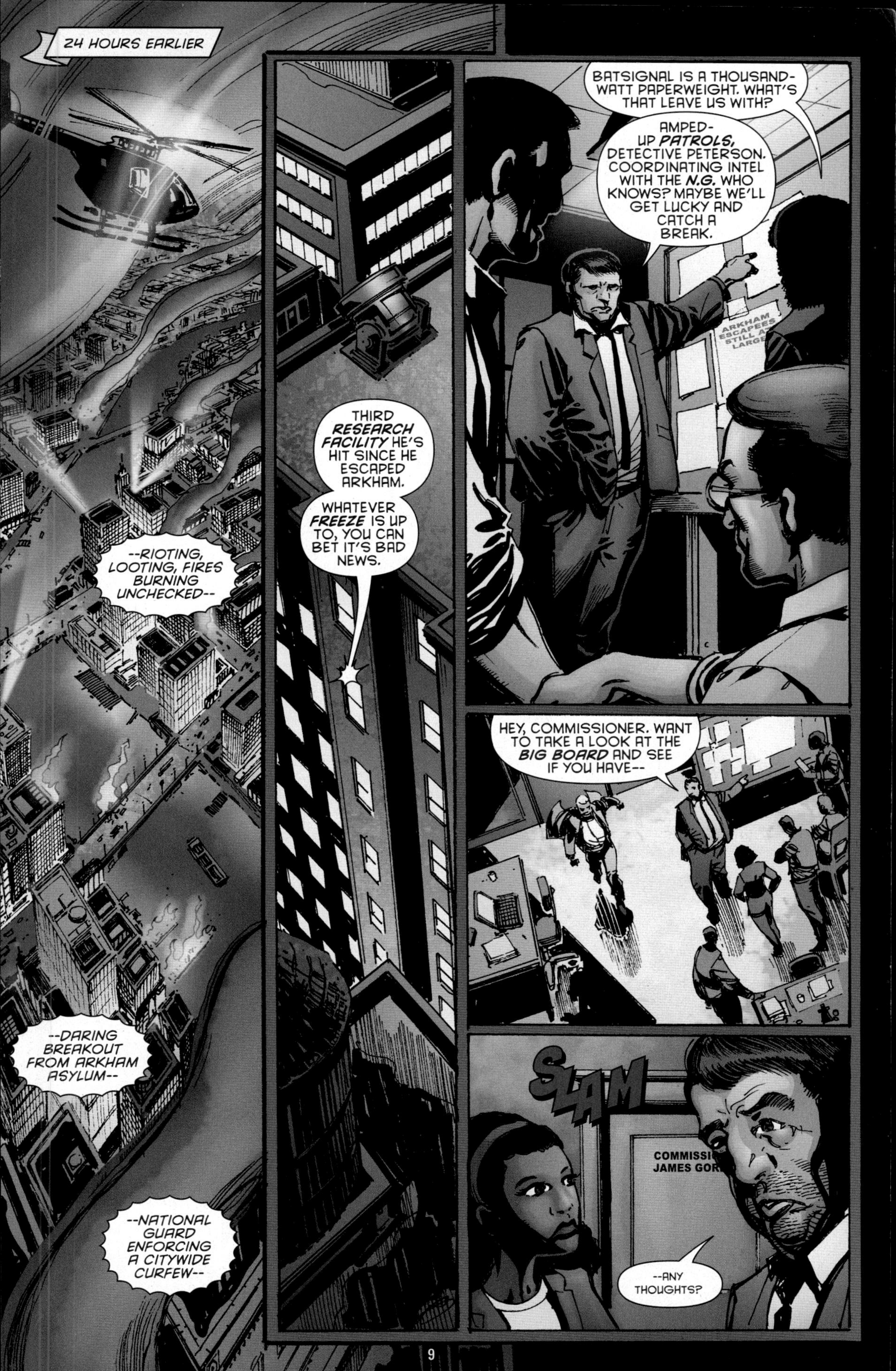
24 HOURS EARLIER
--RIOTING, LOOTING, FIRES BURNING UNCHECKED--
--DARING BREAKOUT FROM ARKHAM ASYLUM--
--NATIONAL GUARD ENFORCING A CITYWIDE CURFEW--
THIRD RESEARCH FACILITY HE'S HIT SINCE HE ESCAPED ARKHAM.
WHATEVER FREEZE IS UP TO, YOU CAN BET IT'S BAD NEWS.
BATSIGNAL IS A THOUSAND-WATT PAPERWEIGHT. WHAT'S THAT LEAVE US WITH?
AMPED-UP PATROLS, DETECTIVE PETERSON. COORDINATING INTEL WITH THE N.G. WHO KNOWS? MAYBE WE'LL GET LUCKY AND CATCH A BREAK.
ARKHAM ESCAPEES STILL AT LARGE
HEY, COMMISSIONER. WANT TO TAKE A LOOK AT THE BIG BOARD AND SEE IF YOU HAVE--
SLAM
COMMISSI
JAMES GOR
--ANY THOUGHTS?

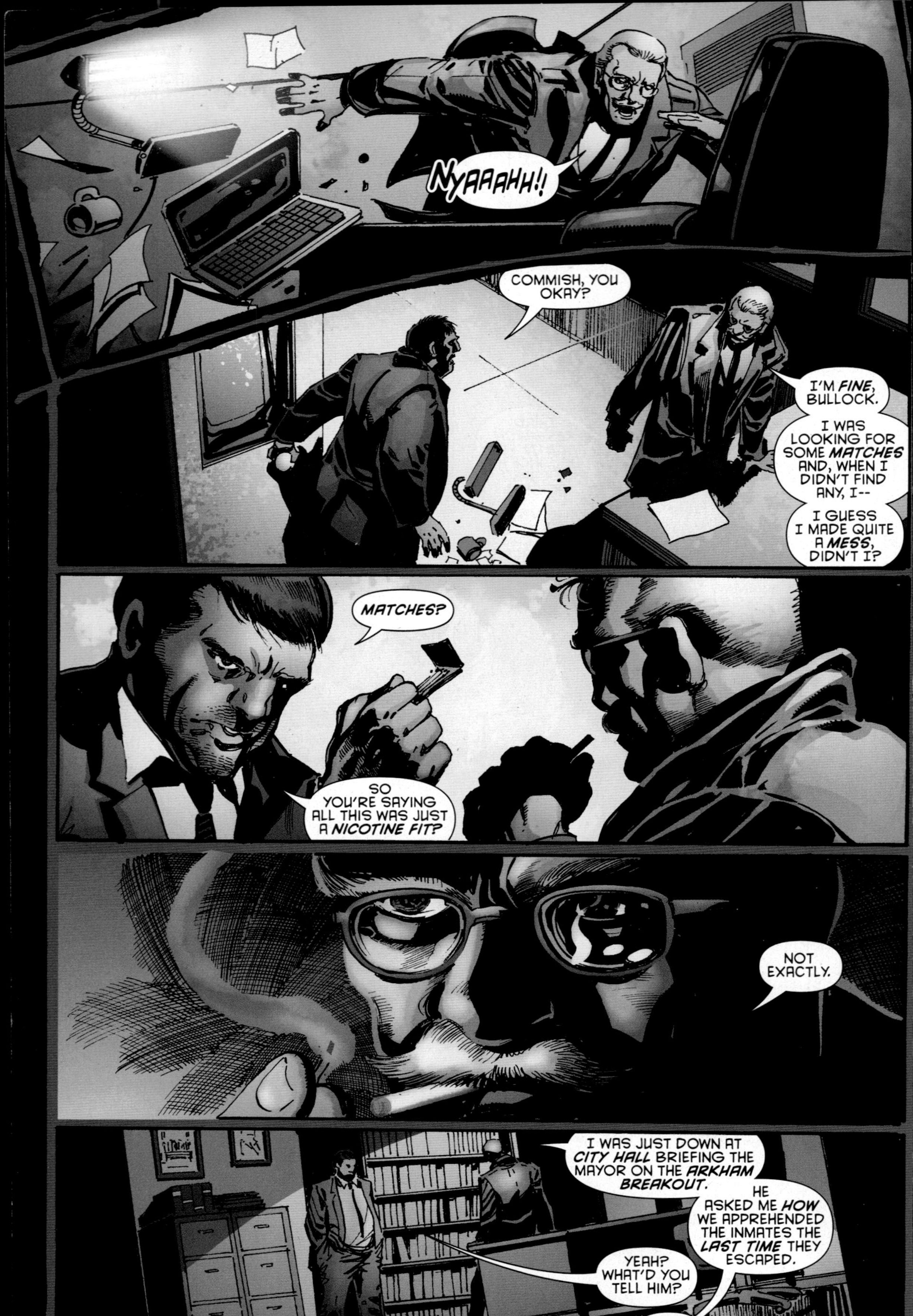
NYAAAHH!!
COMMISH, YOU OKAY?
I'M *FINE*, BULLOCK.
I WAS LOOKING FOR SOME *MATCHES* AND, WHEN I DIDN'T FIND ANY, I--
I GUESS I MADE QUITE A *MESS*, DIDN'T I?
MATCHES?
SO YOU'RE SAYING ALL THIS WAS JUST A *NICOTINE FIT?*
NOT EXACTLY.
I WAS JUST DOWN AT *CITY HALL* BRIEFING THE MAYOR ON THE *ARKHAM BREAKOUT*.
HE ASKED ME *HOW* WE APPREHENDED THE INMATES THE *LAST TIME* THEY ESCAPED.
YEAH? WHAT'D YOU TELL HIM?
THE *TRUTH*.

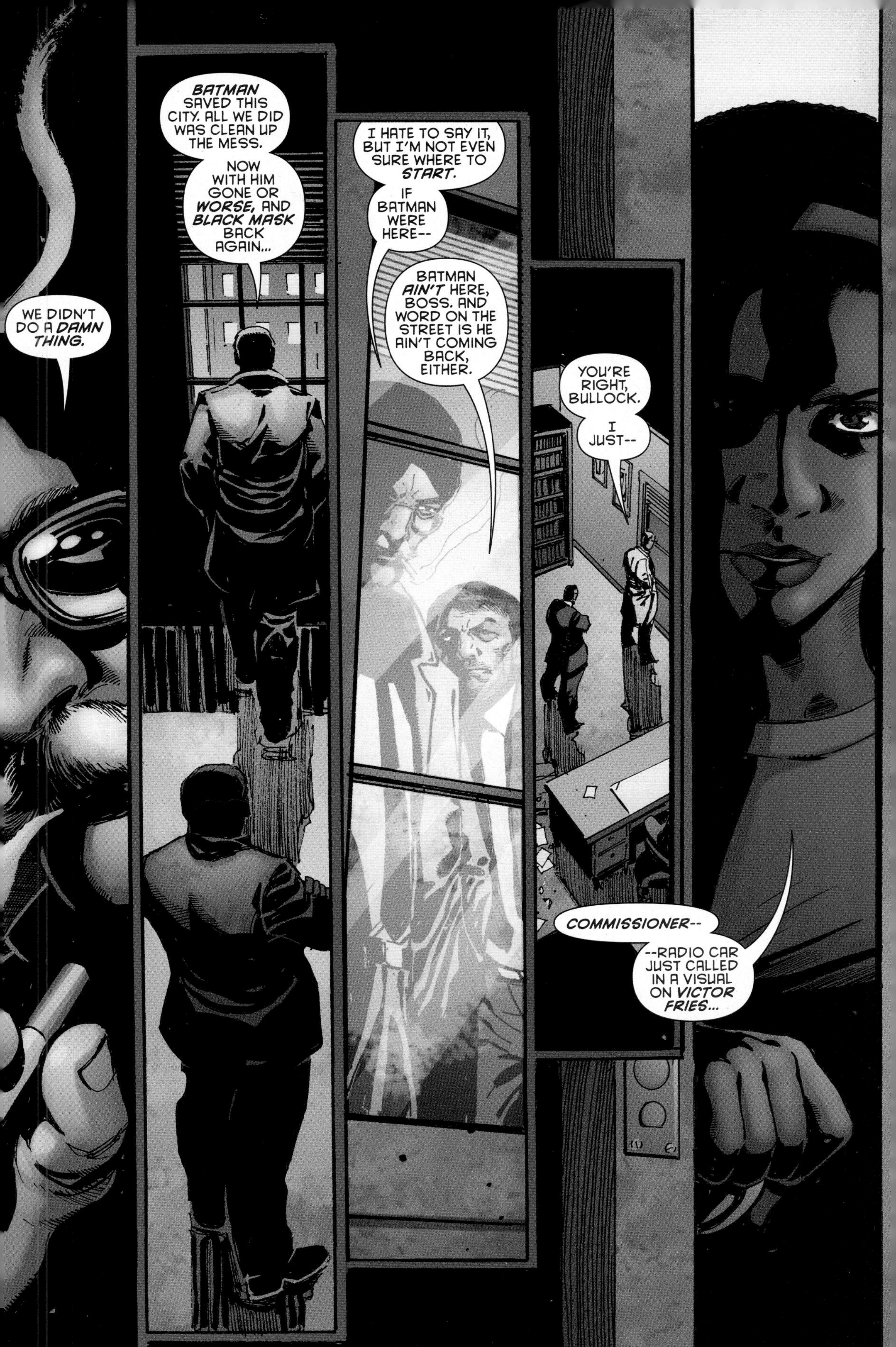
WE DIDN'T DO A *DAMN THING.*
BATMAN SAVED THIS CITY. ALL WE DID WAS CLEAN UP THE MESS.
NOW WITH HIM GONE OR *WORSE,* AND *BLACK MASK* BACK AGAIN...
I HATE TO SAY IT, BUT I'M NOT EVEN SURE WHERE TO *START.*
IF BATMAN WERE HERE--
BATMAN *AIN'T* HERE, BOSS. AND WORD ON THE STREET IS HE AIN'T COMING BACK, EITHER.
YOU'RE RIGHT, BULLOCK.
I JUST--
COMMISSIONER--
--RADIO CAR JUST CALLED IN A VISUAL ON *VICTOR FRIES...*

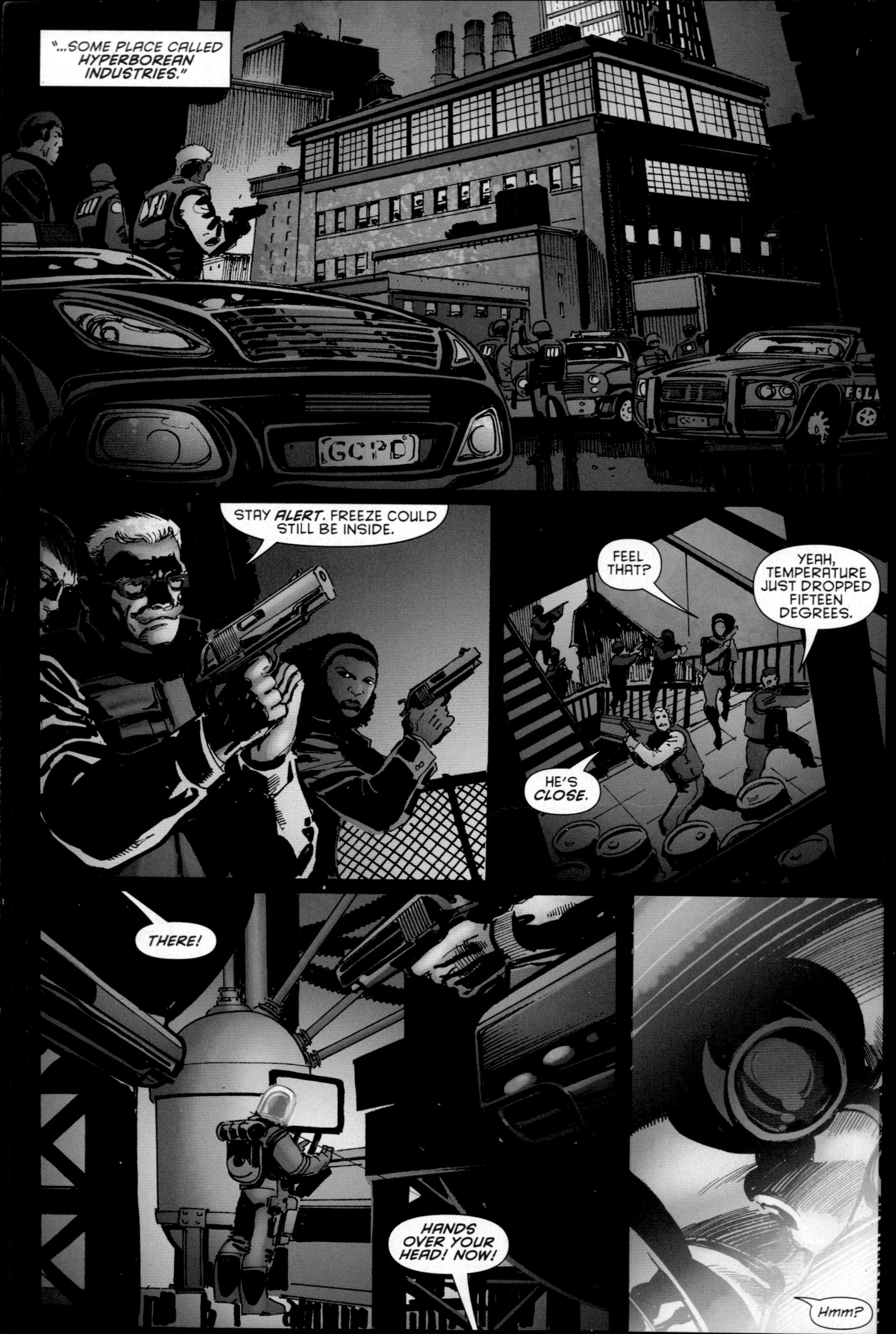
"...SOME PLACE CALLED HYPERBOREAN INDUSTRIES."
GCPD
STAY ALERT. FREEZE COULD STILL BE INSIDE.
FEEL THAT?
YEAH, TEMPERATURE JUST DROPPED FIFTEEN DEGREES.
HE'S CLOSE.
THERE!
HANDS OVER YOUR HEAD! NOW!
Hmm?

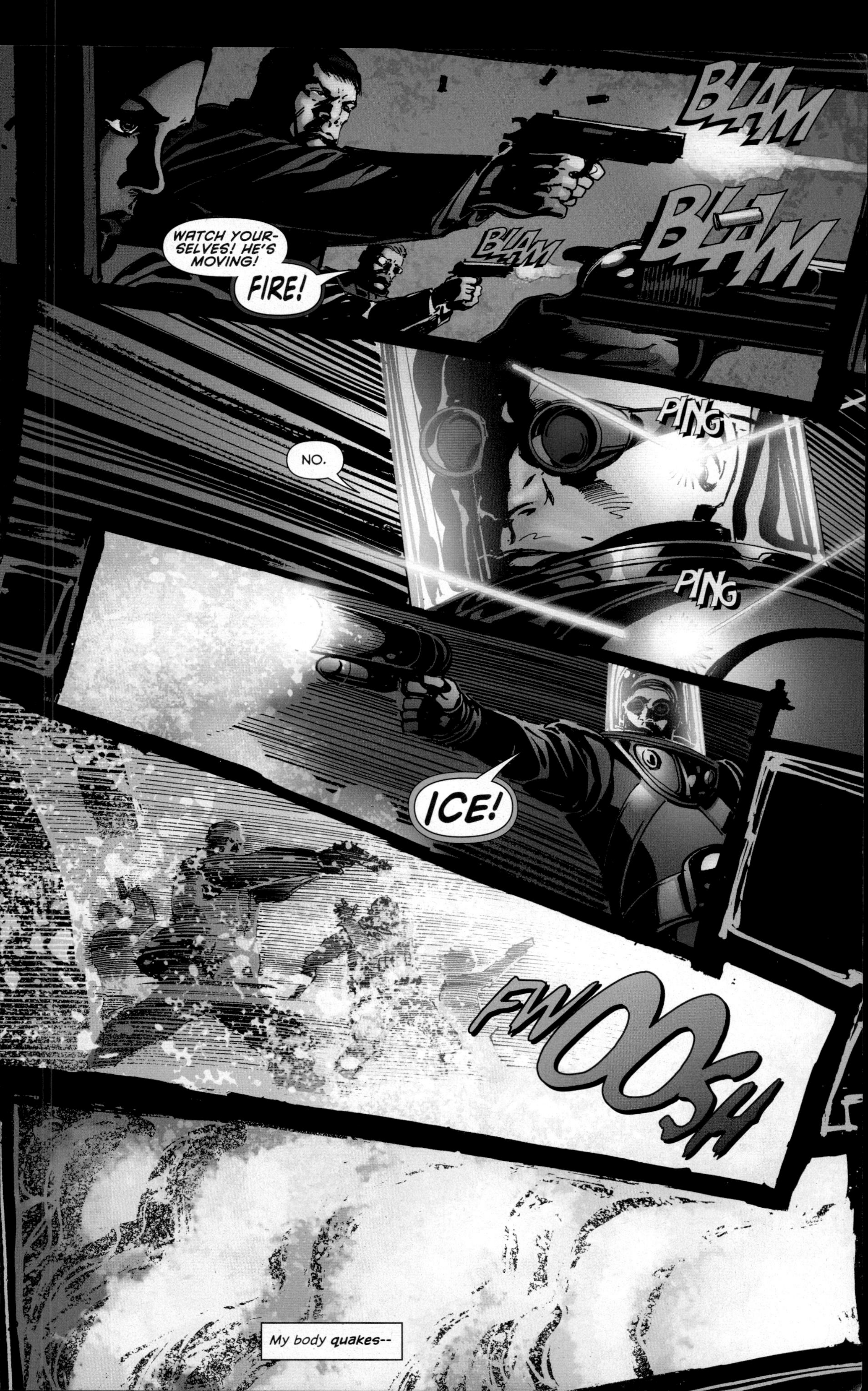
BLAM
BLAM
BLAM
WATCH YOUR-SELVES! HE'S MOVING!
FIRE!
NO.
PING
PING
ICE!
FWOOSH
My body quakes--

--not with *fear*, not with *terror*.

With *cold*.

SPARE THE *THEATRICS.*

IF YOU WERE GOING TO KILL ME, I'D *ALREADY* BE DEAD.

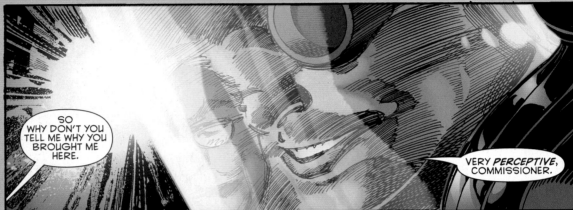

SO WHY DON'T YOU TELL ME WHY YOU BROUGHT ME HERE.

VERY *PERCEPTIVE,* COMMISSIONER.

I INTEND TO FINISH WHAT WE BEGAN THE NIGHT OF THE *COMMENCEMENT.*

YOU MEAN, THE NIGHT YOU TRIED TO MURDER AN AUDITORIUM FULL OF *COLLEGE KIDS?*

IT WAS NEVER ABOUT THE *KILLING.* I THOUGHT YOU *KNEW* THAT.

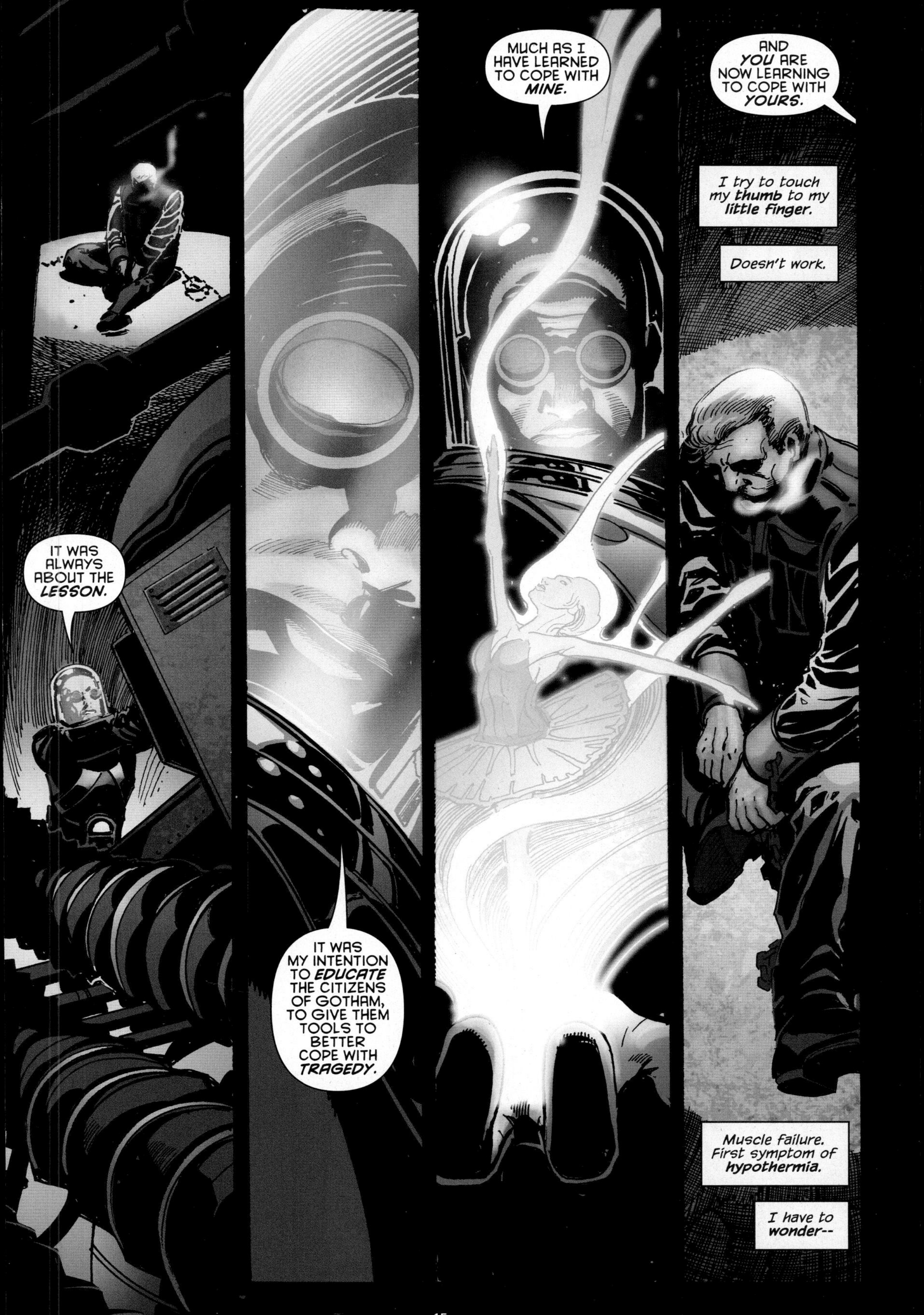
IT WAS ALWAYS ABOUT THE LESSON.
IT WAS MY INTENTION TO EDUCATE THE CITIZENS OF GOTHAM, TO GIVE THEM TOOLS TO BETTER COPE WITH TRAGEDY.
MUCH AS I HAVE LEARNED TO COPE WITH MINE.
AND YOU ARE NOW LEARNING TO COPE WITH YOURS.
I try to touch my thumb to my little finger.
Doesn't work.
Muscle failure. First symptom of hypothermia.
I have to wonder--

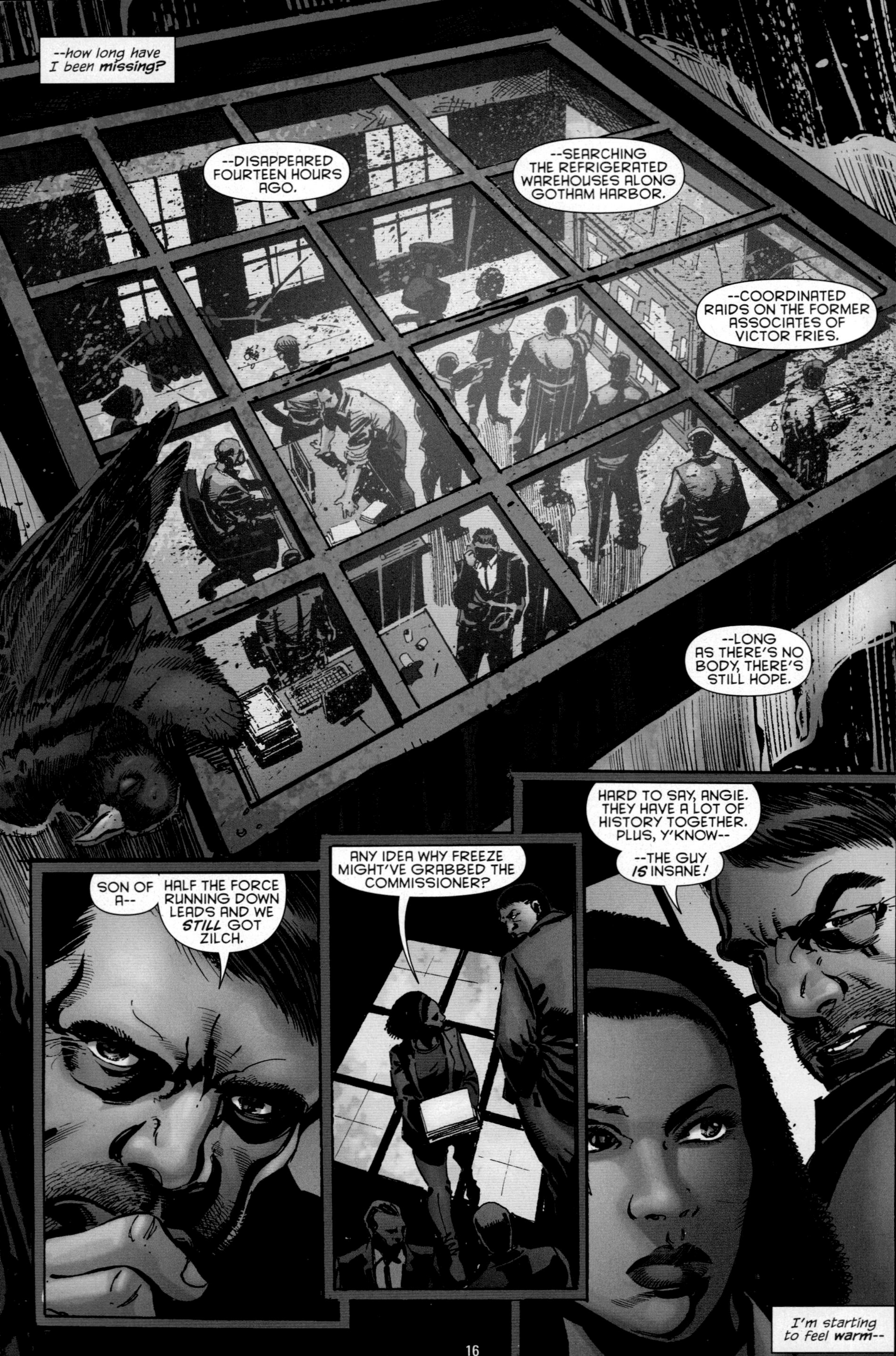
--how long have I been **missing?**
--DISAPPEARED FOURTEEN HOURS AGO.
--SEARCHING THE REFRIGERATED WAREHOUSES ALONG GOTHAM HARBOR.
--COORDINATED RAIDS ON THE FORMER ASSOCIATES OF VICTOR FRIES.
--LONG AS THERE'S NO BODY, THERE'S STILL HOPE.
SON OF A--
HALF THE FORCE RUNNING DOWN LEADS AND WE ***STILL*** GOT ZILCH.
ANY IDEA WHY FREEZE MIGHT'VE GRABBED THE COMMISSIONER?
HARD TO SAY, ANGIE. THEY HAVE A LOT OF HISTORY TOGETHER. PLUS, Y'KNOW--
--THE GUY ***IS*** INSANE!
*I'm starting to feel **warm**--*

my body is starting to give in to the cold...

WH-WHAT ARE YOU TALKING ABOUT? WH-WHAT *TRAGEDY?*

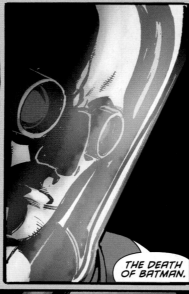

THE DEATH OF BATMAN.

GOTHAM'S PROTECTOR HAS ABANDONED YOU.

HE HAS ABANDONED THIS CITY.

YOU *GRIEVE* YOUR LOSS.

BUT DO NOT DESPAIR, COMMISSIONER. YOU WILL NOT SUFFER ALONE.

WHEN THESE LAST FEW MODIFICATIONS ARE COMPLETE, ALL OF GOTHAM WILL JOIN YOU IN YOUR HOUR OF *MOURNING.*

That *device*--

Freeze must've been stealing *technology* to build it.

Haven't got the first *clue* what it does.

Science was always *his* department. He would know how to *disable* it.

Me? I'm barely *hanging* on.

YOU W-W-WON'T GET AWAY WITH THIS, VICTOR.

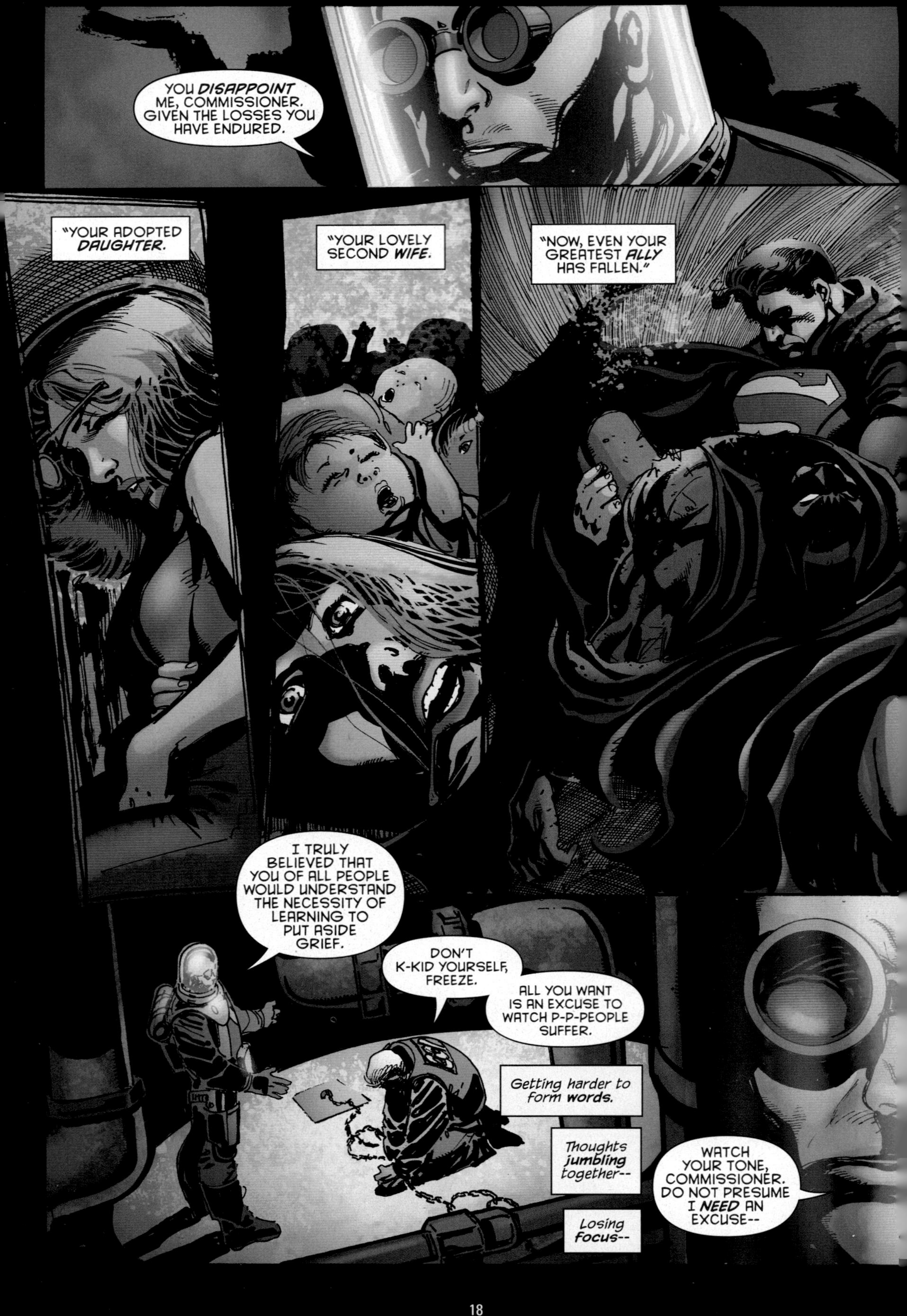
YOU DISAPPOINT ME, COMMISSIONER. GIVEN THE LOSSES YOU HAVE ENDURED.
"YOUR ADOPTED DAUGHTER.
"YOUR LOVELY SECOND WIFE.
"NOW, EVEN YOUR GREATEST ALLY HAS FALLEN."
I TRULY BELIEVED THAT YOU OF ALL PEOPLE WOULD UNDERSTAND THE NECESSITY OF LEARNING TO PUT ASIDE GRIEF.
DON'T K-KID YOURSELF, FREEZE.
ALL YOU WANT IS AN EXCUSE TO WATCH P-P-PEOPLE SUFFER.
Getting harder to form words.
Thoughts jumbling together--
Losing focus--
WATCH YOUR TONE, COMMISSIONER. DO NOT PRESUME I NEED AN EXCUSE--

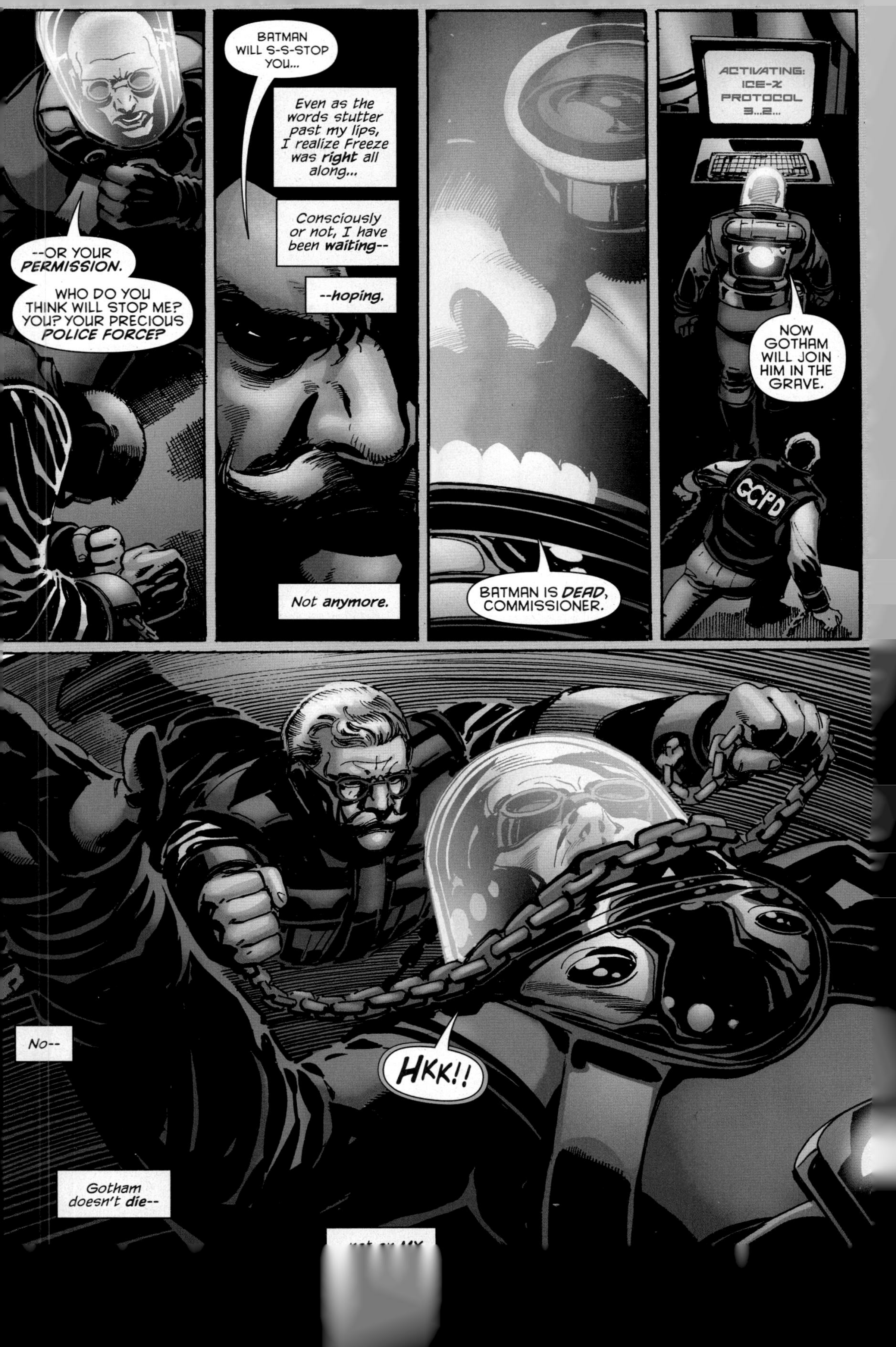
--OR YOUR PERMISSION.
WHO DO YOU THINK WILL STOP ME? YOU? YOUR PRECIOUS POLICE FORCE?
BATMAN WILL S-S-STOP YOU...
Even as the words stutter past my lips, I realize Freeze was right all along...
Consciously or not, I have been waiting--
--hoping.
Not anymore.
BATMAN IS DEAD, COMMISSIONER.
ACTIVATING: ICE-X PROTOCOL 3...2...
NOW GOTHAM WILL JOIN HIM IN THE GRAVE.
No--
HKK!!
Gotham doesn't die--

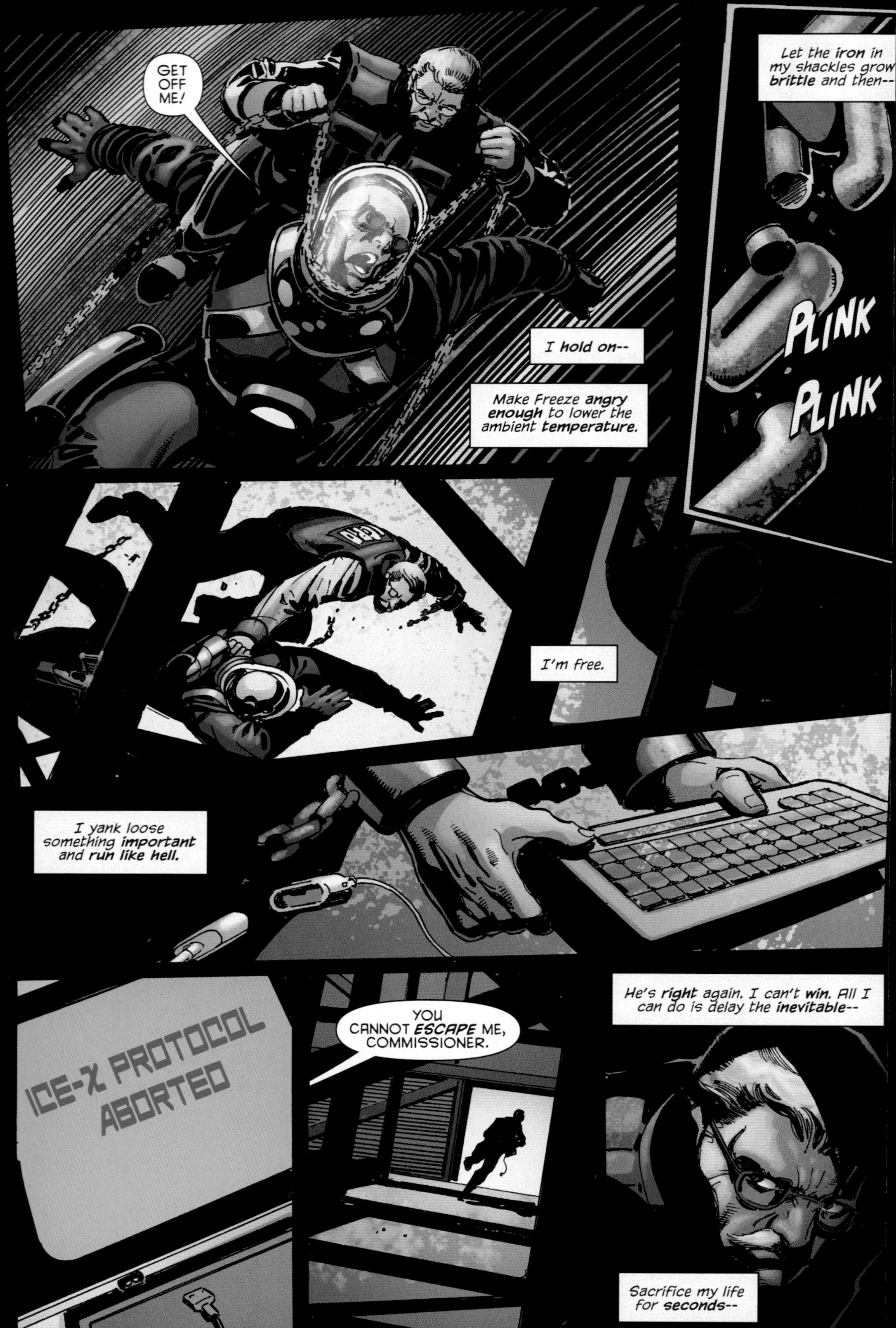
GET OFF ME!
I hold on--
Make Freeze angry enough to lower the ambient temperature.
Let the iron in my shackles grow brittle and then--
PLINK
PLINK
I'm free.
I yank loose something important and run like hell.
ICE-X PROTOCOL ABORTED
YOU CANNOT ESCAPE ME, COMMISSIONER.
He's right again. I can't win. All I can do is delay the inevitable--
Sacrifice my life for seconds--

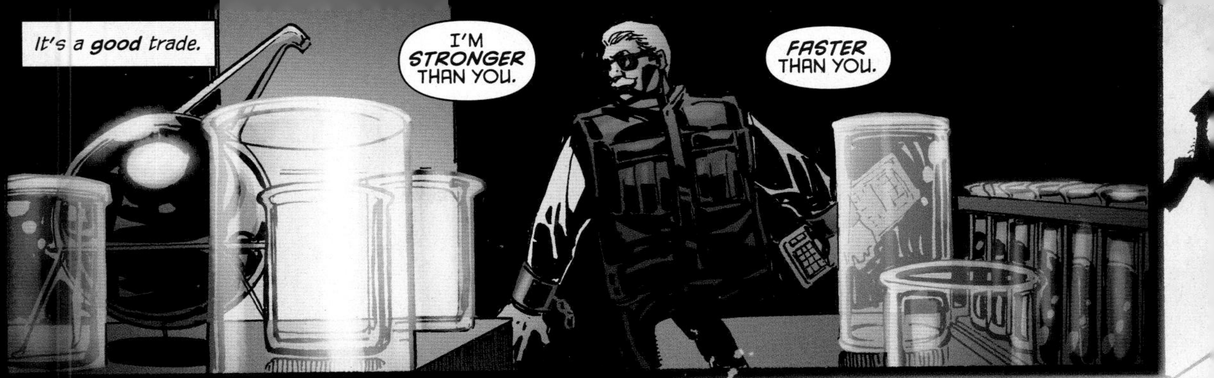
It's a **good** trade.
I'M STRONGER THAN YOU.
FASTER THAN YOU.

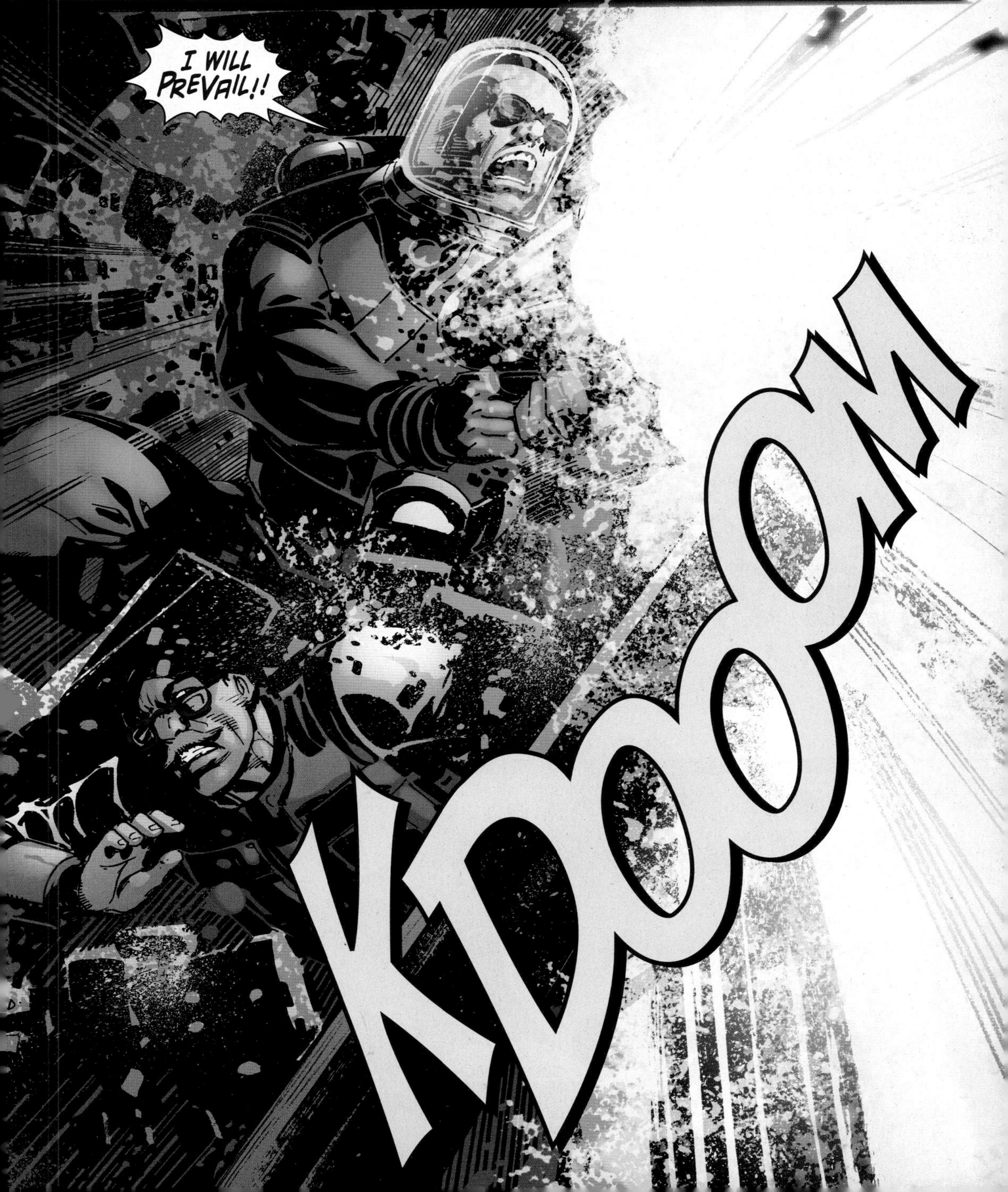
I WILL PREVAIL!!
KDOOOM

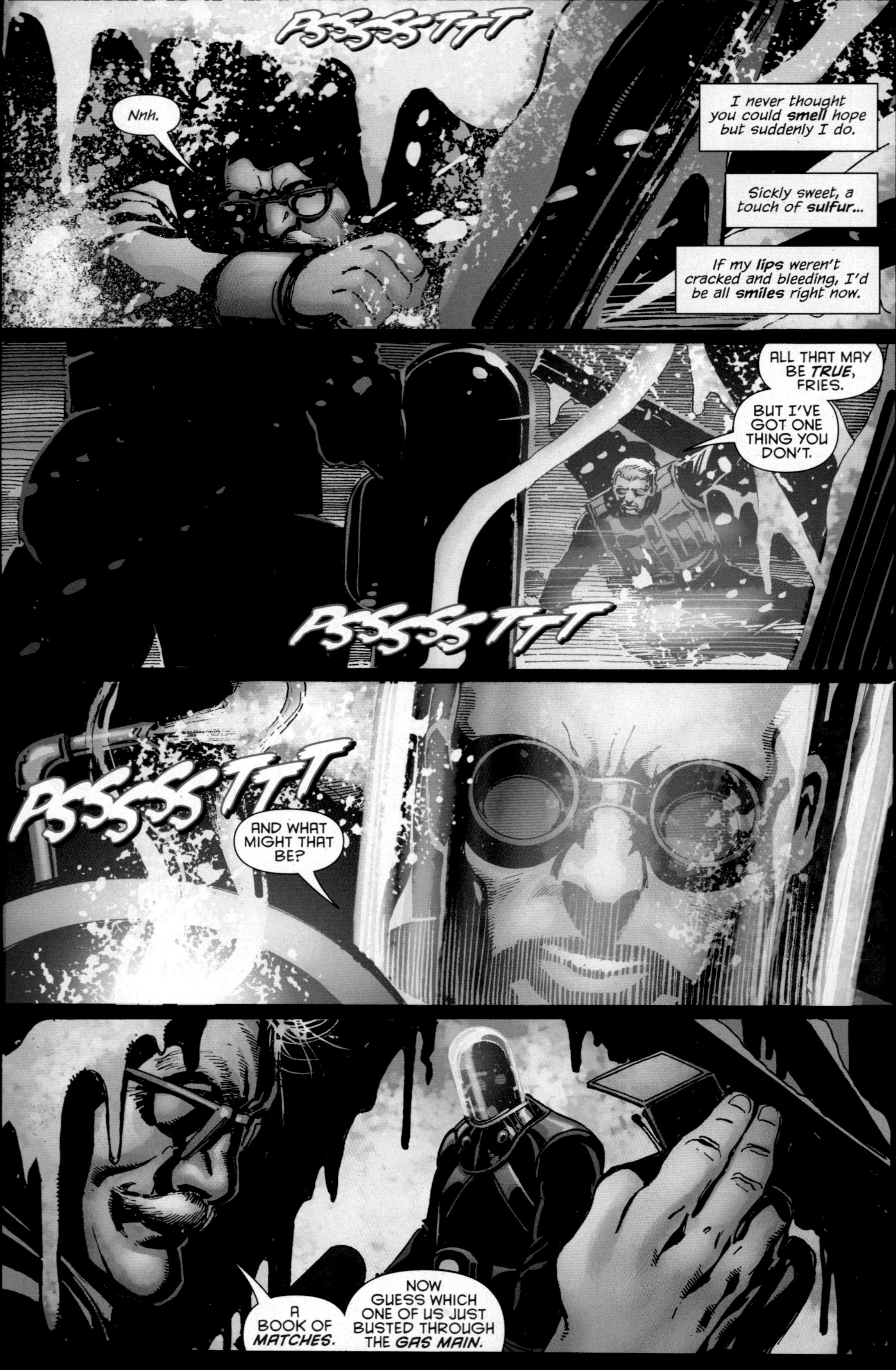
PSSSSSTTT
Nnh.
I never thought you could smell hope but suddenly I do.
Sickly sweet, a touch of sulfur...
If my lips weren't cracked and bleeding, I'd be all smiles right now.
ALL THAT MAY BE TRUE, FRIES.
BUT I'VE GOT ONE THING YOU DON'T.
PSSSSSTTT
PSSSSSTTT
AND WHAT MIGHT THAT BE?
A BOOK OF MATCHES.
NOW GUESS WHICH ONE OF US JUST BUSTED THROUGH THE GAS MAIN.

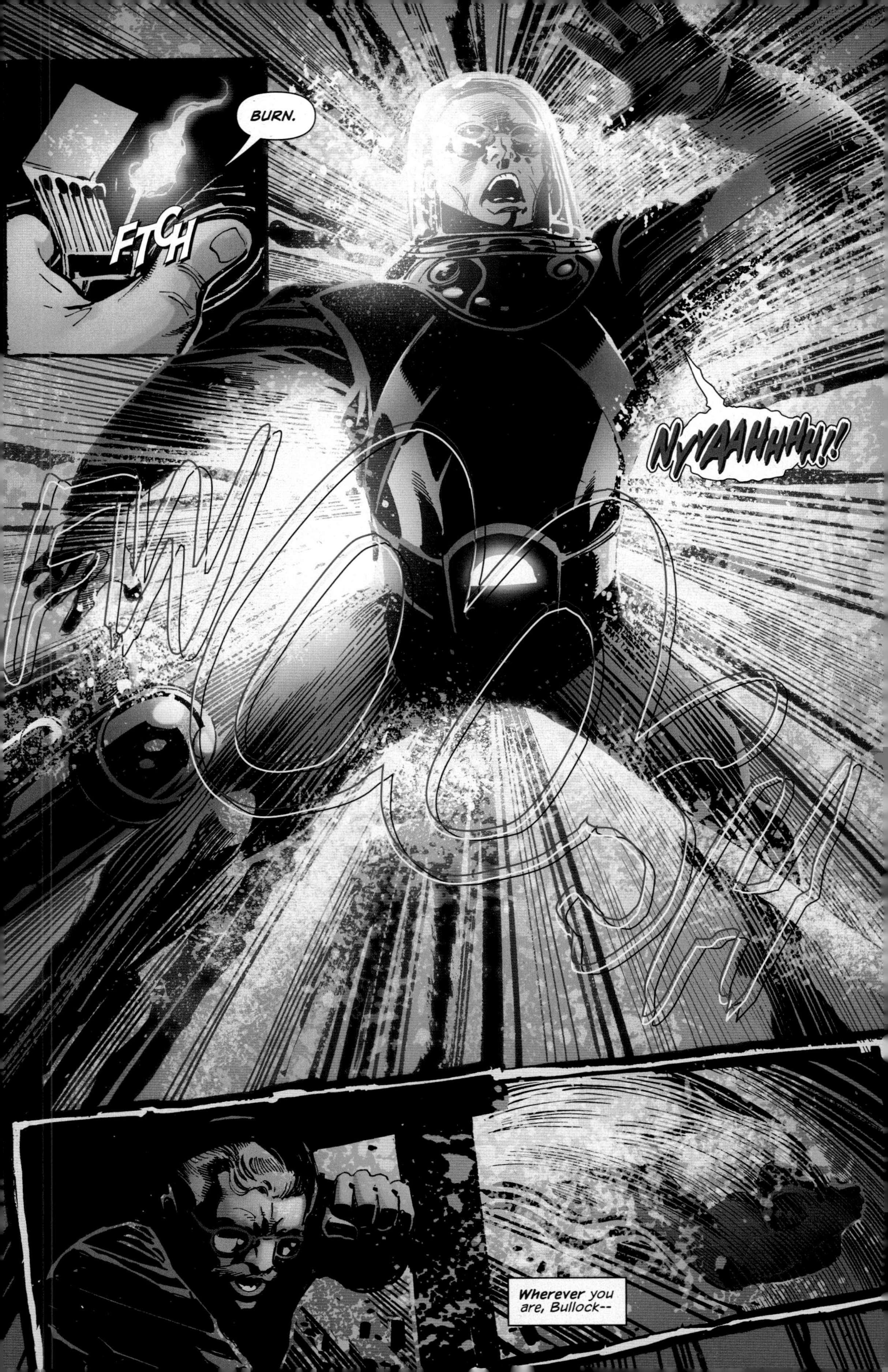
BURN.
FTCH
NYYAAHHHH!!
FWOOOSH
Wherever you are, Bullock--

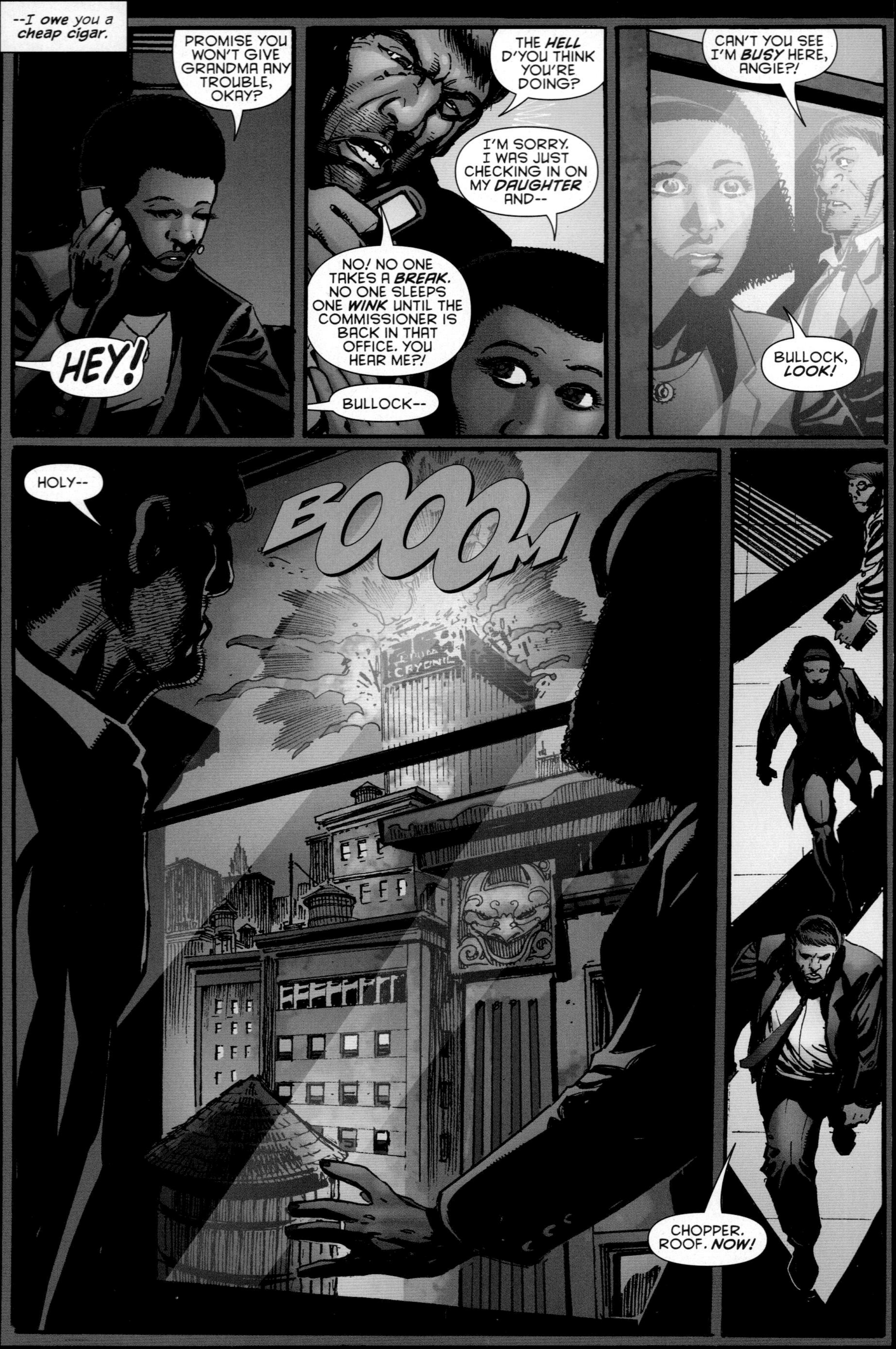
--I *owe* you a *cheap cigar.*
PROMISE YOU WON'T GIVE GRANDMA ANY TROUBLE, OKAY?
HEY!
THE ***HELL*** D'YOU THINK YOU'RE DOING?
I'M SORRY. I WAS JUST CHECKING IN ON MY ***DAUGHTER*** AND--
NO! NO ONE TAKES A ***BREAK.*** NO ONE SLEEPS ONE ***WINK*** UNTIL THE COMMISSIONER IS BACK IN THAT OFFICE. YOU HEAR ME?!
BULLOCK--
CAN'T YOU SEE I'M ***BUSY*** HERE, ANGIE?!
BULLOCK, ***LOOK!***
HOLY--
BOOOOM
CHOPPER. ROOF. ***NOW!***

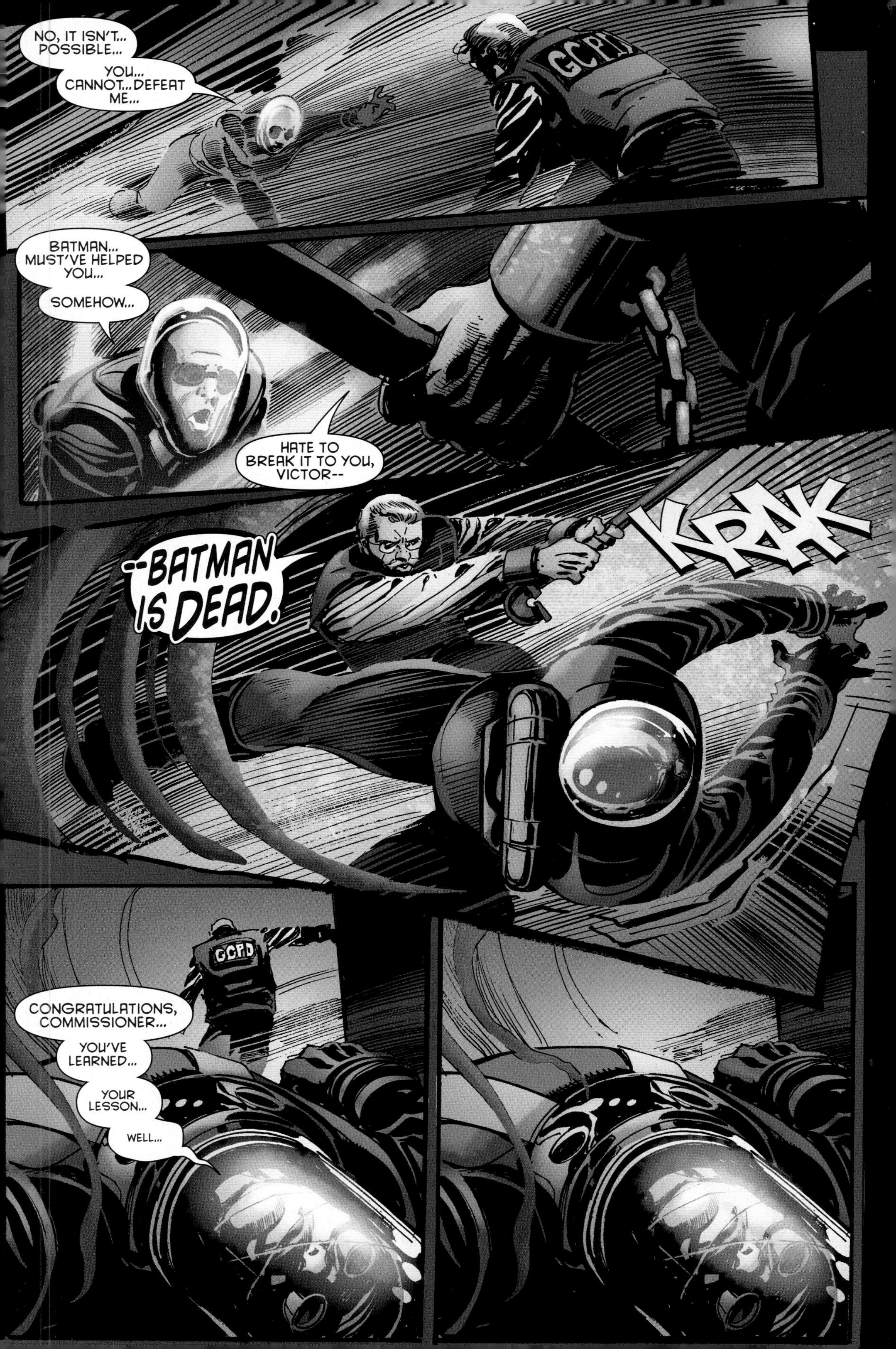
NO, IT ISN'T... POSSIBLE...
YOU... CANNOT...DEFEAT ME...
GCPD
BATMAN... MUST'VE HELPED YOU...
SOMEHOW...
HATE TO BREAK IT TO YOU, VICTOR--
--BATMAN IS DEAD.
KRAK
GCPD
CONGRATULATIONS, COMMISSIONER...
YOU'VE LEARNED...
YOUR LESSON...
WELL...

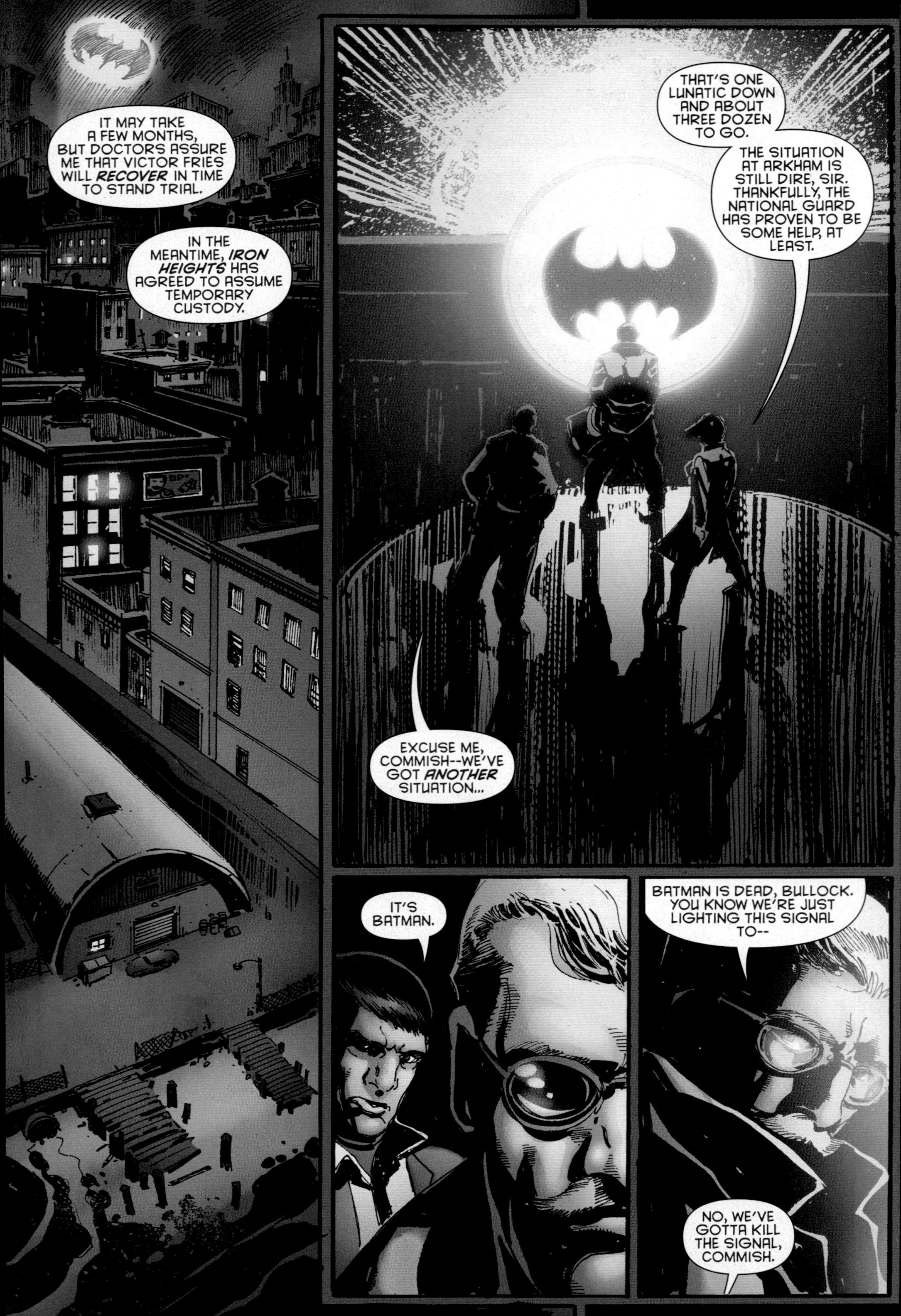
IT MAY TAKE A FEW MONTHS, BUT DOCTORS ASSURE ME THAT VICTOR FRIES WILL *RECOVER* IN TIME TO STAND TRIAL.
IN THE MEANTIME, *IRON HEIGHTS* HAS AGREED TO ASSUME TEMPORARY CUSTODY.
THAT'S ONE LUNATIC DOWN AND ABOUT THREE DOZEN TO GO.
THE SITUATION AT ARKHAM IS STILL DIRE, SIR. THANKFULLY, THE NATIONAL GUARD HAS PROVEN TO BE SOME HELP, AT LEAST.
EXCUSE ME, COMMISH--WE'VE GOT *ANOTHER* SITUATION...
IT'S BATMAN.
BATMAN IS DEAD, BULLOCK. YOU KNOW WE'RE JUST LIGHTING THIS SIGNAL TO--
NO, WE'VE GOTTA KILL THE SIGNAL, COMMISH.

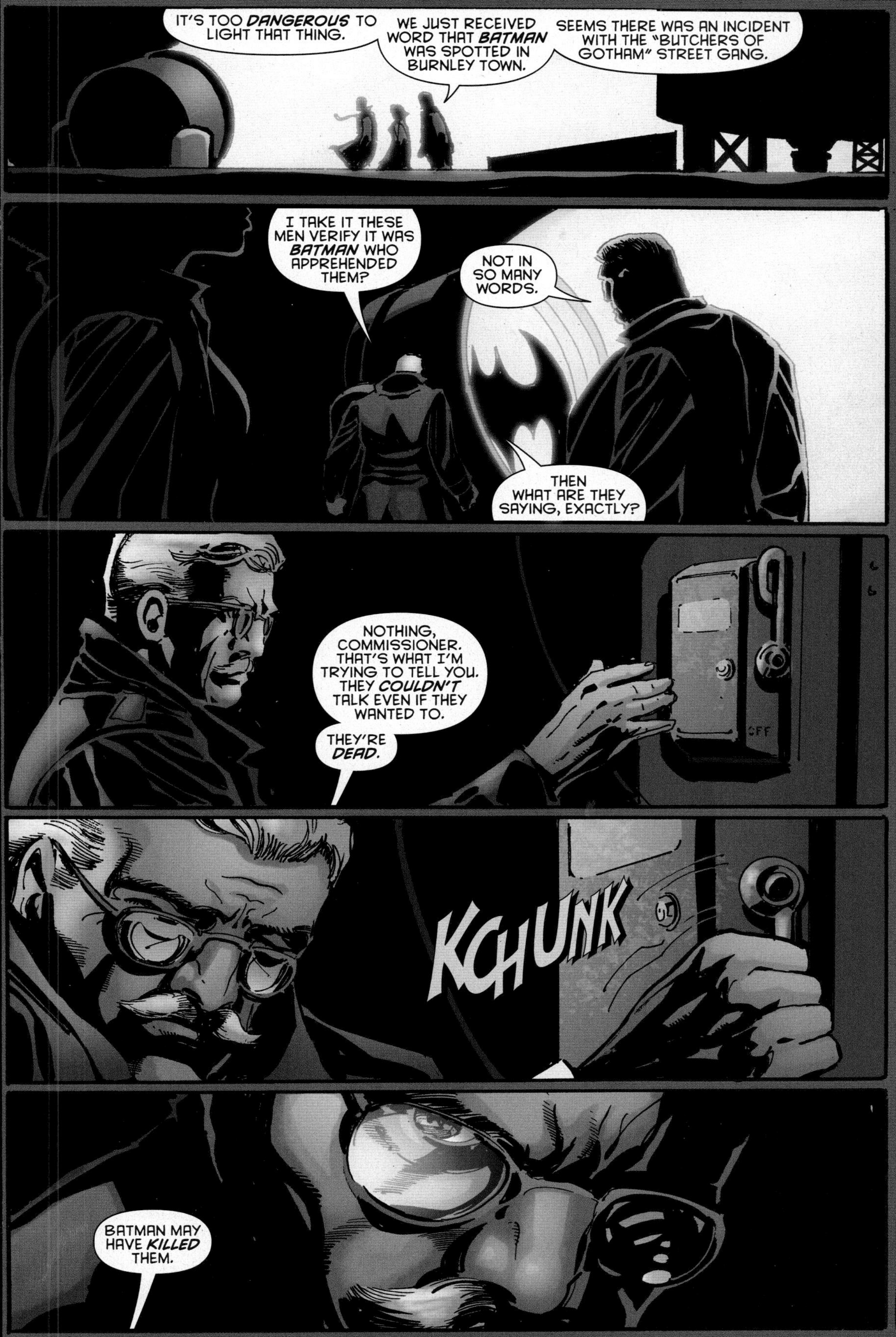

IT'S TOO DANGEROUS TO LIGHT THAT THING.
WE JUST RECEIVED WORD THAT BATMAN WAS SPOTTED IN BURNLEY TOWN.
SEEMS THERE WAS AN INCIDENT WITH THE "BUTCHERS OF GOTHAM" STREET GANG.
I TAKE IT THESE MEN VERIFY IT WAS BATMAN WHO APPREHENDED THEM?
NOT IN SO MANY WORDS.
THEN WHAT ARE THEY SAYING, EXACTLY?
NOTHING, COMMISSIONER. THAT'S WHAT I'M TRYING TO TELL YOU. THEY COULDN'T TALK EVEN IF THEY WANTED TO.
THEY'RE DEAD.
OFF
KCHUNK
BATMAN MAY HAVE KILLED THEM.

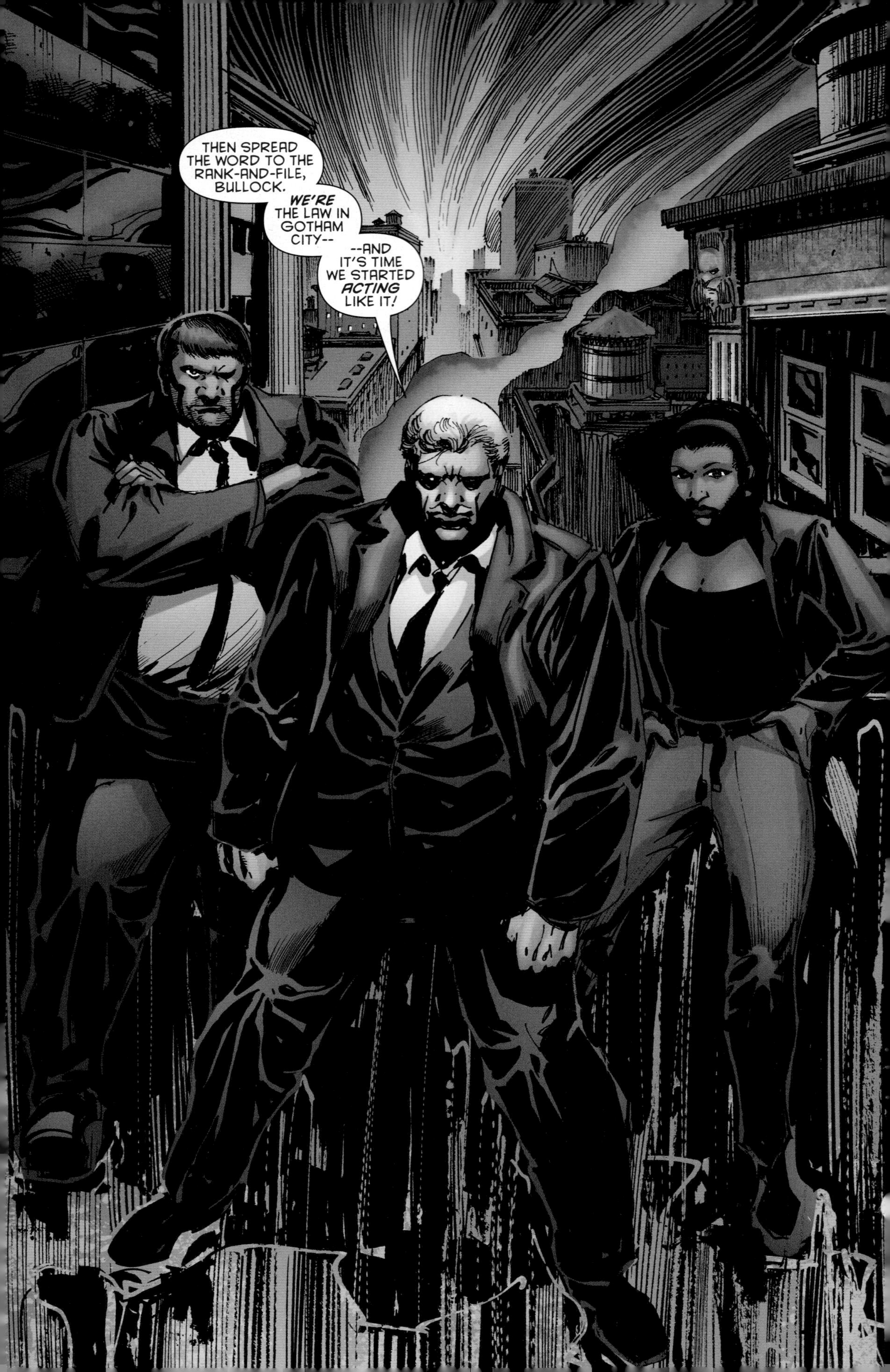
THEN SPREAD THE WORD TO THE RANK-AND-FILE, BULLOCK.
WE'RE THE LAW IN GOTHAM CITY--
--AND IT'S TIME WE STARTED ACTING LIKE IT!

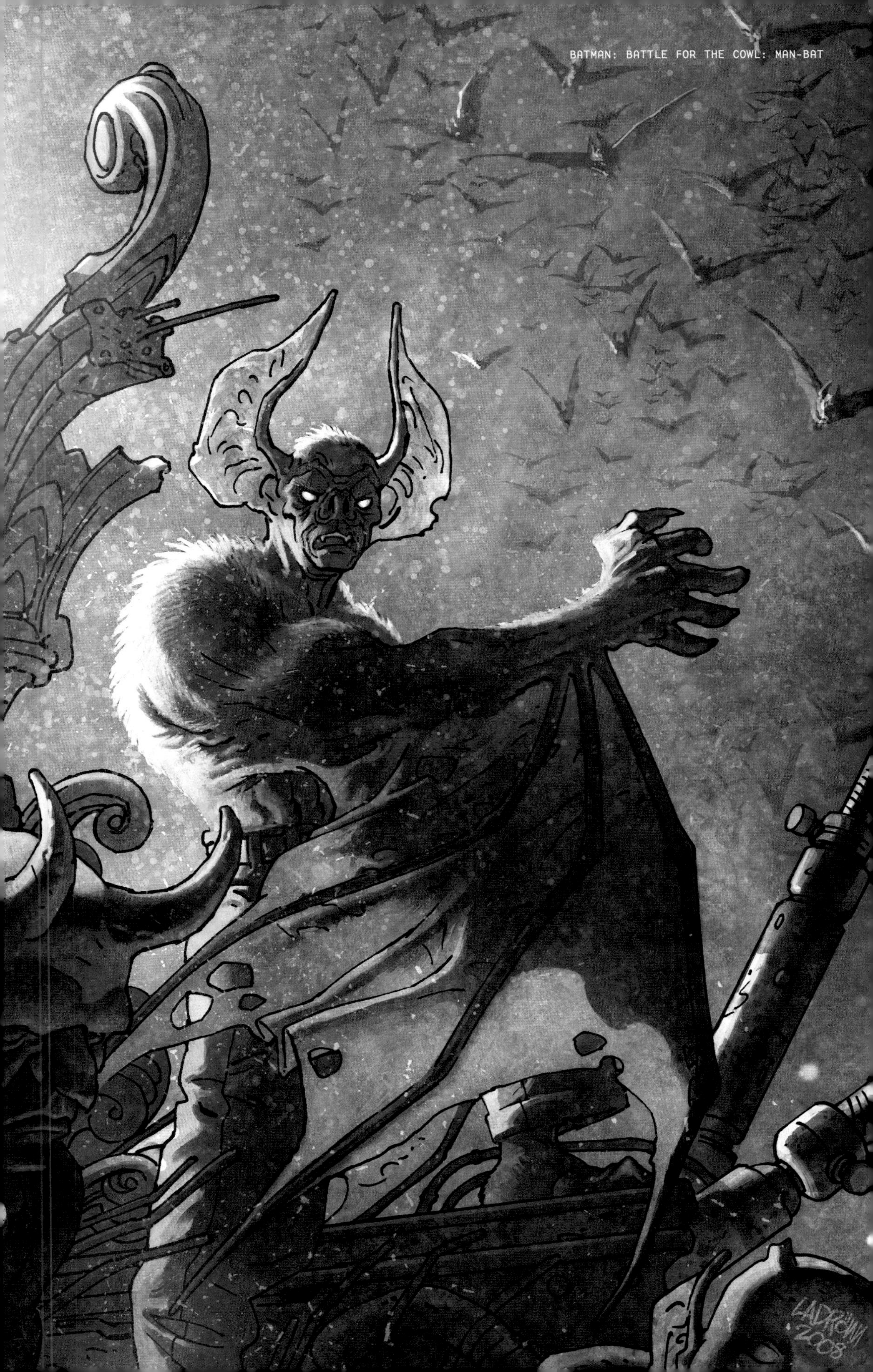
LADRÖNN
2008

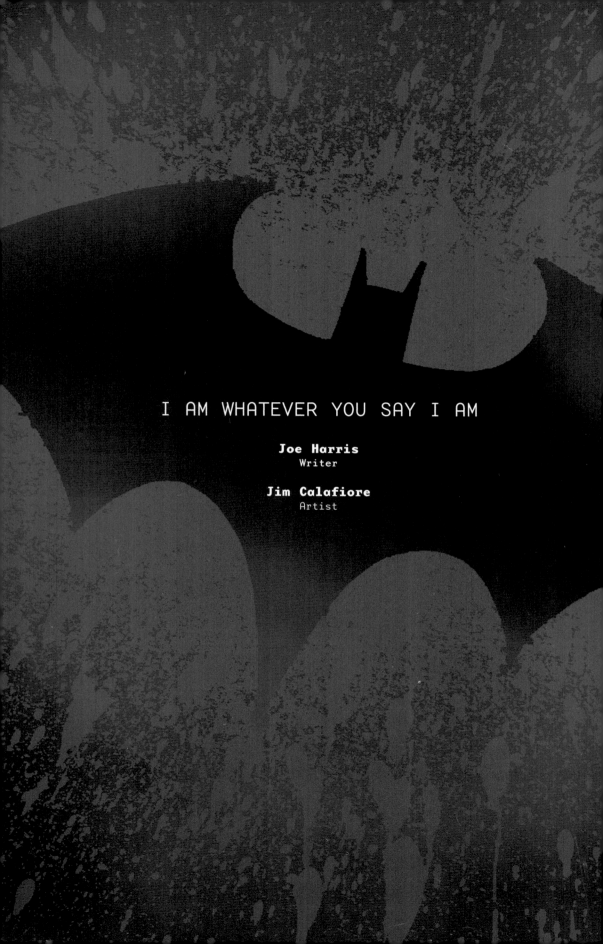

I AM WHATEVER YOU SAY I AM

Joe Harris
Writer

Jim Calafiore
Artist

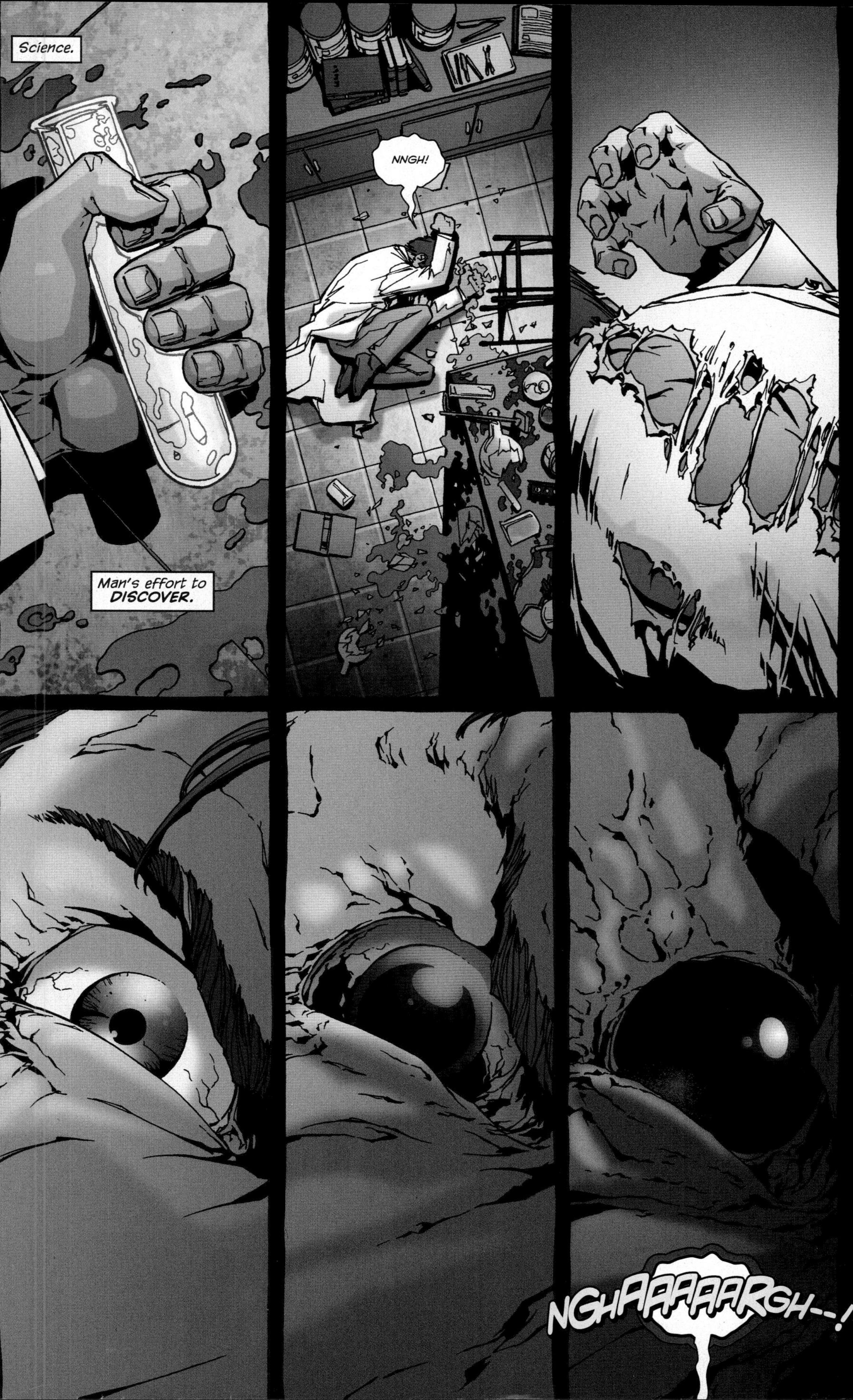
Science.
Man's effort to DISCOVER.
NNGH!
NGHAAAAAARGH--!

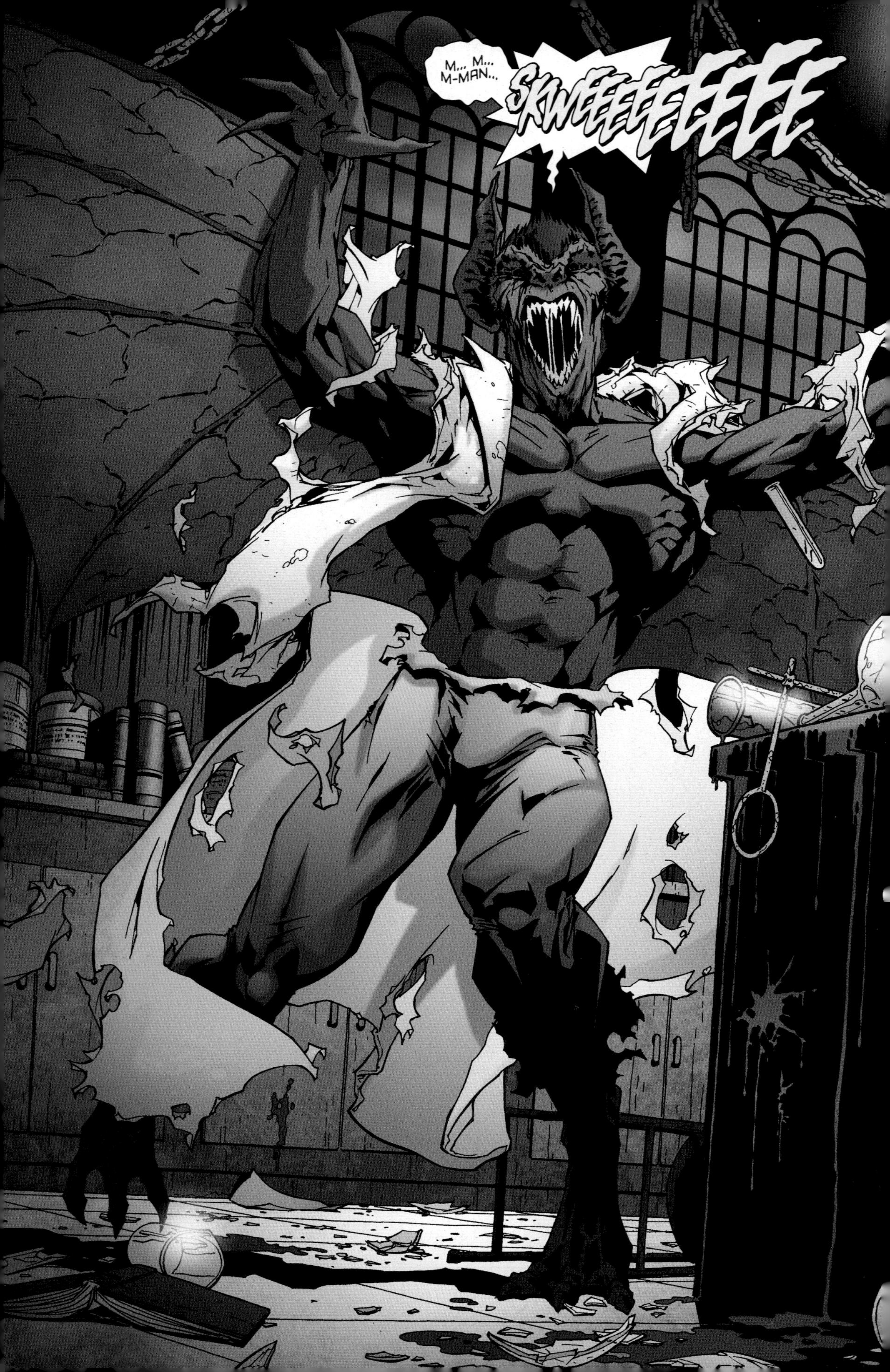
M... M... M-MAN...
SKWEEEEEEEEEE

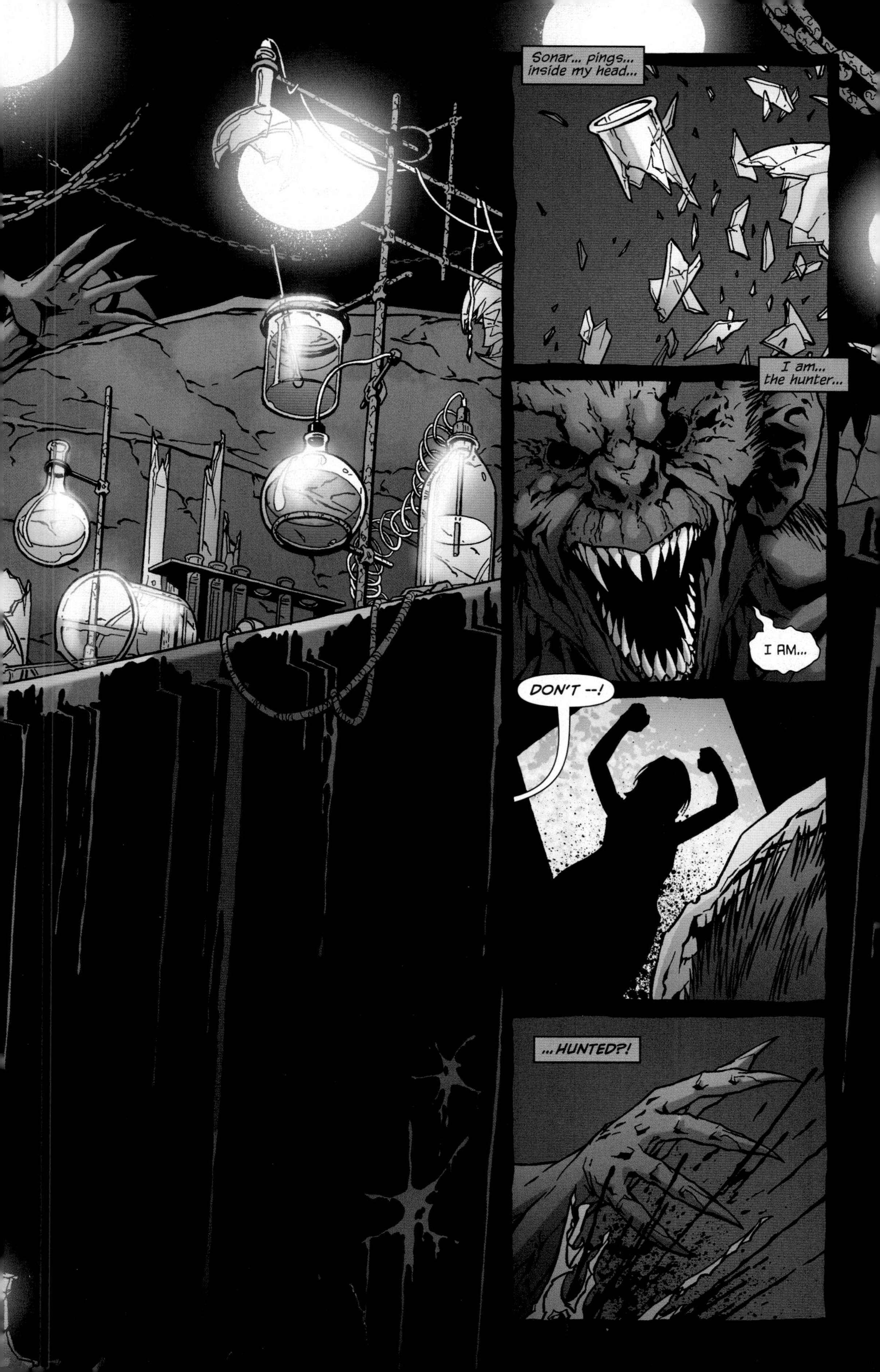
Sonar... pings... inside my head...
I am... the hunter...
I AM...
DON'T --!
...HUNTED?!

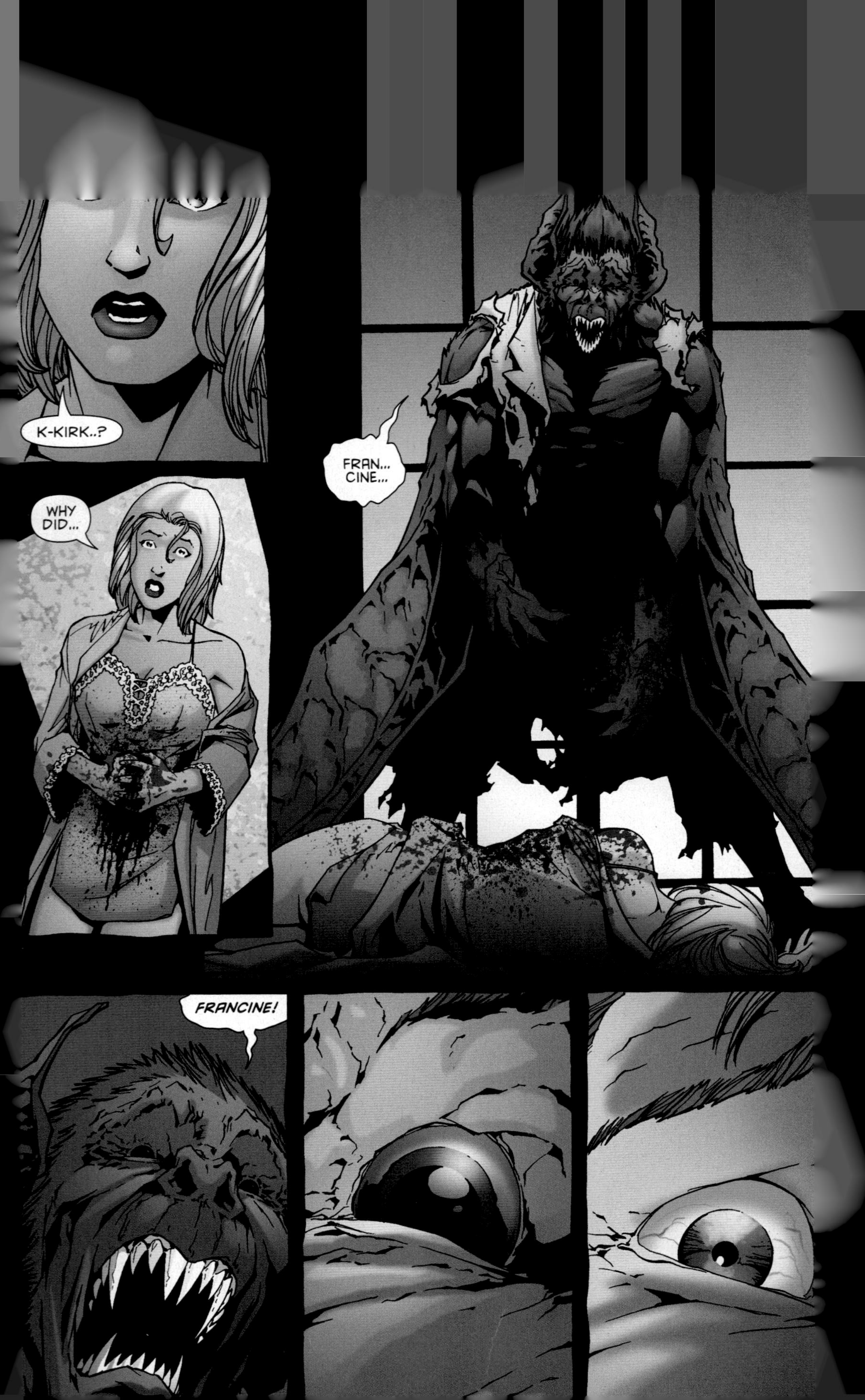
K-KIRK..?
WHY DID...
FRAN... CINE...
FRANCINE!

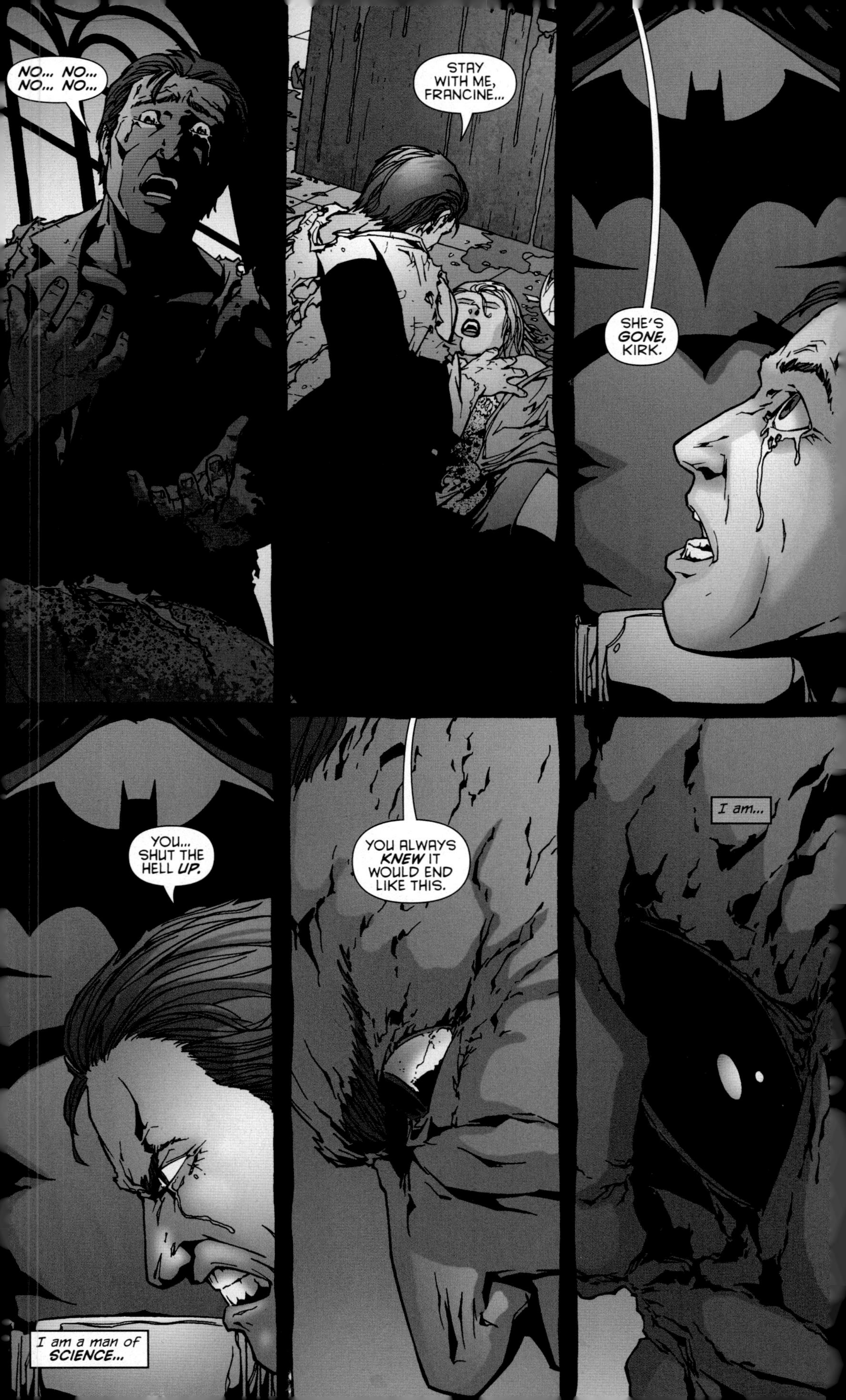
NO... NO... NO... NO...
STAY WITH ME, FRANCINE...
SHE'S GONE, KIRK.
YOU... SHUT THE HELL UP.
I am a man of SCIENCE...
YOU ALWAYS KNEW IT WOULD END LIKE THIS.
I am...

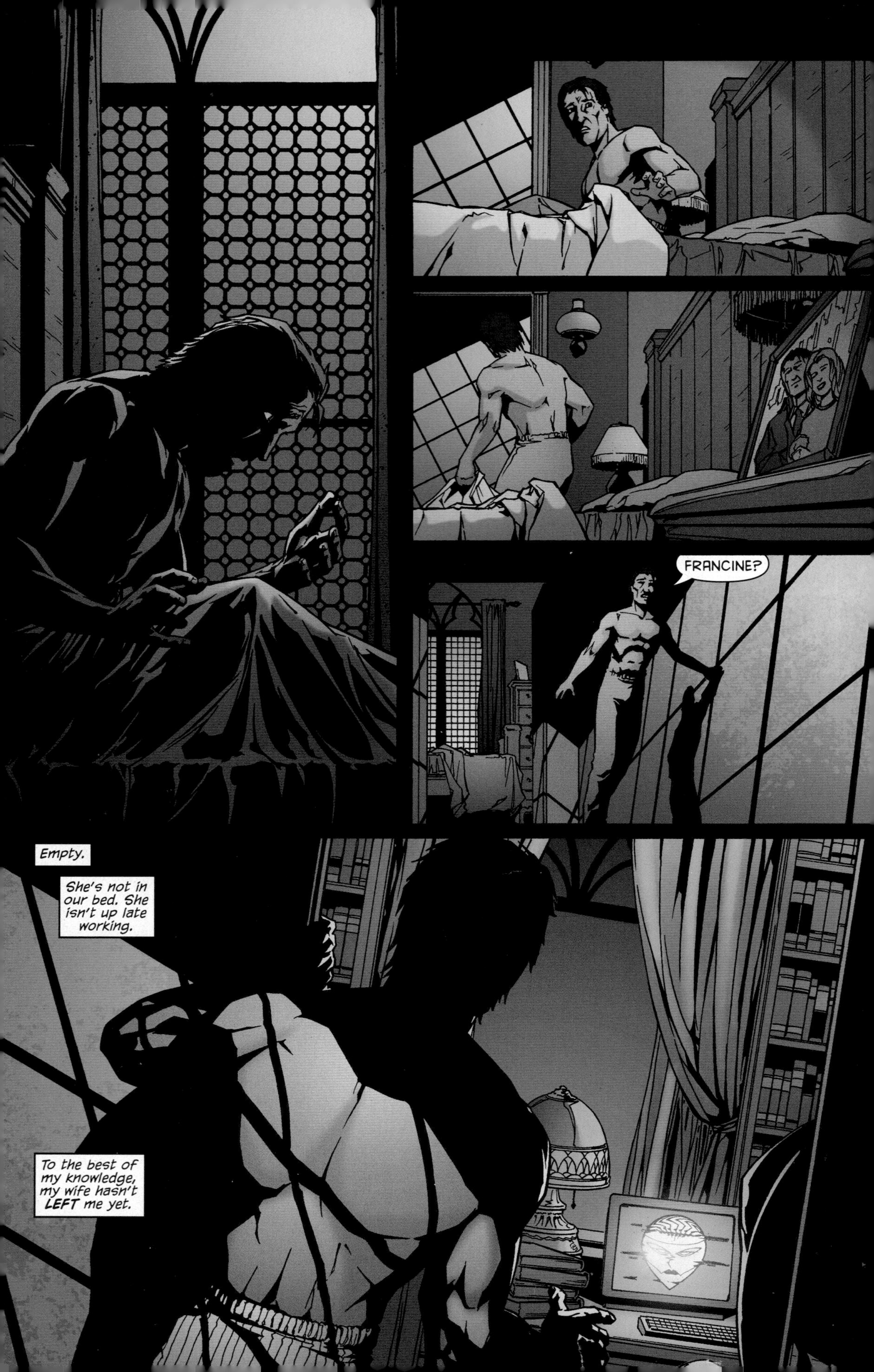
FRANCINE?
Empty.
She's not in our bed. She isn't up late working.
To the best of my knowledge, my wife hasn't LEFT me yet.

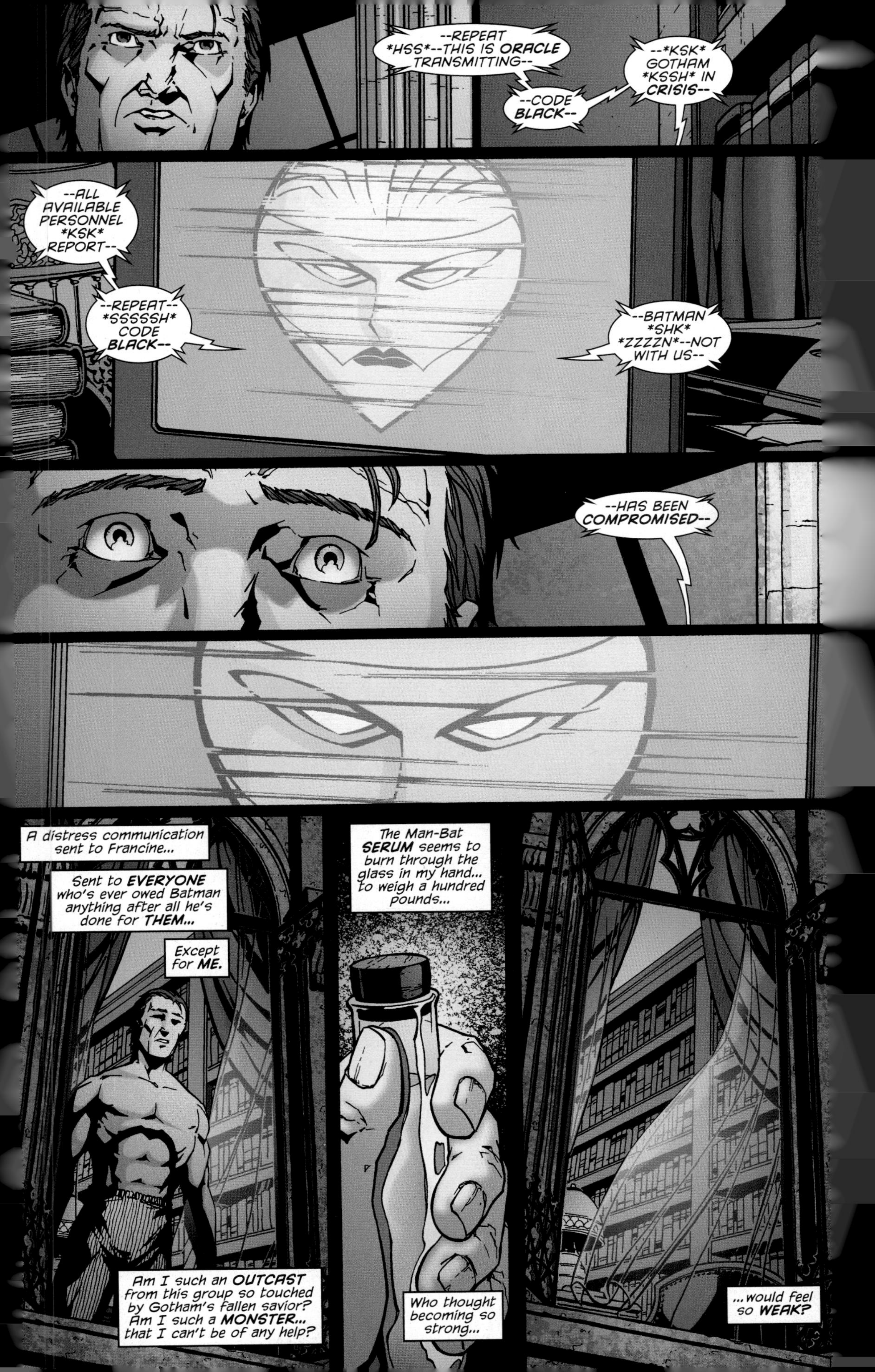
--REPEAT *HSS*--THIS IS ORACLE TRANSMITTING--
--CODE BLACK--
--*KSK* GOTHAM *KSSH* IN CRISIS--
--ALL AVAILABLE PERSONNEL *KSK* REPORT--
--REPEAT-- *SSSSSH* CODE BLACK--
--BATMAN *SHK* *ZZZZN*--NOT WITH US--
--HAS BEEN COMPROMISED--
A distress communication sent to Francine...
Sent to EVERYONE who's ever owed Batman anything after all he's done for THEM...
Except for ME.
Am I such an OUTCAST from this group so touched by Gotham's fallen savior? Am I such a MONSTER... that I can't be of any help?
The Man-Bat SERUM seems to burn through the glass in my hand... to weigh a hundred pounds...
Who thought becoming so strong...
...would feel so WEAK?

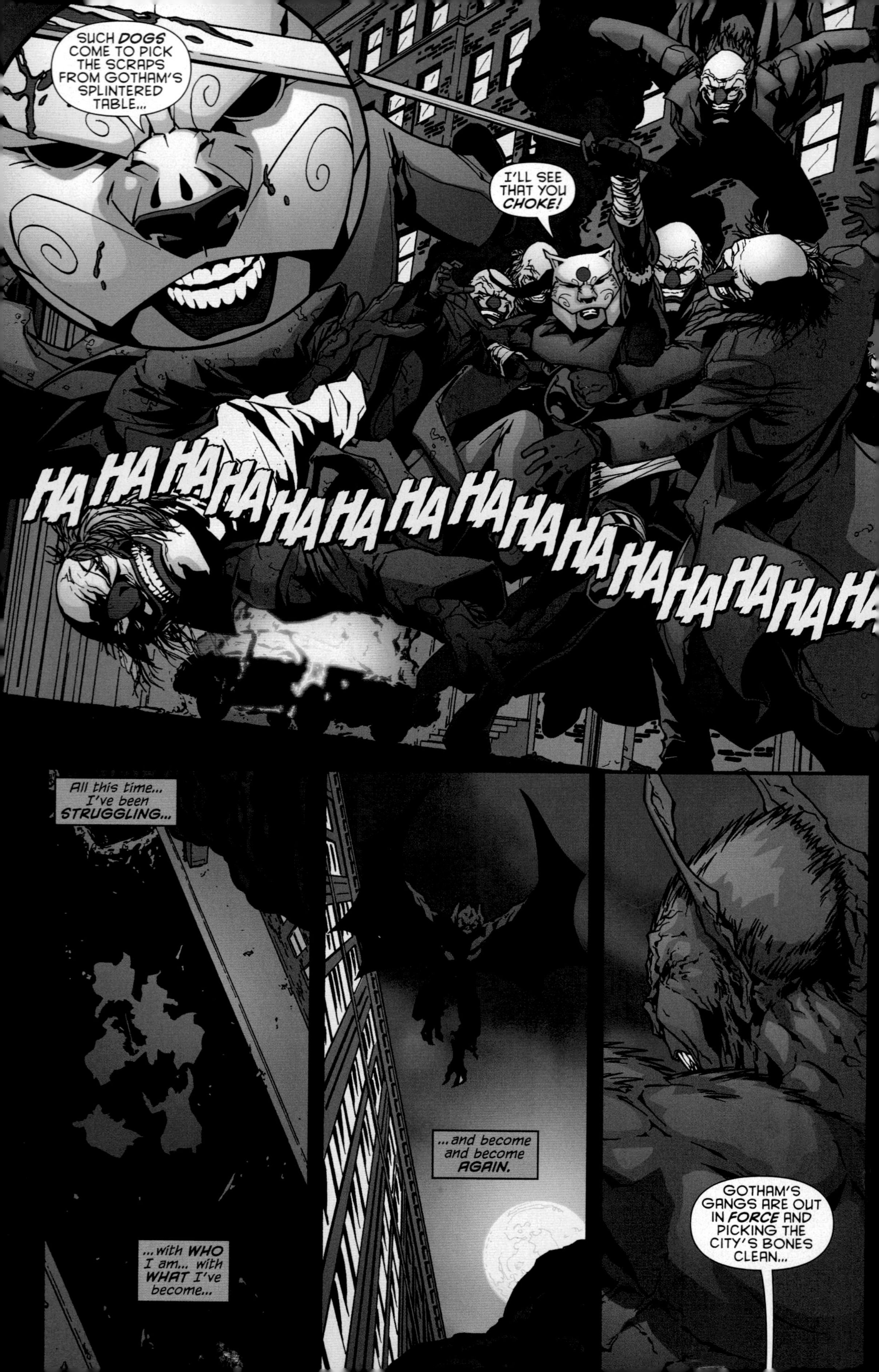
SUCH DOGS COME TO PICK THE SCRAPS FROM GOTHAM'S SPLINTERED TABLE...
I'LL SEE THAT YOU CHOKE!
HA HA HA HA HA HA HA HA HA HA HA HA HA HA HA HA HA
All this time... I've been STRUGGLING...
...with WHO I am... with WHAT I've become...
...and become and become AGAIN.
GOTHAM'S GANGS ARE OUT IN FORCE AND PICKING THE CITY'S BONES CLEAN...

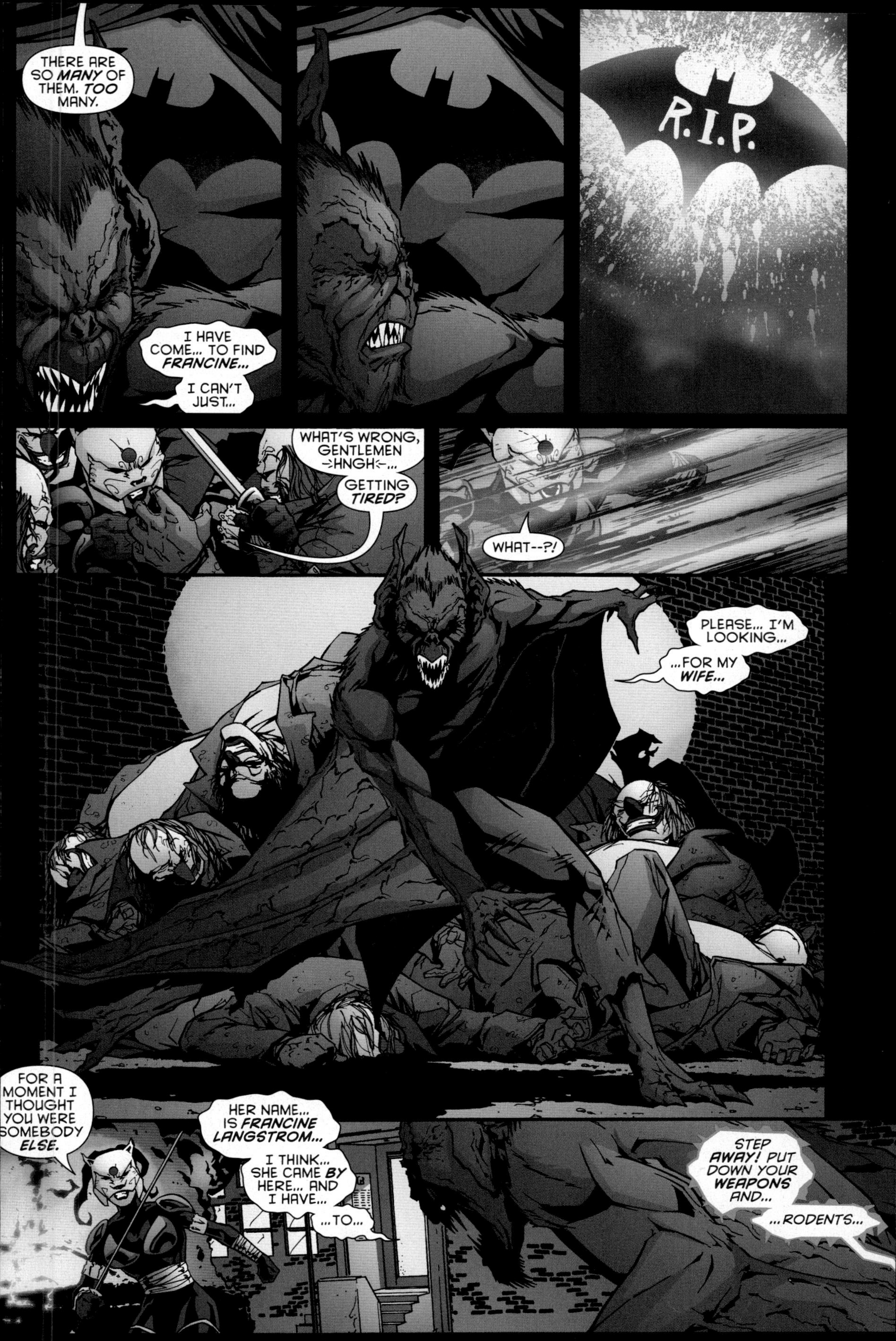
THERE ARE SO MANY OF THEM. TOO MANY.
I HAVE COME... TO FIND FRANCINE...
I CAN'T JUST...
R.I.P.
WHAT'S WRONG, GENTLEMEN =HNGH=...
GETTING TIRED?
WHAT--?!
PLEASE... I'M LOOKING...
...FOR MY WIFE...
FOR A MOMENT I THOUGHT YOU WERE SOMEBODY ELSE.
HER NAME... IS FRANCINE LANGSTROM...
I THINK... SHE CAME BY HERE... AND I HAVE...
...TO...
STEP AWAY! PUT DOWN YOUR WEAPONS AND...
...RODENTS...

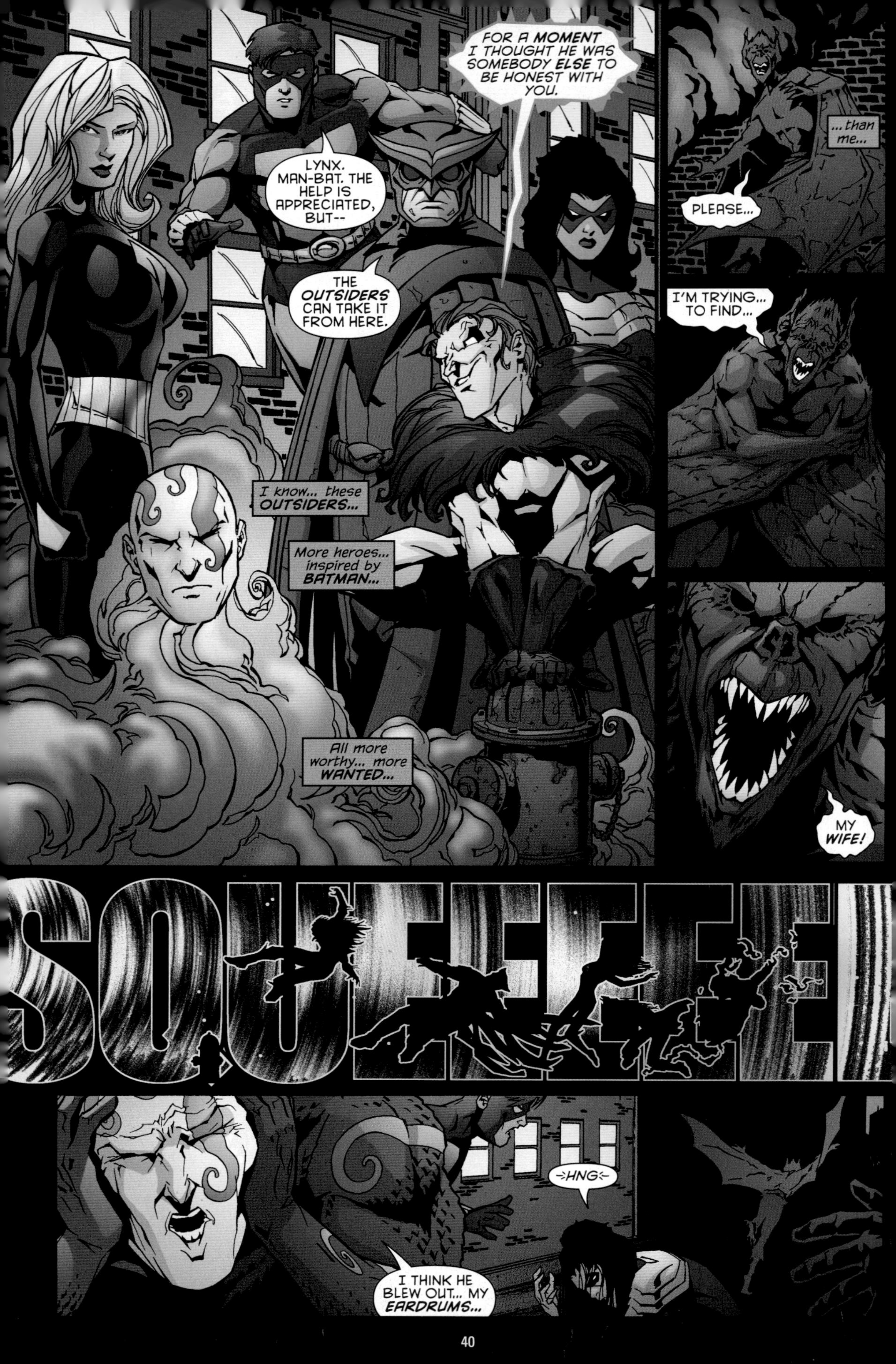
LYNX. MAN-BAT. THE HELP IS APPRECIATED, BUT--
THE OUTSIDERS CAN TAKE IT FROM HERE.
FOR A MOMENT I THOUGHT HE WAS SOMEBODY ELSE TO BE HONEST WITH YOU.
I know... these OUTSIDERS...
More heroes... inspired by BATMAN...
All more worthy... more WANTED...
...than me...
PLEASE...
I'M TRYING... TO FIND...
MY WIFE!
SQUEEE
-HNG-
I THINK HE BLEW OUT... MY EARDRUMS...

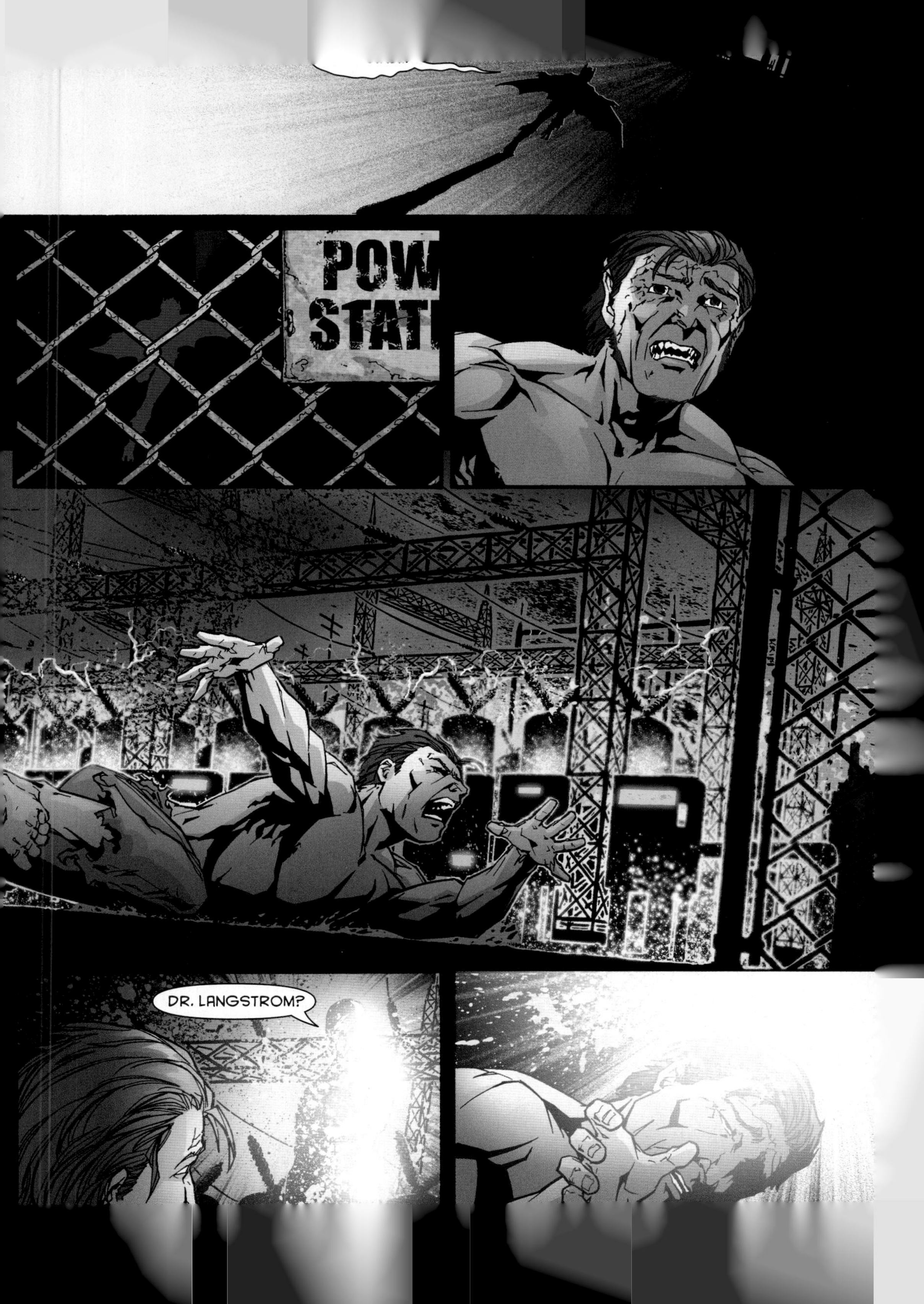
POW
STAT
DR. LANGSTROM?

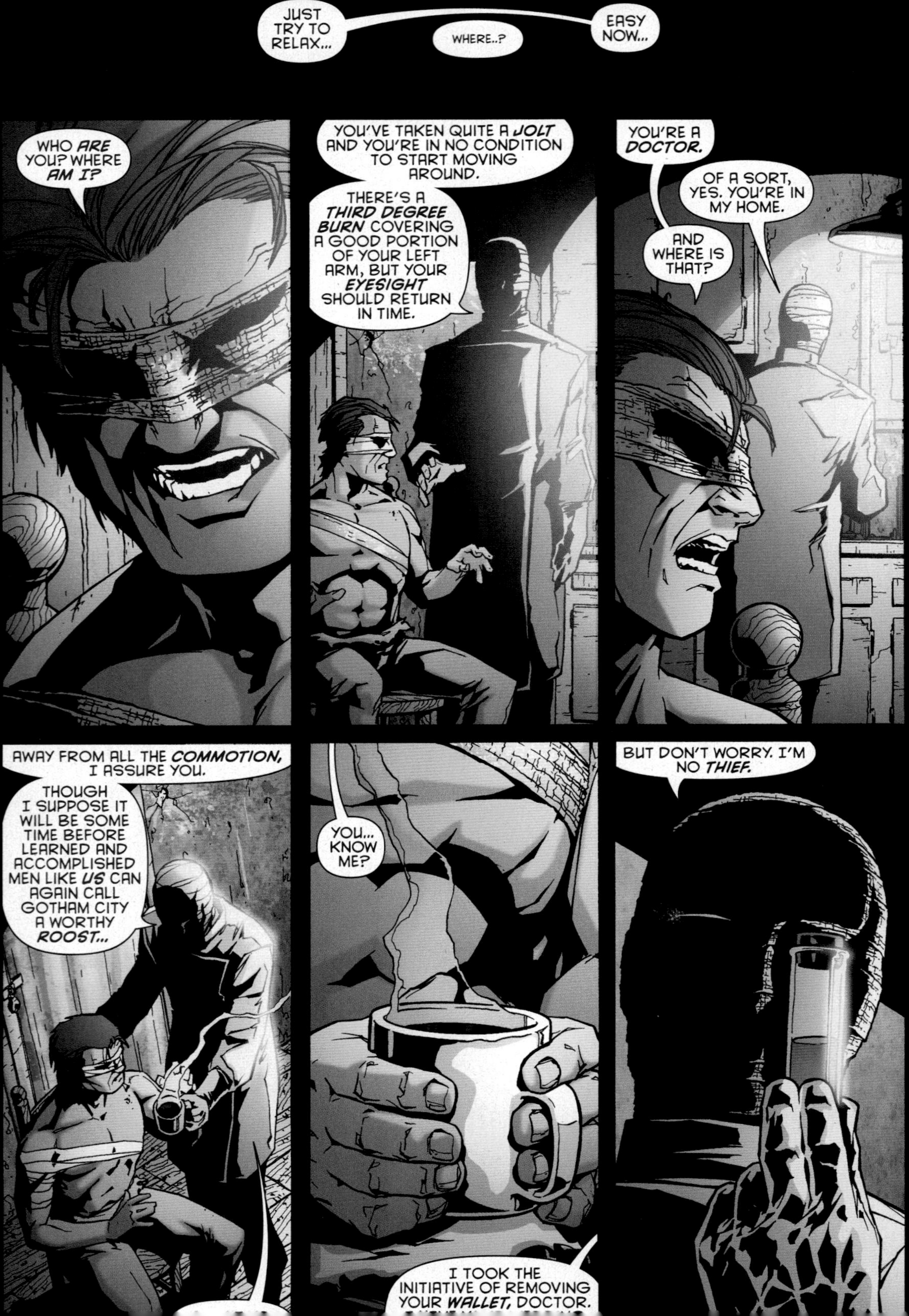

JUST TRY TO RELAX...
WHERE..?
EASY NOW...
WHO *ARE* YOU? WHERE *AM I?*
YOU'VE TAKEN QUITE A *JOLT* AND YOU'RE IN NO CONDITION TO START MOVING AROUND.
THERE'S A *THIRD DEGREE BURN* COVERING A GOOD PORTION OF YOUR LEFT ARM, BUT YOUR *EYESIGHT* SHOULD RETURN IN TIME.
YOU'RE A *DOCTOR.*
OF A SORT, YES. YOU'RE IN MY HOME.
AND WHERE IS THAT?
AWAY FROM ALL THE *COMMOTION,* I ASSURE YOU.
THOUGH I SUPPOSE IT WILL BE SOME TIME BEFORE LEARNED AND ACCOMPLISHED MEN LIKE *US* CAN AGAIN CALL GOTHAM CITY A WORTHY *ROOST...*
YOU... KNOW ME?
I TOOK THE INITIATIVE OF REMOVING YOUR *WALLET,* DOCTOR.
BUT DON'T WORRY. I'M NO *THIEF.*

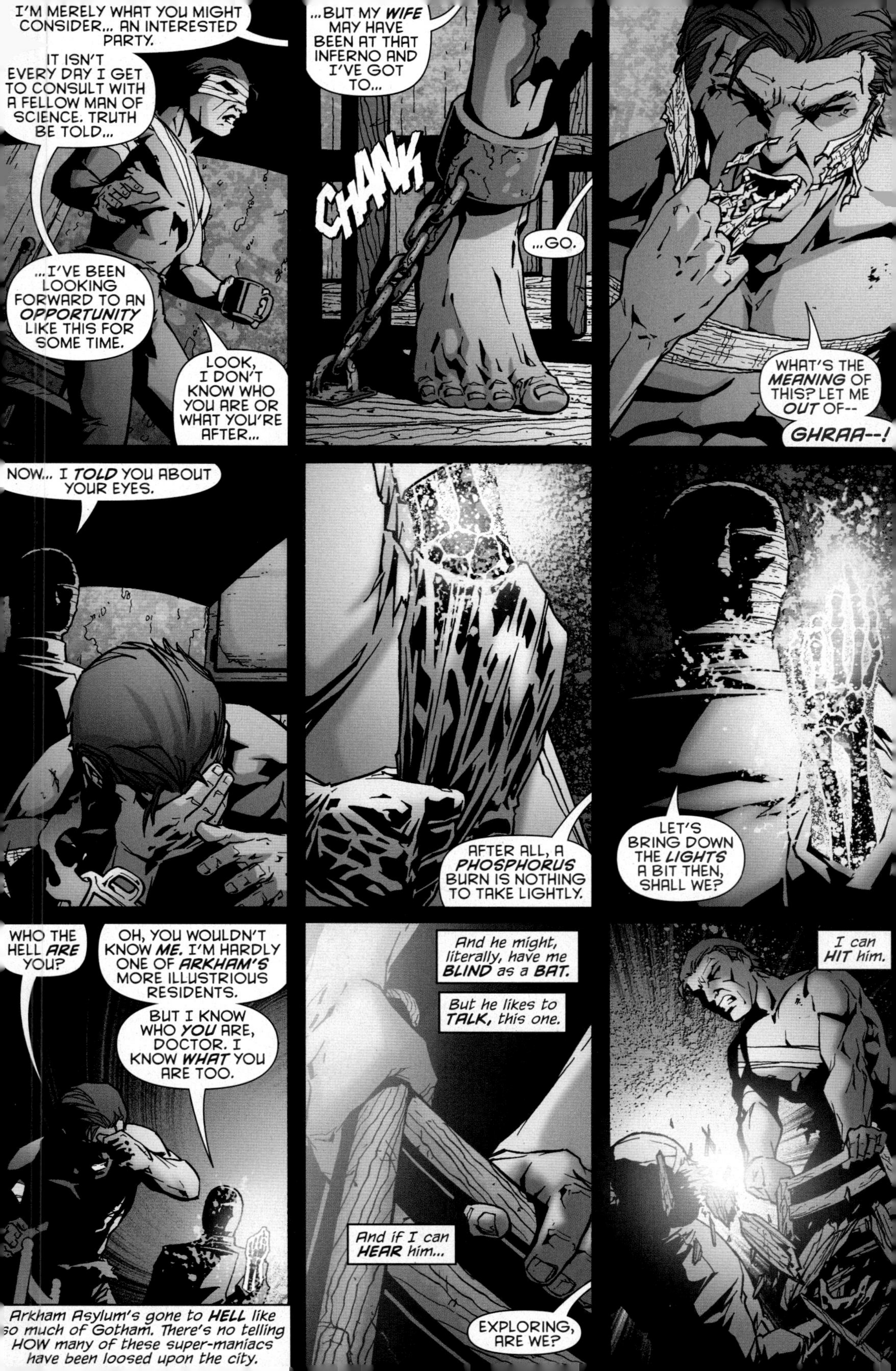
I'M MERELY WHAT YOU MIGHT CONSIDER... AN INTERESTED PARTY.
IT ISN'T EVERY DAY I GET TO CONSULT WITH A FELLOW MAN OF SCIENCE. TRUTH BE TOLD...
...I'VE BEEN LOOKING FORWARD TO AN OPPORTUNITY LIKE THIS FOR SOME TIME.
LOOK, I DON'T KNOW WHO YOU ARE OR WHAT YOU'RE AFTER...
...BUT MY WIFE MAY HAVE BEEN AT THAT INFERNO AND I'VE GOT TO...
CHANK
...GO.
WHAT'S THE MEANING OF THIS? LET ME OUT OF--
GHRAA--!
NOW... I TOLD YOU ABOUT YOUR EYES.
AFTER ALL, A PHOSPHORUS BURN IS NOTHING TO TAKE LIGHTLY.
LET'S BRING DOWN THE LIGHTS A BIT THEN, SHALL WE?
WHO THE HELL ARE YOU?
OH, YOU WOULDN'T KNOW ME. I'M HARDLY ONE OF ARKHAM'S MORE ILLUSTRIOUS RESIDENTS.
BUT I KNOW WHO YOU ARE, DOCTOR. I KNOW WHAT YOU ARE TOO.
Arkham Asylum's gone to HELL like so much of Gotham. There's no telling HOW many of these super-maniacs have been loosed upon the city.
And he might, literally, have me BLIND as a BAT.
But he likes to TALK, this one.
And if I can HEAR him...
EXPLORING, ARE WE?
I can HIT him.

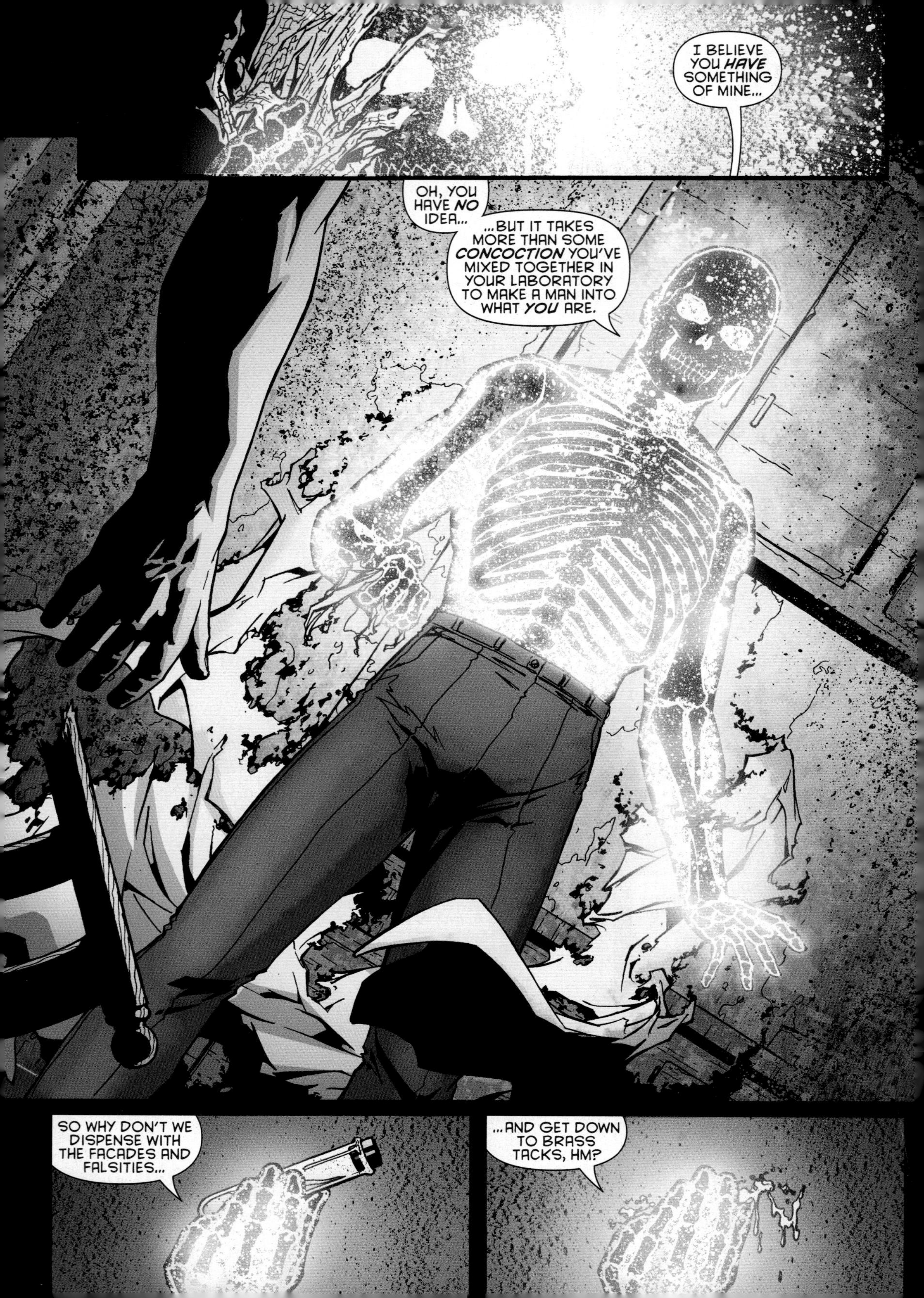
I BELIEVE YOU HAVE SOMETHING OF MINE...
OH, YOU HAVE NO IDEA...
...BUT IT TAKES MORE THAN SOME CONCOCTION YOU'VE MIXED TOGETHER IN YOUR LABORATORY TO MAKE A MAN INTO WHAT YOU ARE.
SO WHY DON'T WE DISPENSE WITH THE FACADES AND FALSITIES...
...AND GET DOWN TO BRASS TACKS, HM?

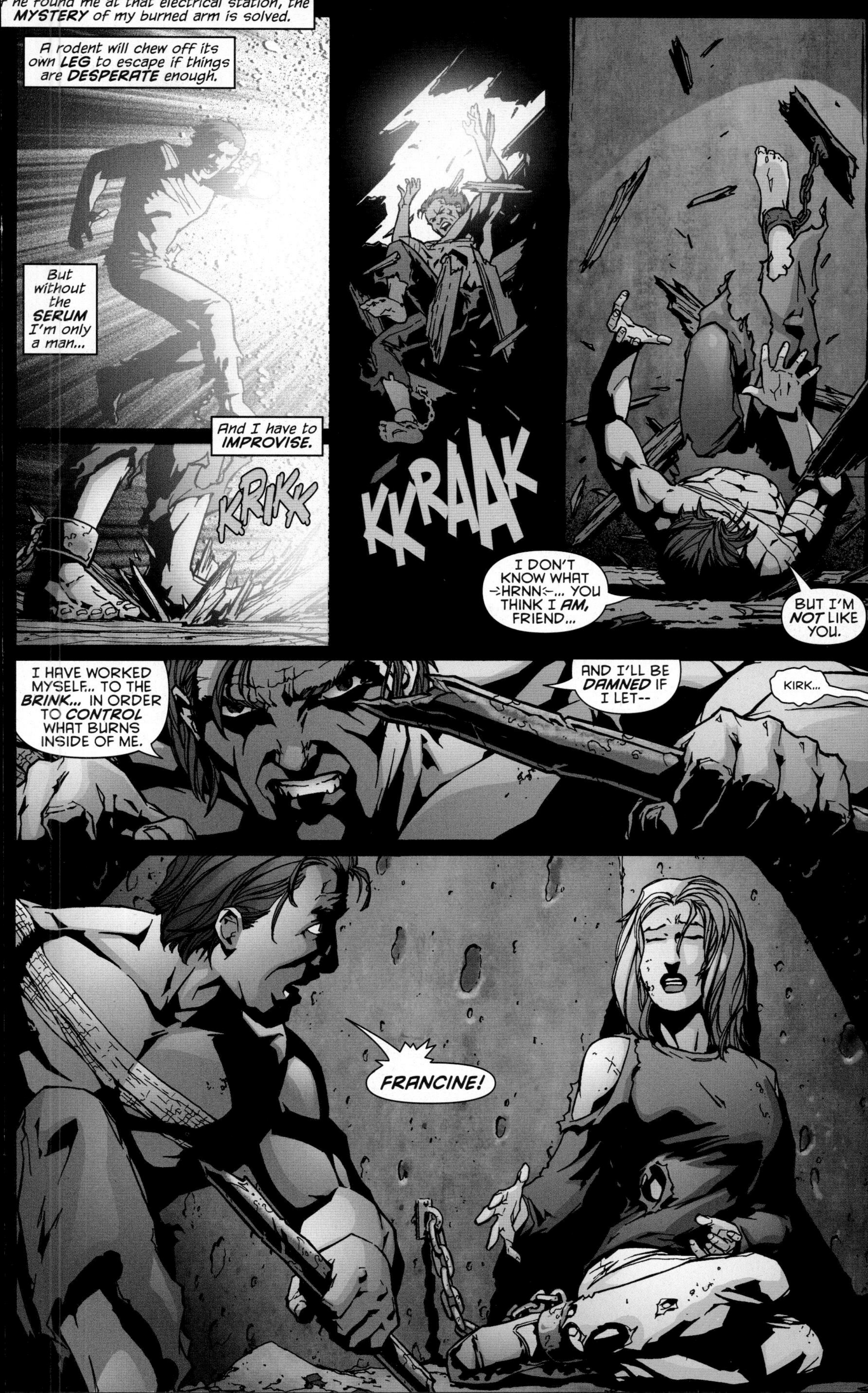

f he found me at that electrical station, the MYSTERY of my burned arm is solved.
A rodent will chew off its own LEG to escape if things are DESPERATE enough.
But without the SERUM I'm only a man...
And I have to IMPROVISE.
KRIKK
KKRAAK
I DON'T KNOW WHAT -HRNN-... YOU THINK I AM, FRIEND...
BUT I'M NOT LIKE YOU.
I HAVE WORKED MYSELF... TO THE BRINK... IN ORDER TO CONTROL WHAT BURNS INSIDE OF ME.
AND I'LL BE DAMNED IF I LET--
KIRK...
FRANCINE!

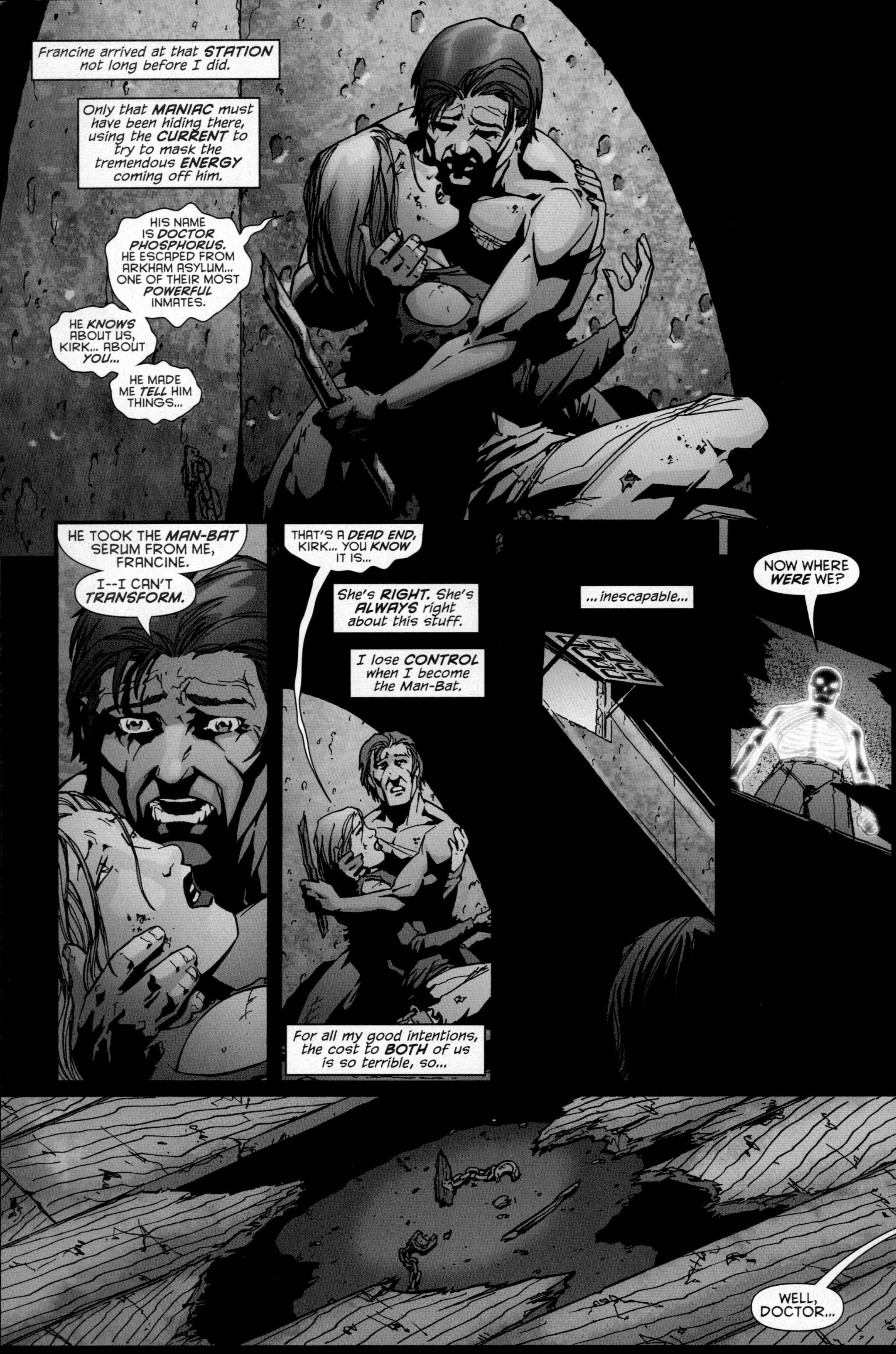
Francine arrived at that **STATION** not long before I did.
Only that **MANIAC** must have been hiding there, using the **CURRENT** to try to mask the tremendous **ENERGY** coming off him.
HIS NAME IS ***DOCTOR PHOSPHORUS.*** HE ESCAPED FROM ARKHAM ASYLUM... ONE OF THEIR MOST ***POWERFUL*** INMATES.
HE ***KNOWS*** ABOUT US, KIRK... ABOUT ***YOU...***
HE MADE ME ***TELL*** HIM THINGS...
HE TOOK THE ***MAN-BAT*** SERUM FROM ME, FRANCINE.
I--I CAN'T ***TRANSFORM.***
THAT'S A ***DEAD END,*** KIRK... YOU ***KNOW*** IT IS...
She's **RIGHT.** She's **ALWAYS** right about this stuff.
I lose **CONTROL** when I become the Man-Bat.
For all my good intentions, the cost to **BOTH** of us is so terrible, so...
...inescapable...
NOW WHERE ***WERE*** WE?
WELL, DOCTOR...

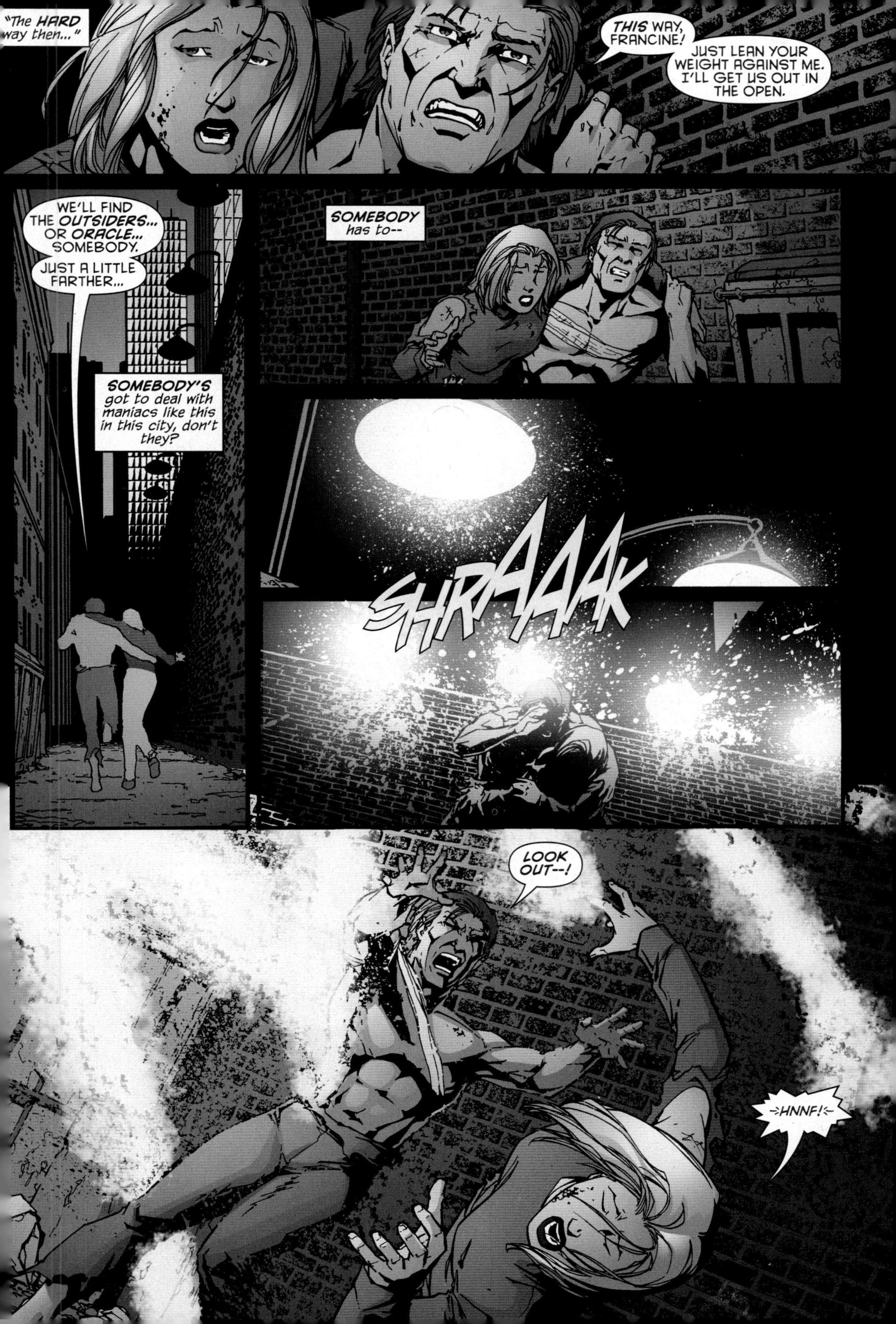
"The HARD way then..."
THIS WAY, FRANCINE!
JUST LEAN YOUR WEIGHT AGAINST ME. I'LL GET US OUT IN THE OPEN.
WE'LL FIND THE OUTSIDERS... OR ORACLE... SOMEBODY.
JUST A LITTLE FARTHER...
SOMEBODY'S got to deal with maniacs like this in this city, don't they?
SOMEBODY has to--
SHRAAAK
LOOK OUT--!
HNNF!

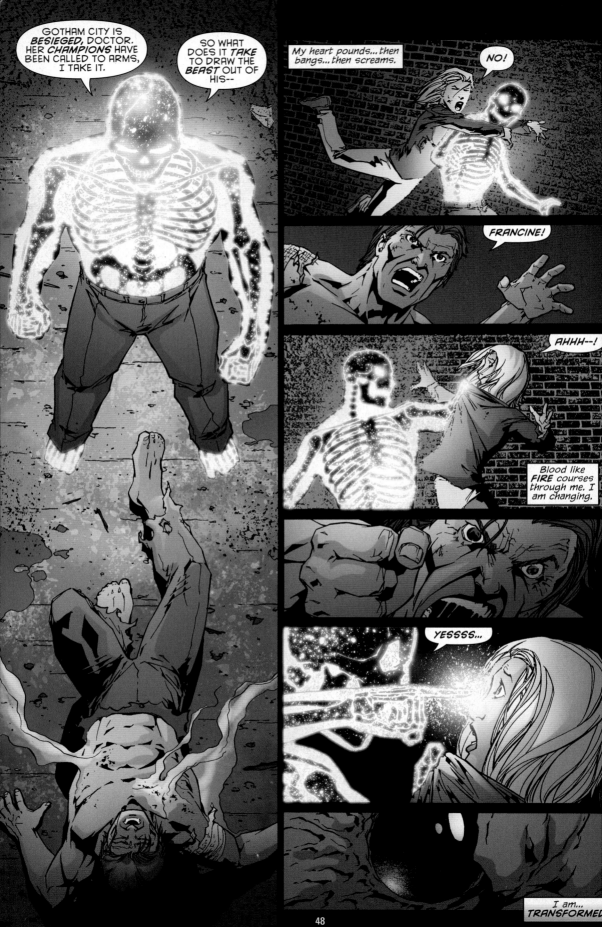

GOTHAM CITY IS *BESIEGED*, DOCTOR. HER *CHAMPIONS* HAVE BEEN CALLED TO ARMS, I TAKE IT.

SO WHAT DOES IT *TAKE* TO DRAW THE *BEAST* OUT OF HIS--

My heart pounds...then bangs...then screams.

NO!

FRANCINE!

AHHH--!

Blood like *FIRE* courses through me. I am changing.

YESSSS...

I am... *TRANSFORMED!*

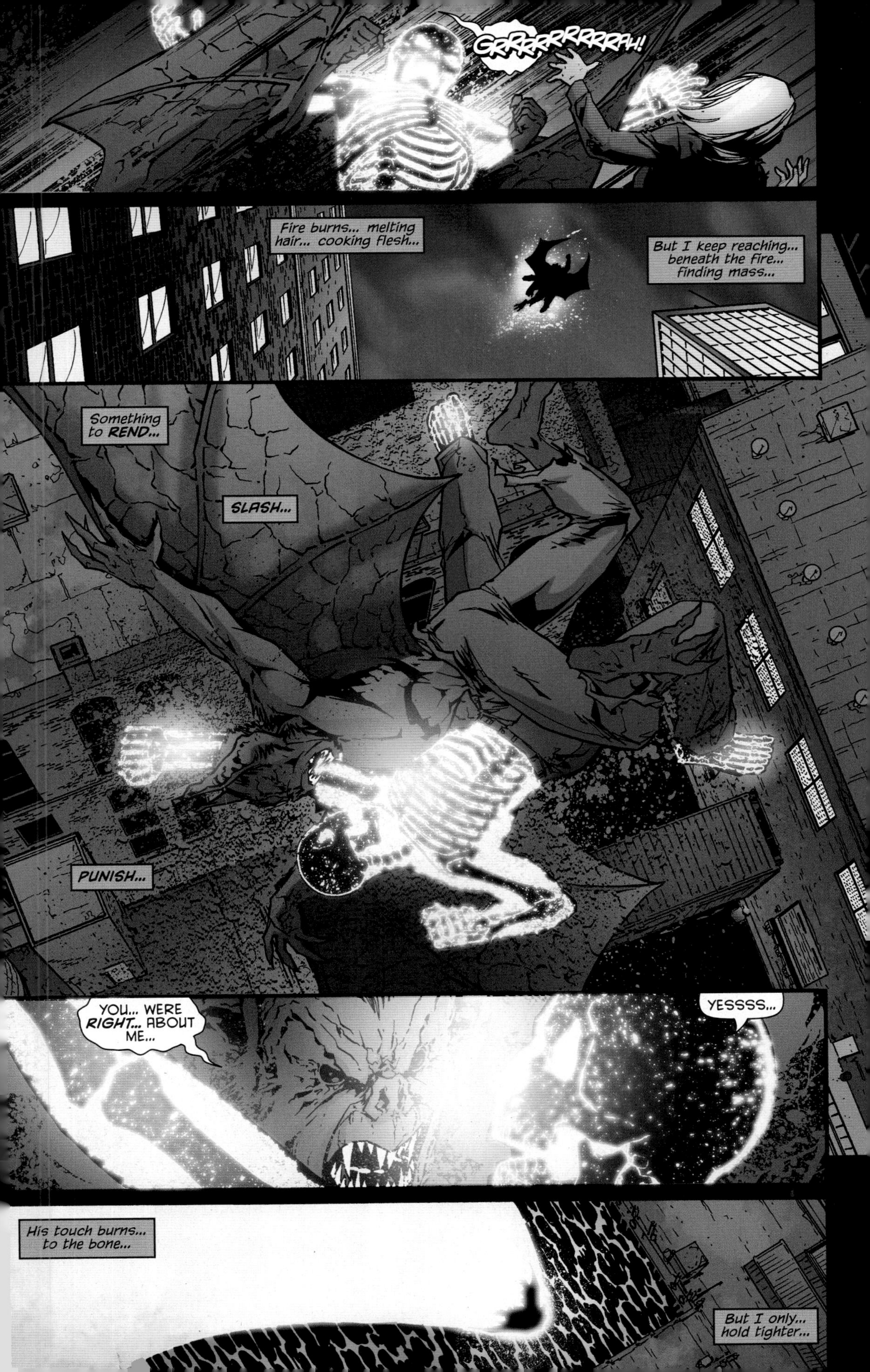
GRRRRRRRRRAH!
Fire burns... melting hair... cooking flesh...
But I keep reaching... beneath the fire... finding mass...
Something to REND...
SLASH...
PUNISH...
YOU... WERE RIGHT... ABOUT ME...
YESSSS...
His touch burns... to the bone...
But I only... hold tighter...

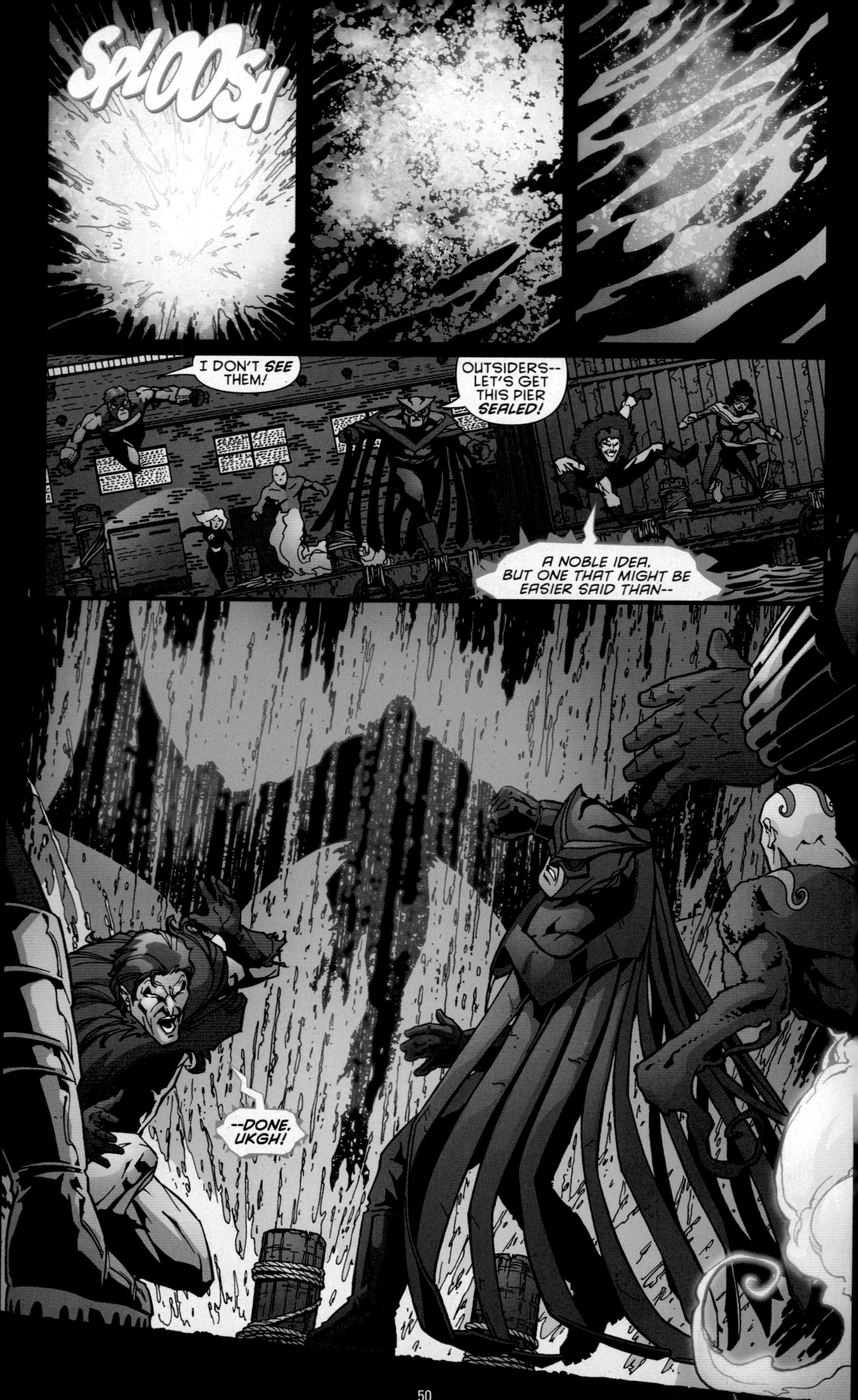
SPLOOSH
I DON'T SEE THEM!
OUTSIDERS-- LET'S GET THIS PIER SEALED!
A NOBLE IDEA. BUT ONE THAT MIGHT BE EASIER SAID THAN--
--DONE. UKGH!

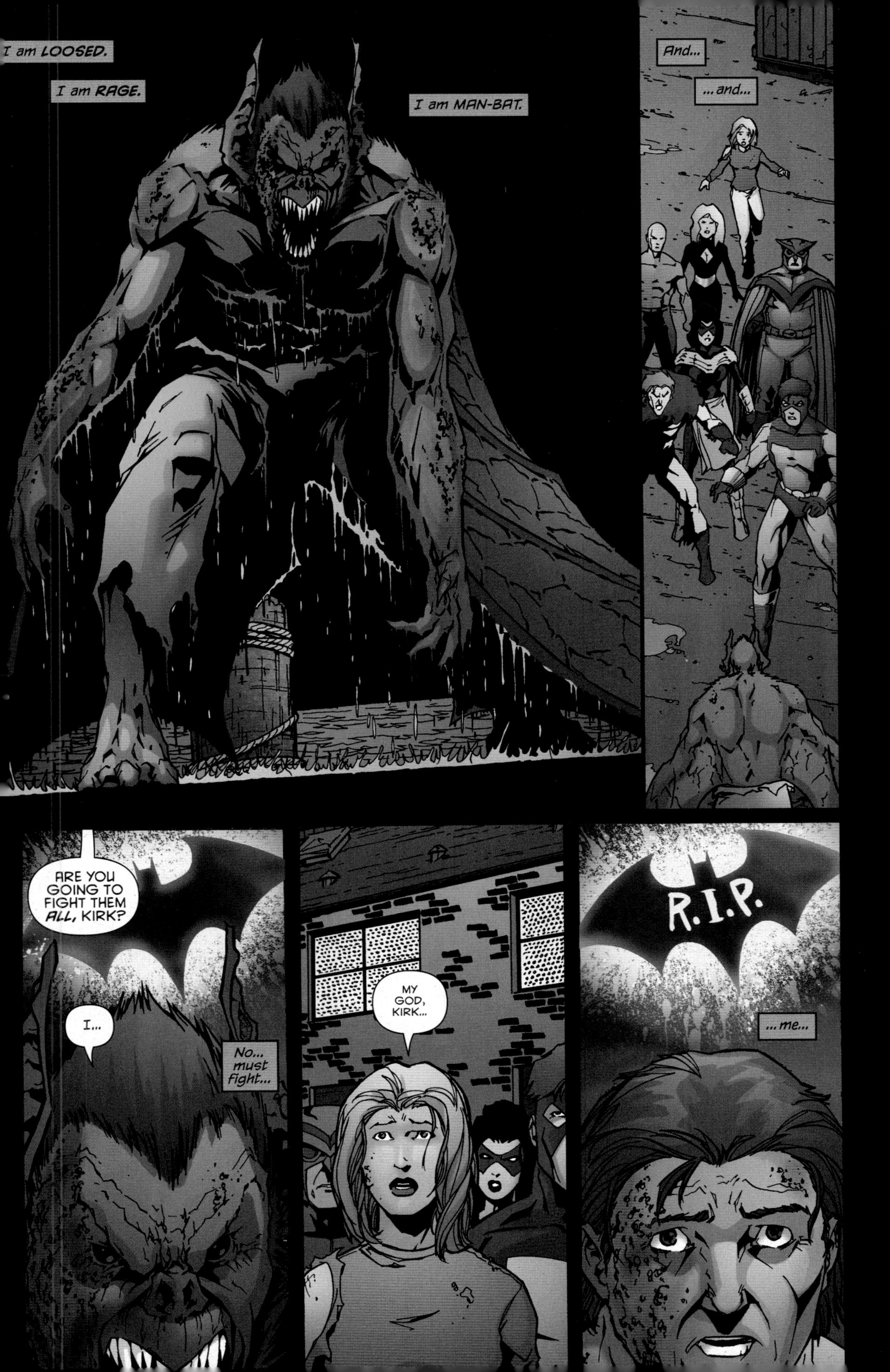

I am LOOSED.
I am RAGE.
I am MAN-BAT.
And...
...and...
ARE YOU GOING TO FIGHT THEM ALL, KIRK?
I...
No... must fight...
MY GOD, KIRK...
R.I.P.
...me...

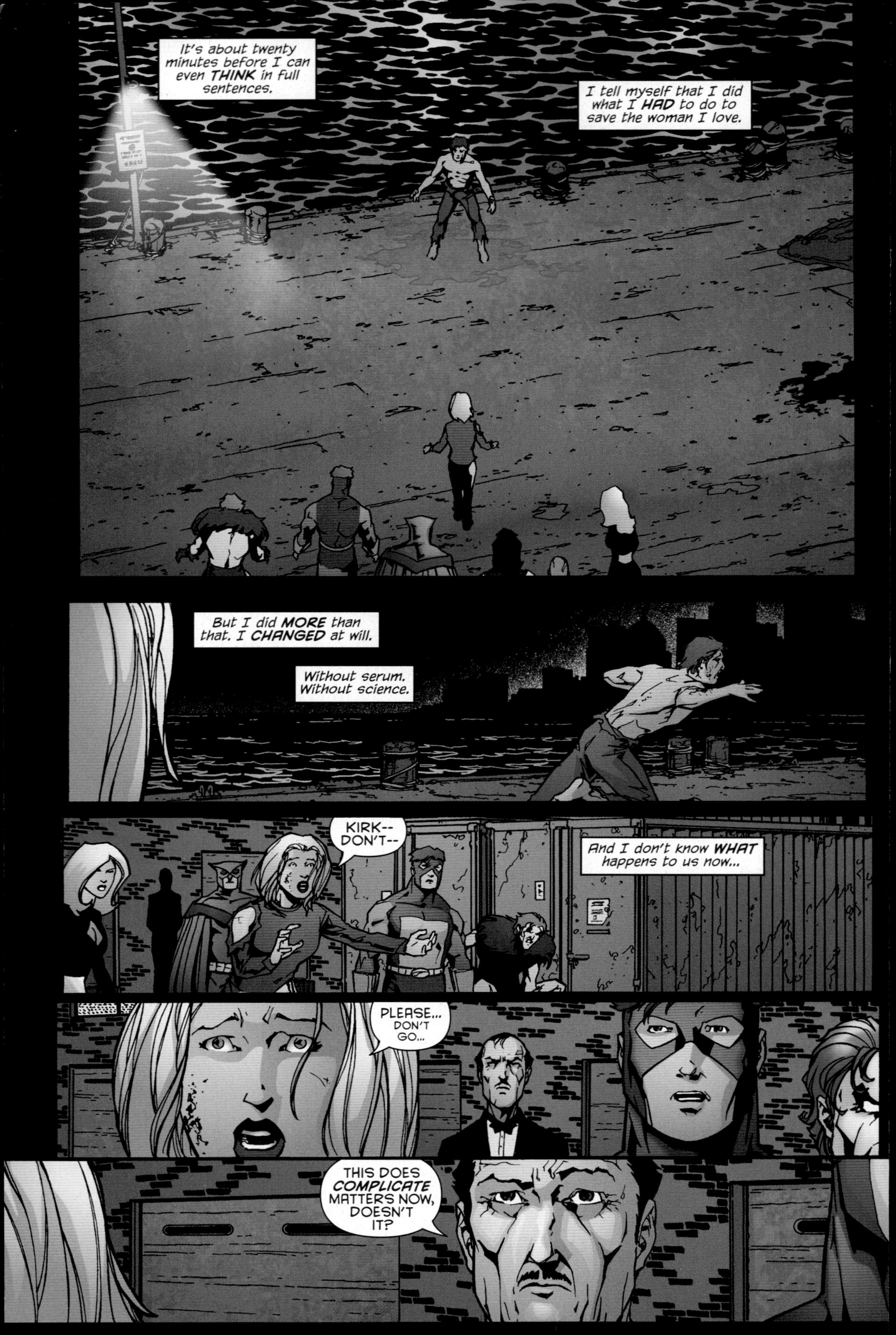
It's about twenty minutes before I can even THINK in full sentences.
I tell myself that I did what I HAD to do to save the woman I love.
But I did MORE than that. I CHANGED at will.
Without serum. Without science.
KIRK-- DON'T--
And I don't know WHAT happens to us now...
PLEASE... DON'T GO...
THIS DOES COMPLICATE MATTERS NOW, DOESN'T IT?

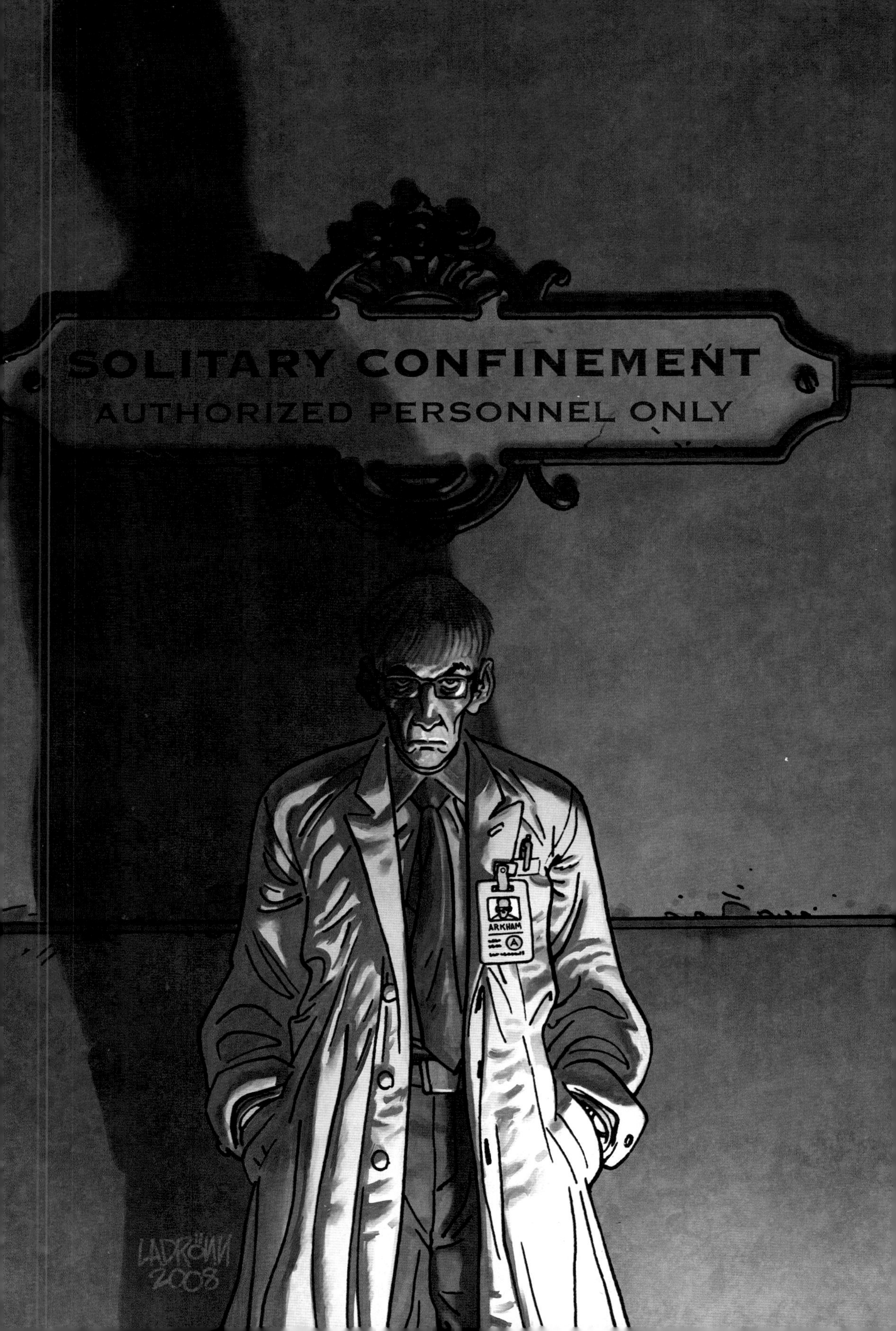
SOLITARY CONFINEMENT
AUTHORIZED PERSONNEL ONLY
ARKHAM
LADRÖNN
2008

THE PLACE WHERE BEAUTY LIES

David Hine
Writer

Jeremy Haun
Artist

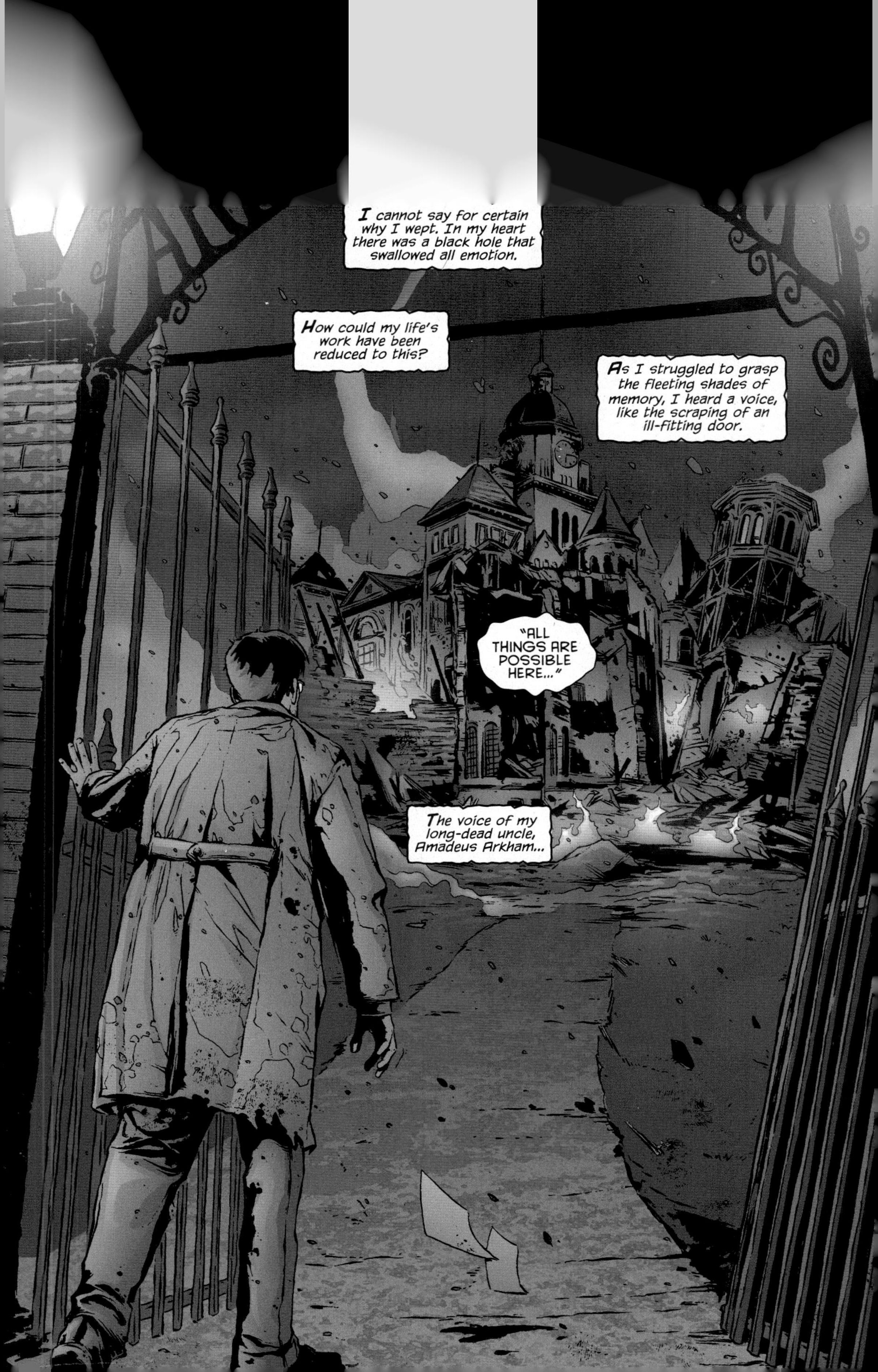

I cannot say for certain why I wept. In my heart there was a black hole that swallowed all emotion.
How could my life's work have been reduced to this?
As I struggled to grasp the fleeting shades of memory, I heard a voice, like the scraping of an ill-fitting door.
"ALL THINGS ARE POSSIBLE HERE..."
The voice of my long-dead uncle, Amadeus Arkham...

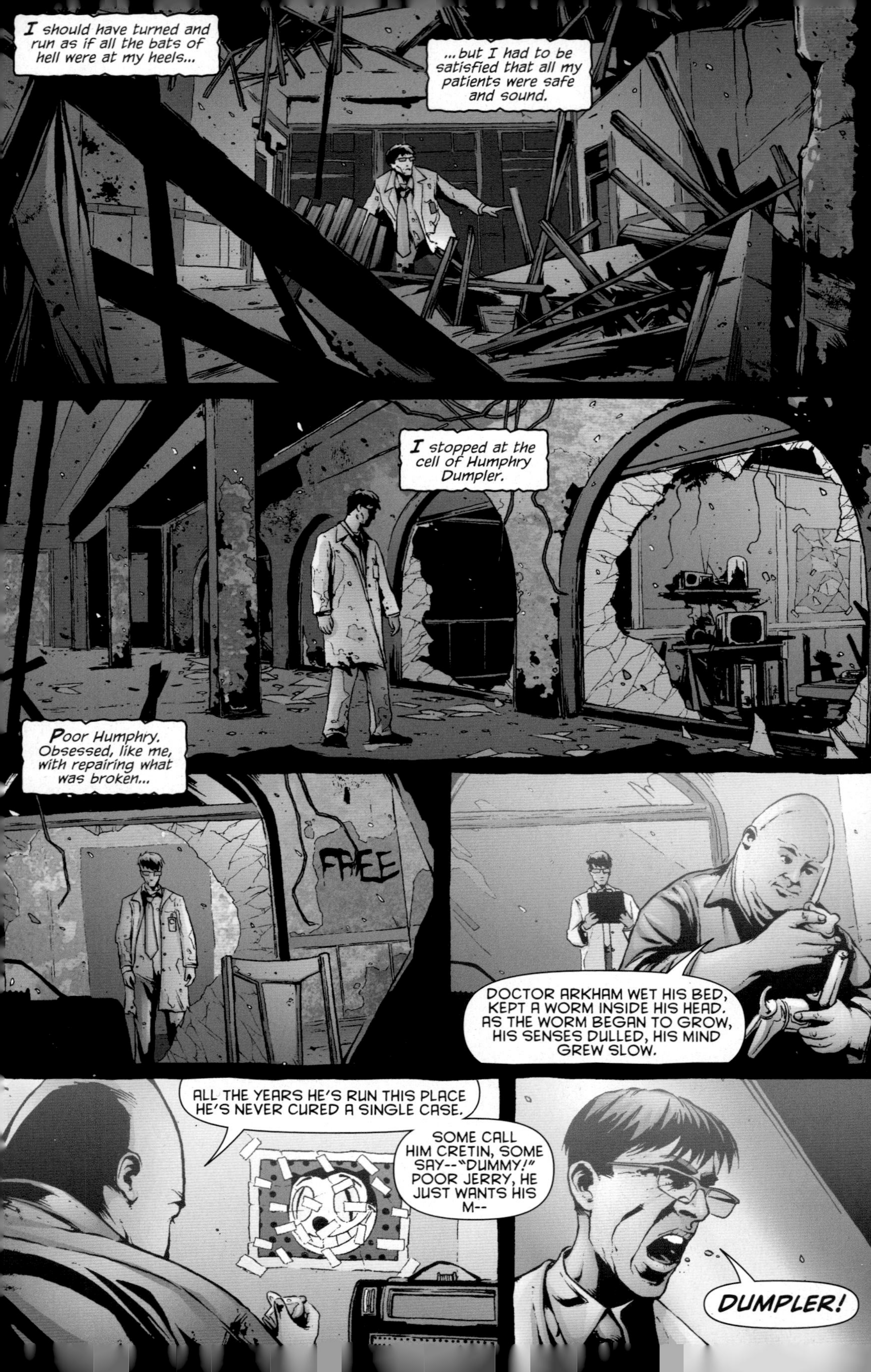
I should have turned and run as if all the bats of hell were at my heels...
...but I had to be satisfied that all my patients were safe and sound.
I stopped at the cell of Humphry Dumpler.
Poor Humphry. Obsessed, like me, with repairing what was broken...
FREE
DOCTOR ARKHAM WET HIS BED, KEPT A WORM INSIDE HIS HEAD. AS THE WORM BEGAN TO GROW, HIS SENSES DULLED, HIS MIND GREW SLOW.
ALL THE YEARS HE'S RUN THIS PLACE HE'S NEVER CURED A SINGLE CASE.
SOME CALL HIM CRETIN, SOME SAY--"DUMMY!" POOR JERRY, HE JUST WANTS HIS M--
DUMPLER!

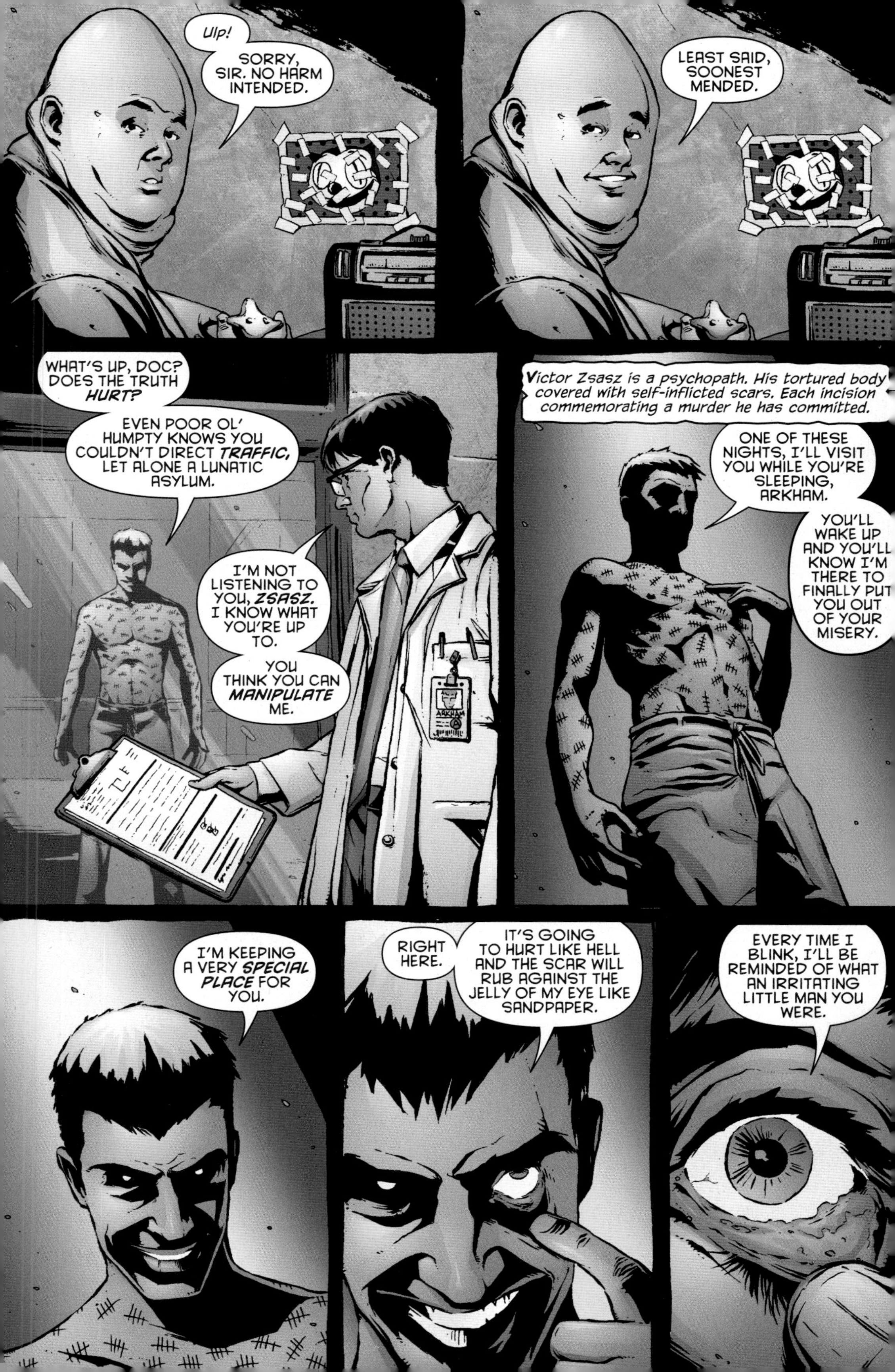
Ulp!
SORRY, SIR. NO HARM INTENDED.
LEAST SAID, SOONEST MENDED.
WHAT'S UP, DOC? DOES THE TRUTH HURT?
EVEN POOR OL' HUMPTY KNOWS YOU COULDN'T DIRECT TRAFFIC, LET ALONE A LUNATIC ASYLUM.
I'M NOT LISTENING TO YOU, ZSASZ. I KNOW WHAT YOU'RE UP TO.
YOU THINK YOU CAN MANIPULATE ME.
ARKHAM
Victor Zsasz is a psychopath. His tortured body covered with self-inflicted scars. Each incision commemorating a murder he has committed.
ONE OF THESE NIGHTS, I'LL VISIT YOU WHILE YOU'RE SLEEPING, ARKHAM.
YOU'LL WAKE UP AND YOU'LL KNOW I'M THERE TO FINALLY PUT YOU OUT OF YOUR MISERY.
I'M KEEPING A VERY SPECIAL PLACE FOR YOU.
RIGHT HERE.
IT'S GOING TO HURT LIKE HELL AND THE SCAR WILL RUB AGAINST THE JELLY OF MY EYE LIKE SANDPAPER.
EVERY TIME I BLINK, I'LL BE REMINDED OF WHAT AN IRRITATING LITTLE MAN YOU WERE.

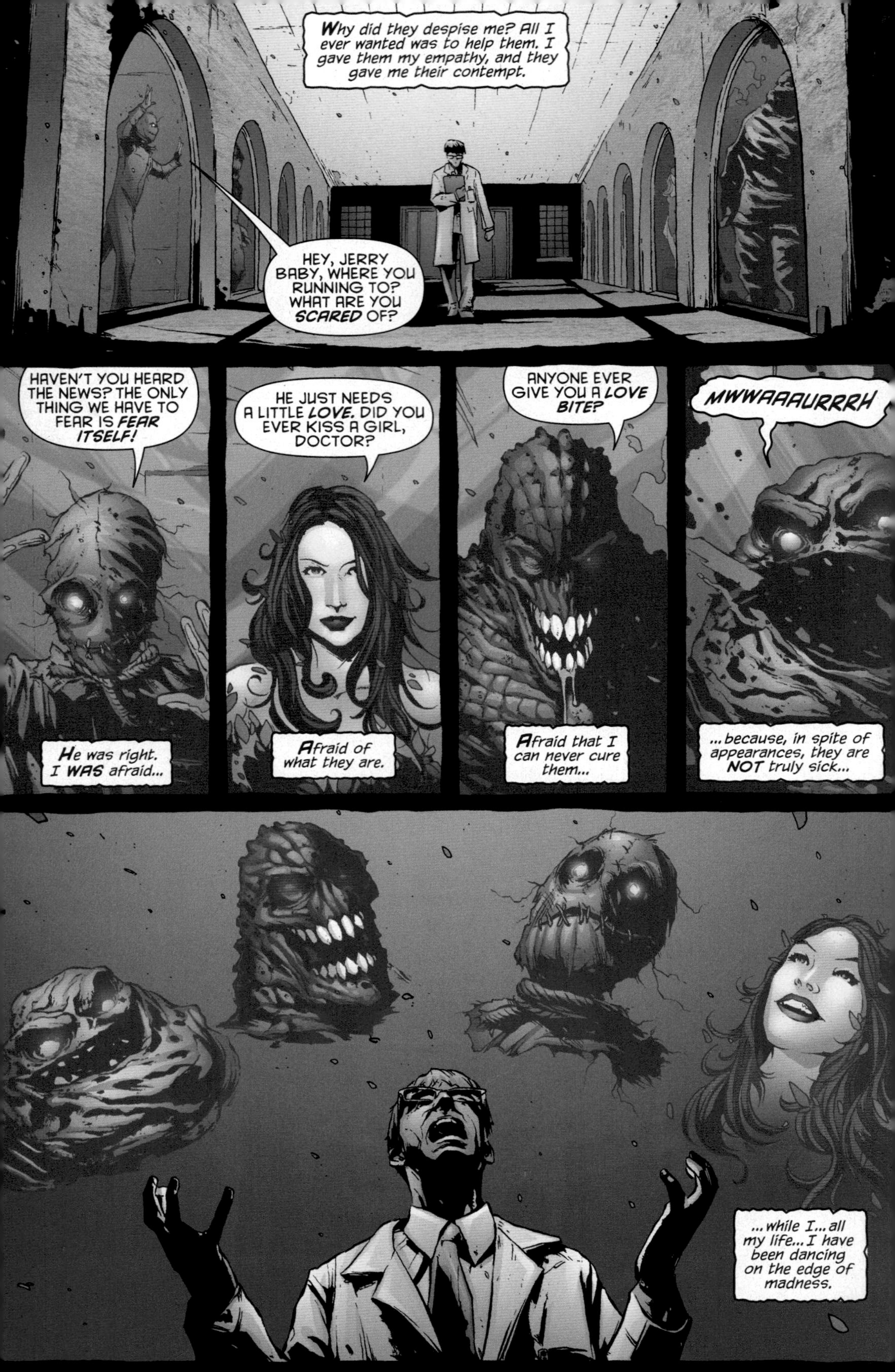
Why did they despise me? All I ever wanted was to help them. I gave them my empathy, and they gave me their contempt.
HEY, JERRY BABY, WHERE YOU RUNNING TO? WHAT ARE YOU SCARED OF?
HAVEN'T YOU HEARD THE NEWS? THE ONLY THING WE HAVE TO FEAR IS FEAR ITSELF!
He was right. I WAS afraid...
HE JUST NEEDS A LITTLE LOVE. DID YOU EVER KISS A GIRL, DOCTOR?
Afraid of what they are.
ANYONE EVER GIVE YOU A LOVE BITE?
Afraid that I can never cure them...
MWWAAAAURRRH
...because, in spite of appearances, they are NOT truly sick...
...while I... all my life... I have been dancing on the edge of madness.

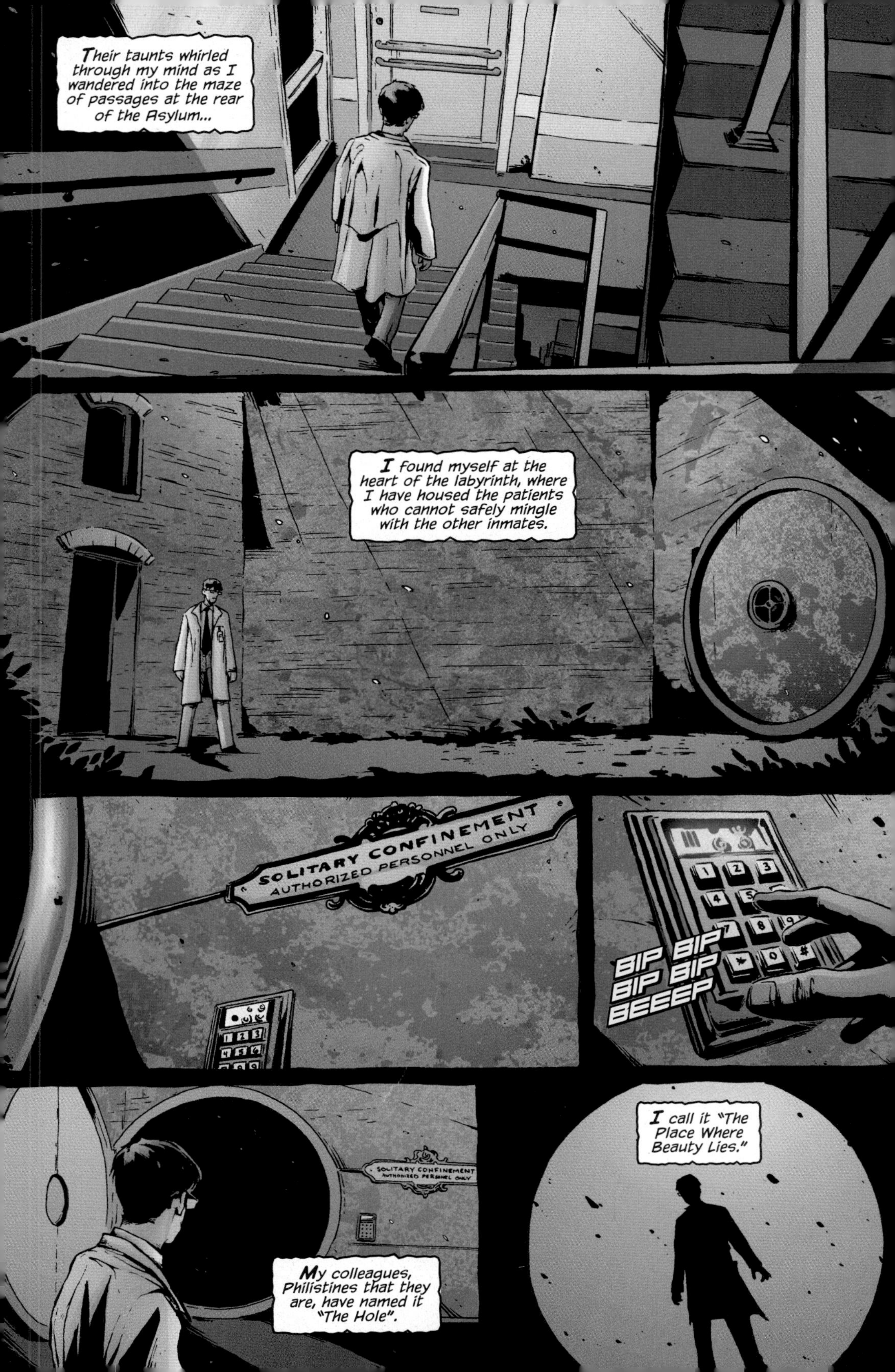
Their taunts whirled through my mind as I wandered into the maze of passages at the rear of the Asylum...
I found myself at the heart of the labyrinth, where I have housed the patients who cannot safely mingle with the other inmates.
SOLITARY CONFINEMENT
AUTHORIZED PERSONNEL ONLY
BIP BIP
BIP BIP
BEEEP
SOLITARY CONFINEMENT
AUTHORIZED PERSONNEL ONLY
My colleagues, Philistines that they are, have named it "The Hole".
I call it "The Place Where Beauty Lies."

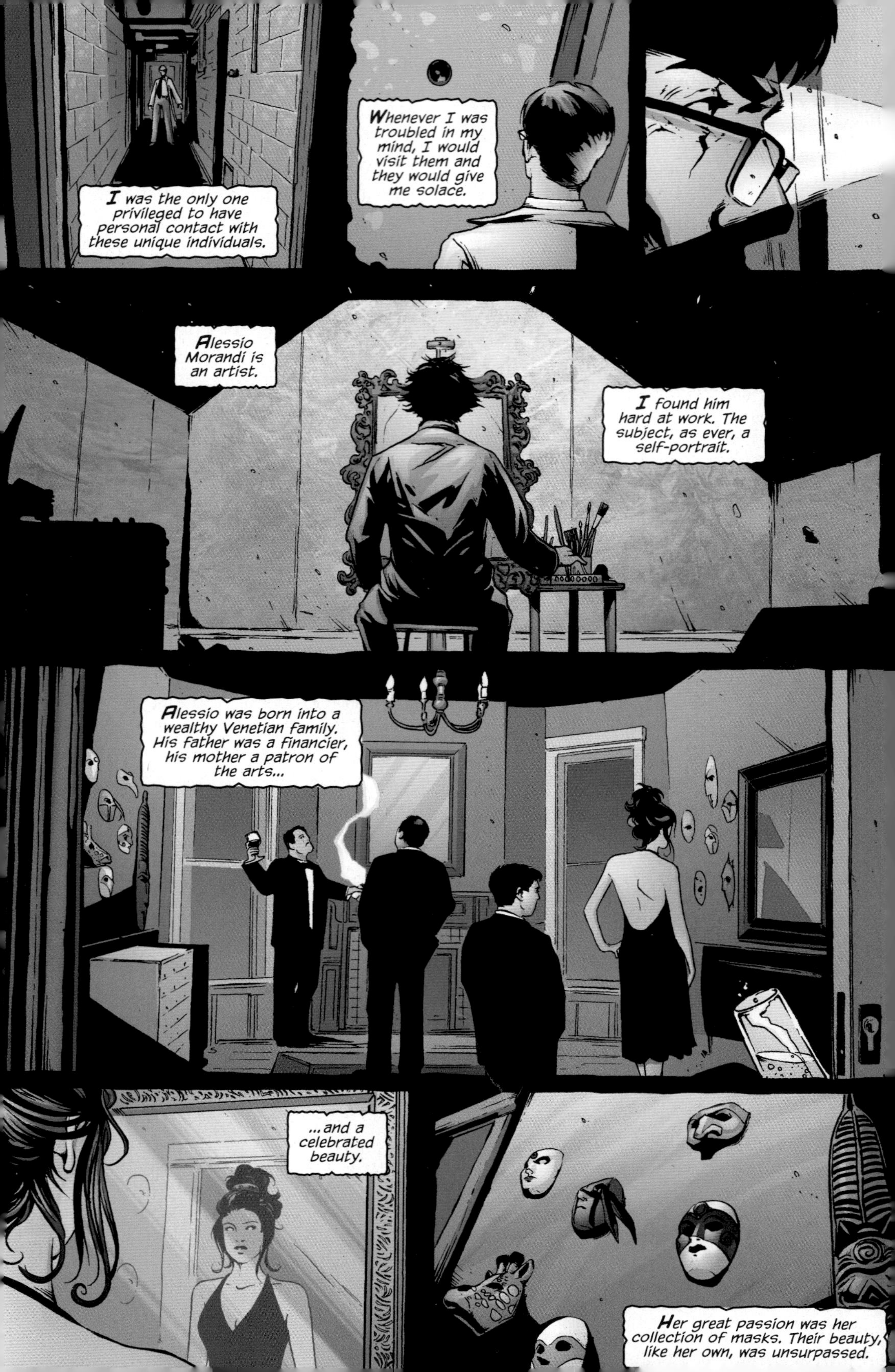
I was the only one privileged to have personal contact with these unique individuals.
Whenever I was troubled in my mind, I would visit them and they would give me solace.
Alessio Morandi is an artist.
I found him hard at work. The subject, as ever, a self-portrait.
Alessio was born into a wealthy Venetian family. His father was a financier, his mother a patron of the arts...
...and a celebrated beauty.
Her great passion was her collection of masks. Their beauty, like her own, was unsurpassed.

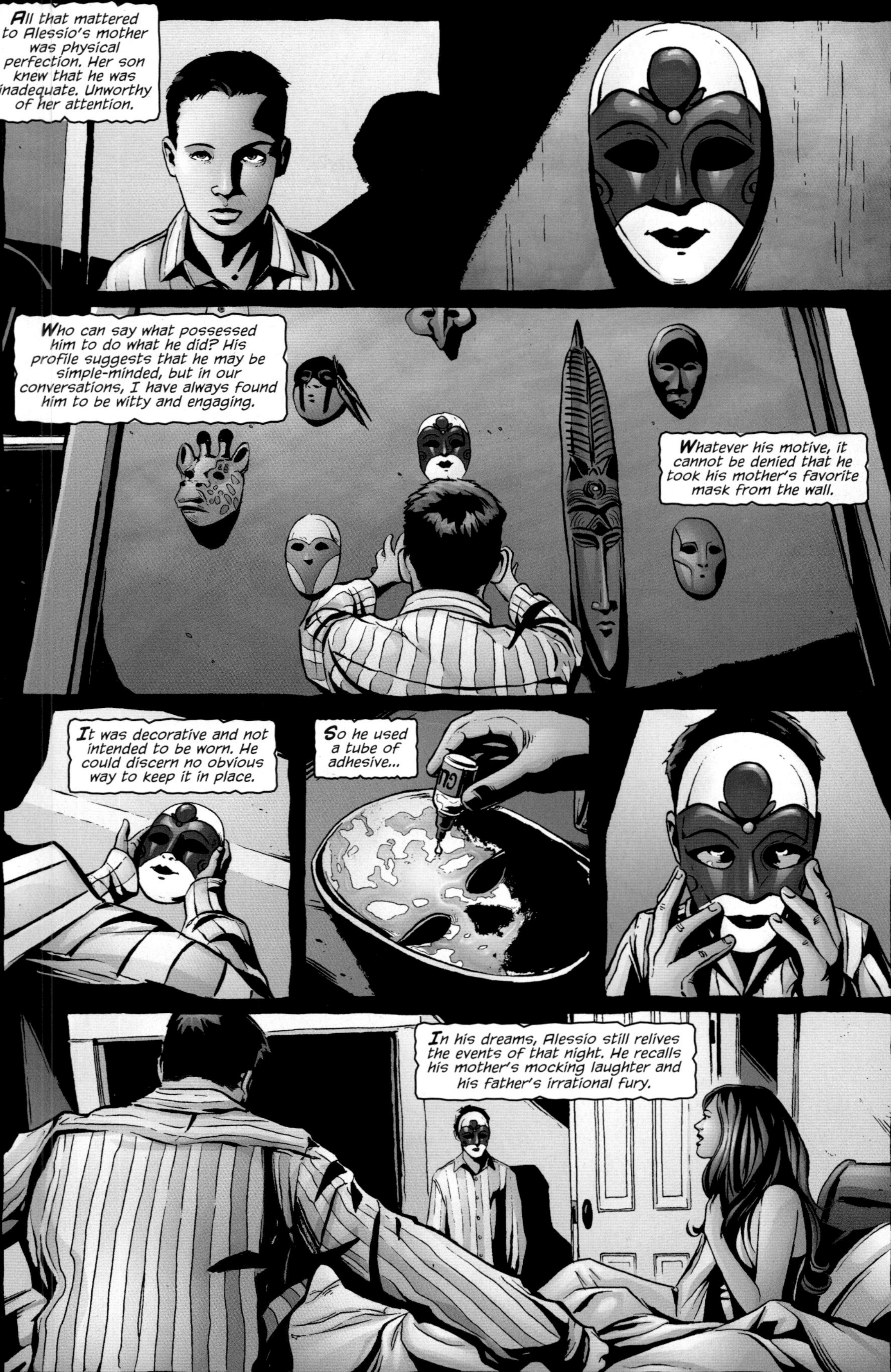
All that mattered to Alessio's mother was physical perfection. Her son knew that he was inadequate. Unworthy of her attention.
Who can say what possessed him to do what he did? His profile suggests that he may be simple-minded, but in our conversations, I have always found him to be witty and engaging.
Whatever his motive, it cannot be denied that he took his mother's favorite mask from the wall.
It was decorative and not intended to be worn. He could discern no obvious way to keep it in place.
So he used a tube of adhesive...
In his dreams, Alessio still relives the events of that night. He recalls his mother's mocking laughter and his father's irrational fury.

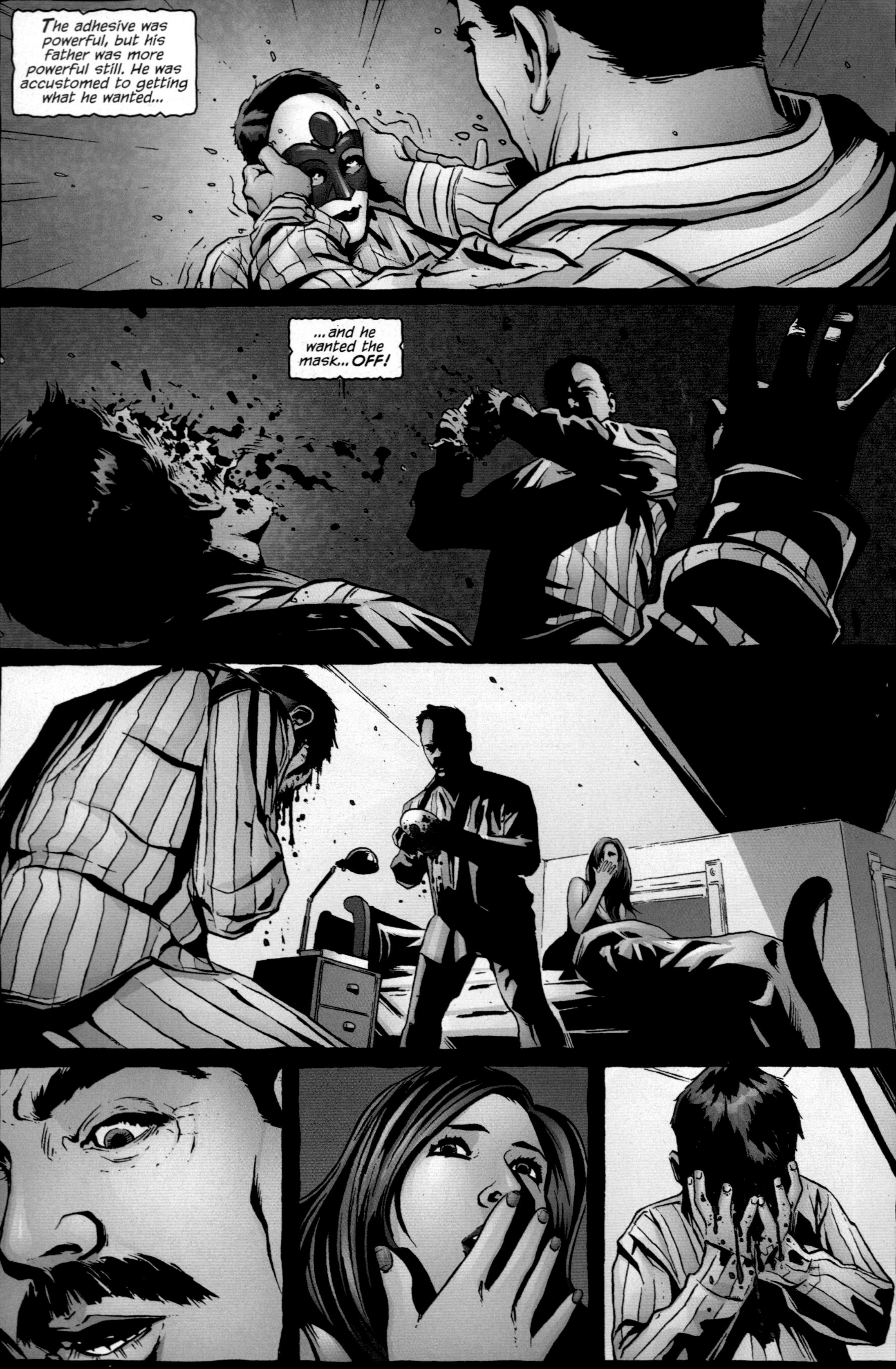
The adhesive was powerful, but his father was more powerful still. He was accustomed to getting what he wanted...
...and he wanted the mask... OFF!

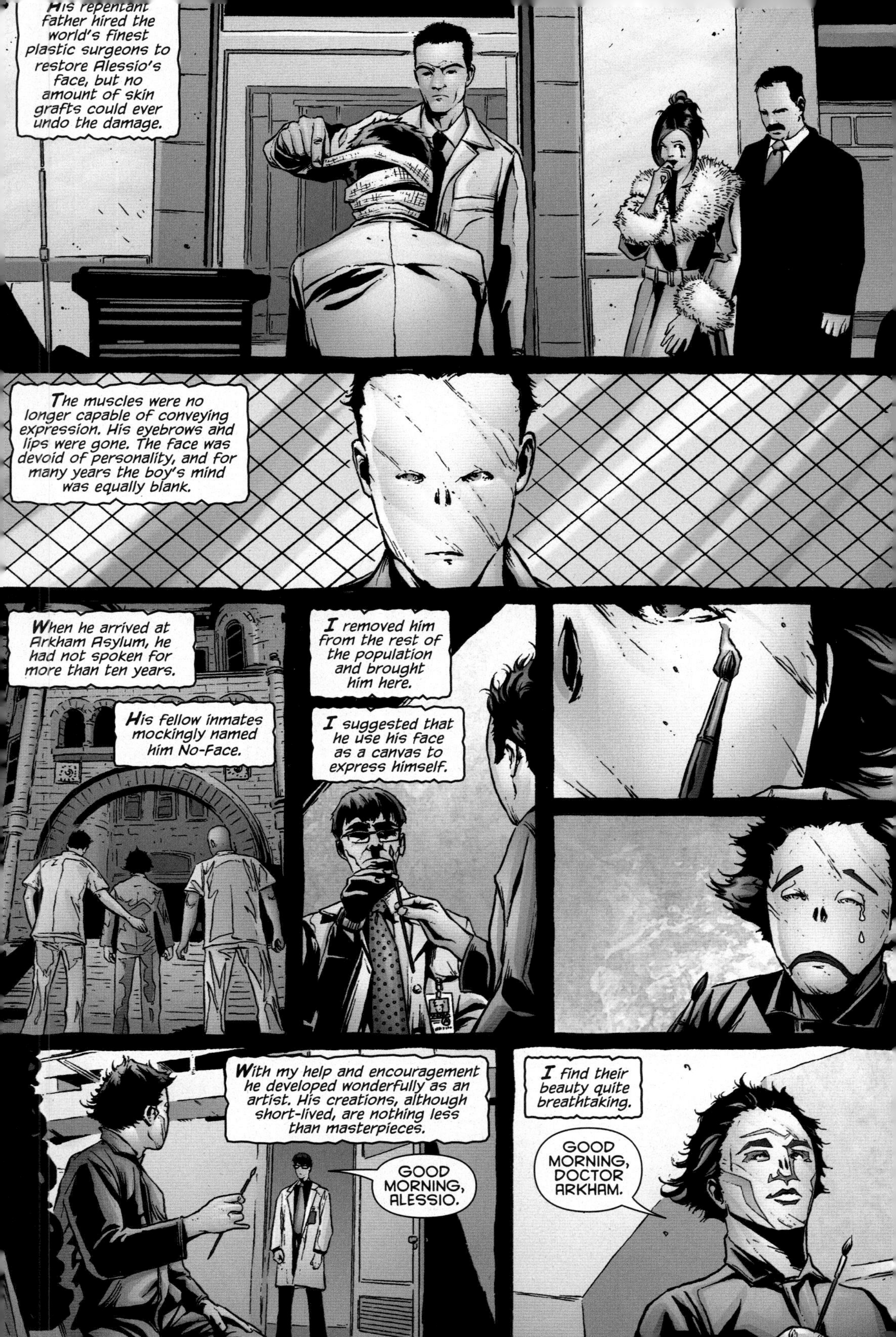
His repentant father hired the world's finest plastic surgeons to restore Alessio's face, but no amount of skin grafts could ever undo the damage.
The muscles were no longer capable of conveying expression. His eyebrows and lips were gone. The face was devoid of personality, and for many years the boy's mind was equally blank.
When he arrived at Arkham Asylum, he had not spoken for more than ten years.
His fellow inmates mockingly named him No-Face.
I removed him from the rest of the population and brought him here.
I suggested that he use his face as a canvas to express himself.
With my help and encouragement he developed wonderfully as an artist. His creations, although short-lived, are nothing less than masterpieces.
GOOD MORNING, ALESSIO.
I find their beauty quite breathtaking.
GOOD MORNING, DOCTOR ARKHAM.

My second visit, that fateful day, was to the Mirror Man.

He came to us without a name, but I called him Narcissus, for like the mythological hero, he spends his time in idle contemplation of his own reflection.

He whispers to himself endlessly in a language that no one can identify and he truly appears to adore himself with the passion of a lover.

Five years ago, Narcissus walked out of the forest in Haiti.

There are no clues to his past. The only intelligible words he speaks are those he repeats like an echo.

YOU'RE LOOKING SPLENDID TODAY.

...SPLENDID...

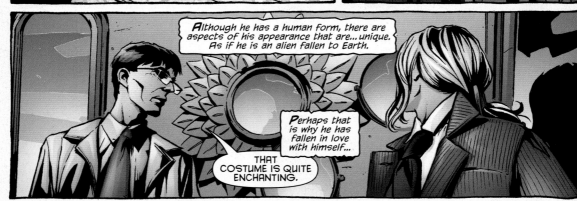

Although he has a human form, there are aspects of his appearance that are... unique. As if he is an alien fallen to Earth.

Perhaps that is why he has fallen in love with himself...

THAT COSTUME IS QUITE ENCHANTING.

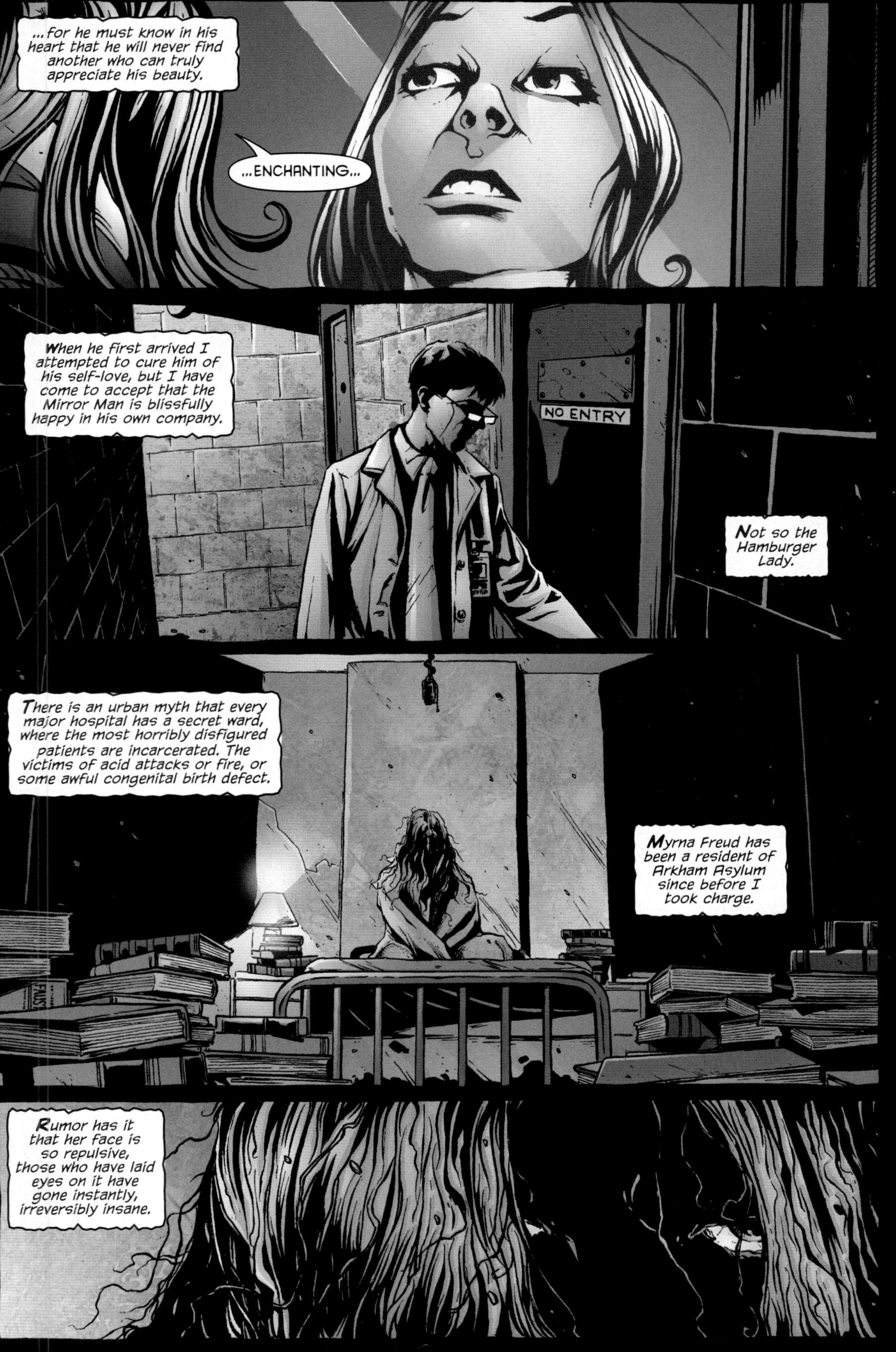
...for he must know in his heart that he will never find another who can truly appreciate his beauty.
...ENCHANTING...
When he first arrived I attempted to cure him of his self-love, but I have come to accept that the Mirror Man is blissfully happy in his own company.
NO ENTRY
Not so the Hamburger Lady.
There is an urban myth that every major hospital has a secret ward, where the most horribly disfigured patients are incarcerated. The victims of acid attacks or fire, or some awful congenital birth defect.
Myrna Freud has been a resident of Arkham Asylum since before I took charge.
Rumor has it that her face is so repulsive, those who have laid eyes on it have gone instantly, irreversibly insane.

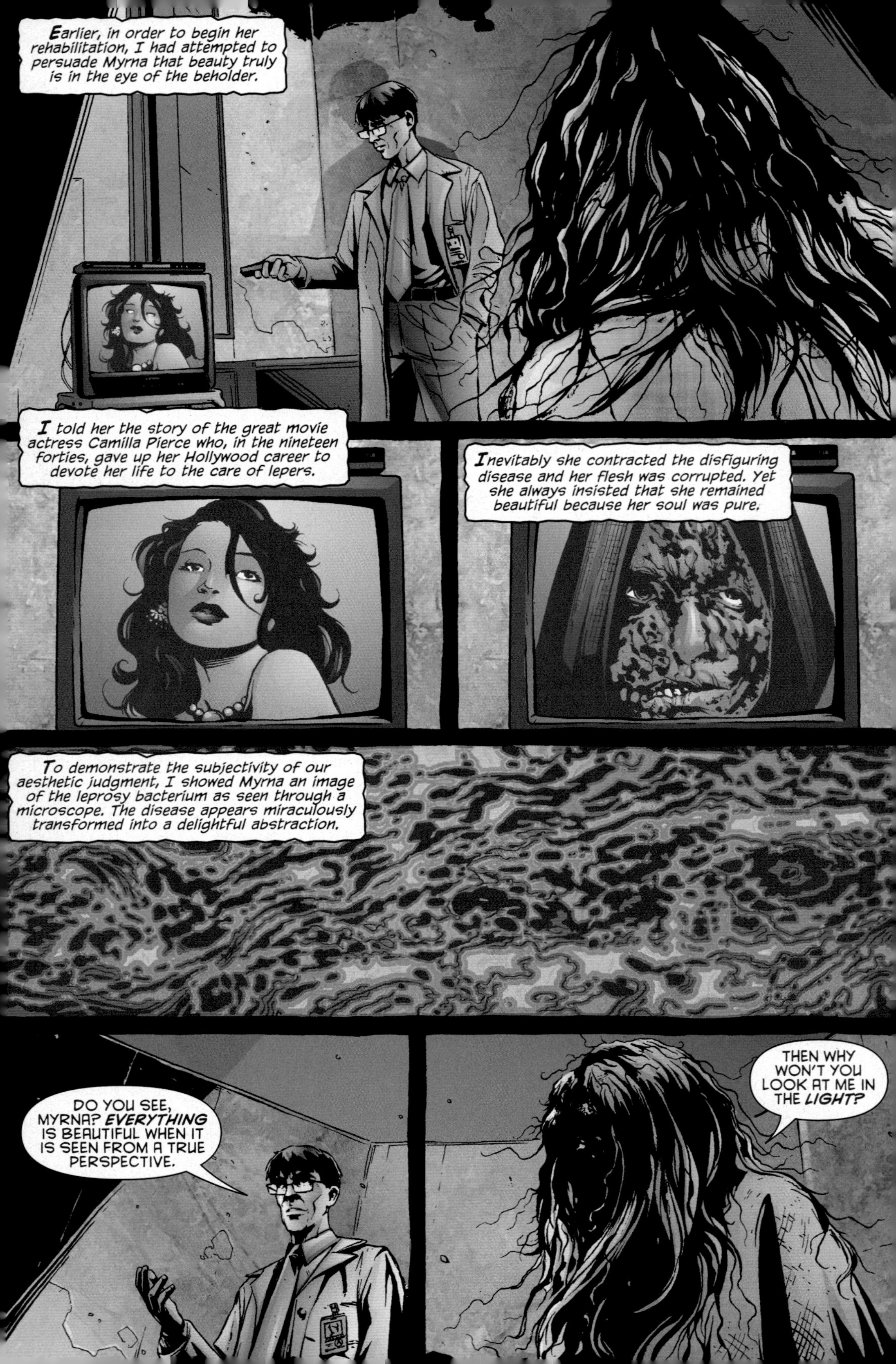

Earlier, in order to begin her rehabilitation, I had attempted to persuade Myrna that beauty truly is in the eye of the beholder.
I told her the story of the great movie actress Camilla Pierce who, in the nineteen forties, gave up her Hollywood career to devote her life to the care of lepers.
Inevitably she contracted the disfiguring disease and her flesh was corrupted. Yet she always insisted that she remained beautiful because her soul was pure.
To demonstrate the subjectivity of our aesthetic judgment, I showed Myrna an image of the leprosy bacterium as seen through a microscope. The disease appears miraculously transformed into a delightful abstraction.
DO YOU SEE, MYRNA? EVERYTHING IS BEAUTIFUL WHEN IT IS SEEN FROM A TRUE PERSPECTIVE.
THEN WHY WON'T YOU LOOK AT ME IN THE LIGHT?

She had a point, of course. And so I finally decided to practice what I preach.

WHAT ARE YOU DOING?

IT'S TIME YOU HAD SOME DECENT ILLUMINATION IN HERE.

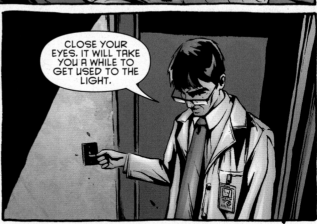

CLOSE YOUR EYES. IT WILL TAKE YOU A WHILE TO GET USED TO THE LIGHT.

Then she lifted her head, and her hair fell away from her ravaged features.

WELL?

As I gazed upon that dreadful face, I felt as if the scales had fallen from my eyes. It was a revelation that would change my life forever.

The following day, I entered my office in a state of exhilaration, to find that some mysterious intruder had penetrated my sanctum.

PERVERTED TWISTED CRIPPLED

PERVERTED TWISTED CRIPPLED

Who was the message intended for? Myself? The inmates of the Asylum? Or was it a comment on the entire human race?

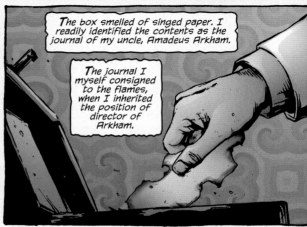

The box smelled of singed paper. I readily identified the contents as the journal of my uncle, Amadeus Arkham.

The journal I myself consigned to the flames, when I inherited the position of director of Arkham.

The house is an organism, hungry for madness.

Madness is born in the blood. It is my birthright.

Who could have rescued the pages from the flames? And why did they choose to leave them here now?

As I read the brief passages that had survived, I saw that my uncle, although deeply troubled, perceived the world with a clarity that rivaled my own.

He had a vision for the Asylum.

"SEE THE TRUTH THAT LIES BEHIND REFLECTION."

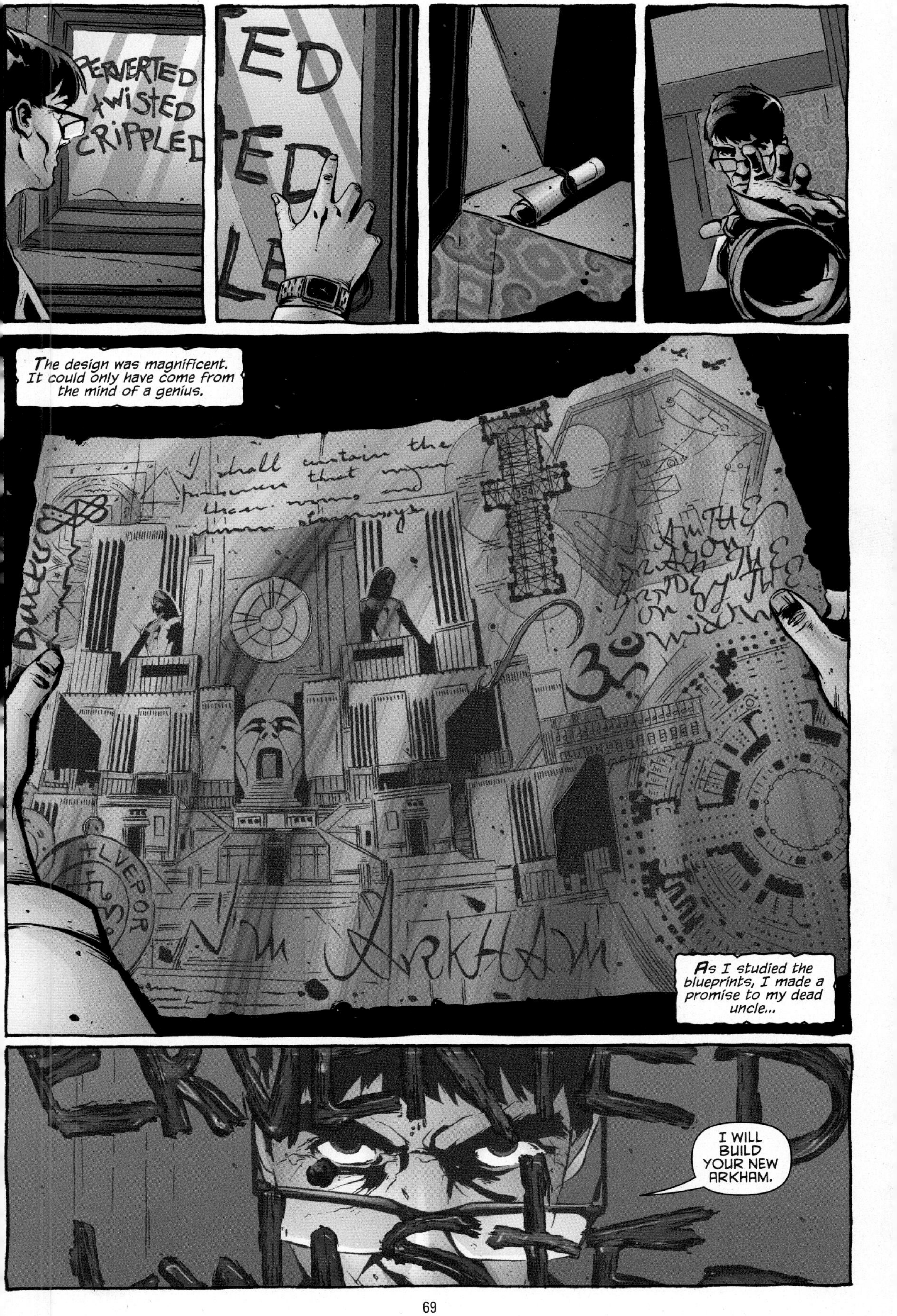
PERVERTED
twisted
CRIPPLED
The design was magnificent. It could only have come from the mind of a genius.
As I studied the blueprints, I made a promise to my dead uncle...
I WILL BUILD YOUR NEW ARKHAM.

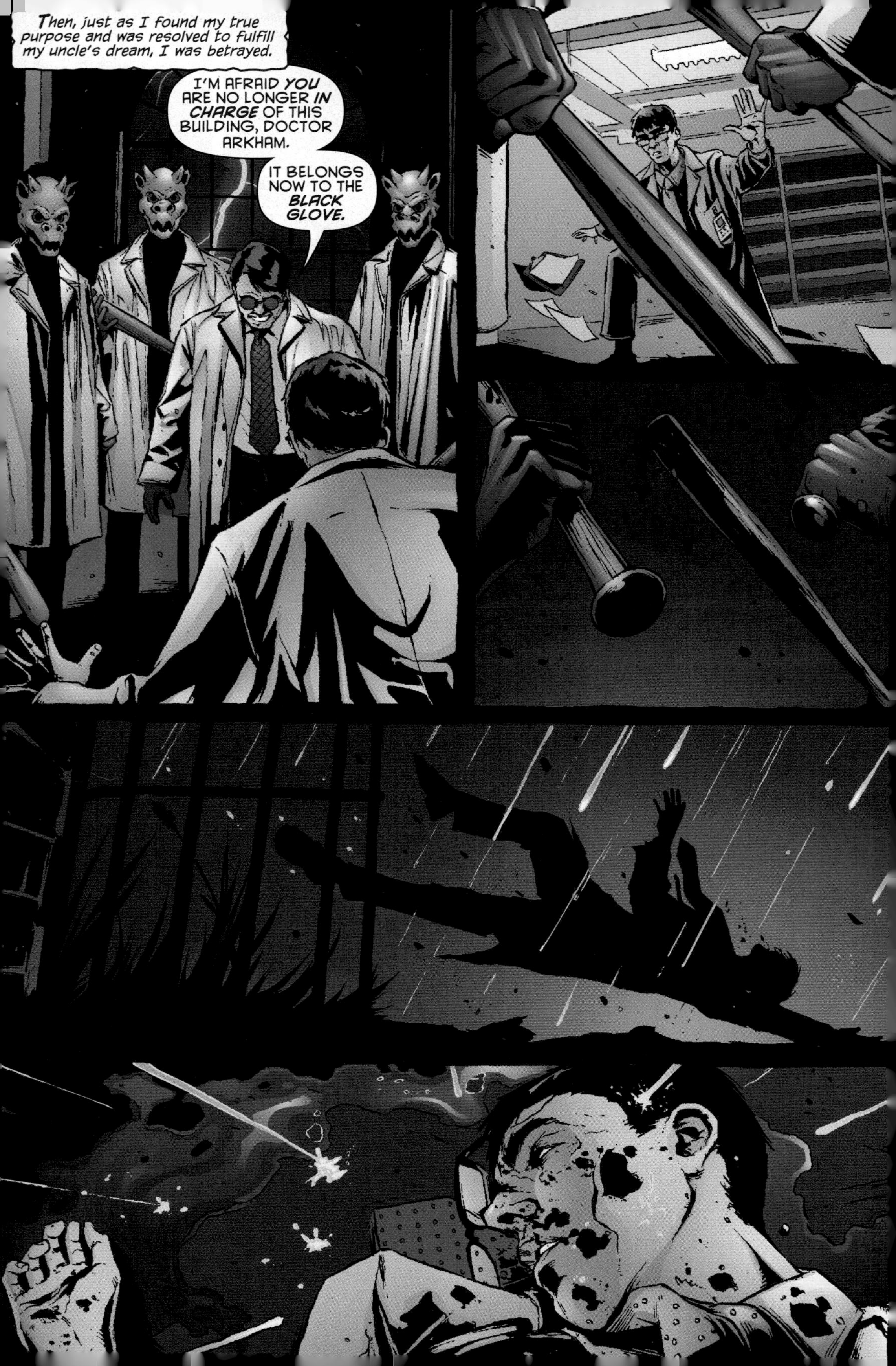
Then, just as I found my true purpose and was resolved to fulfill my uncle's dream, I was betrayed.
I'M AFRAID YOU ARE NO LONGER IN CHARGE OF THIS BUILDING, DOCTOR ARKHAM.
IT BELONGS NOW TO THE BLACK GLOVE.

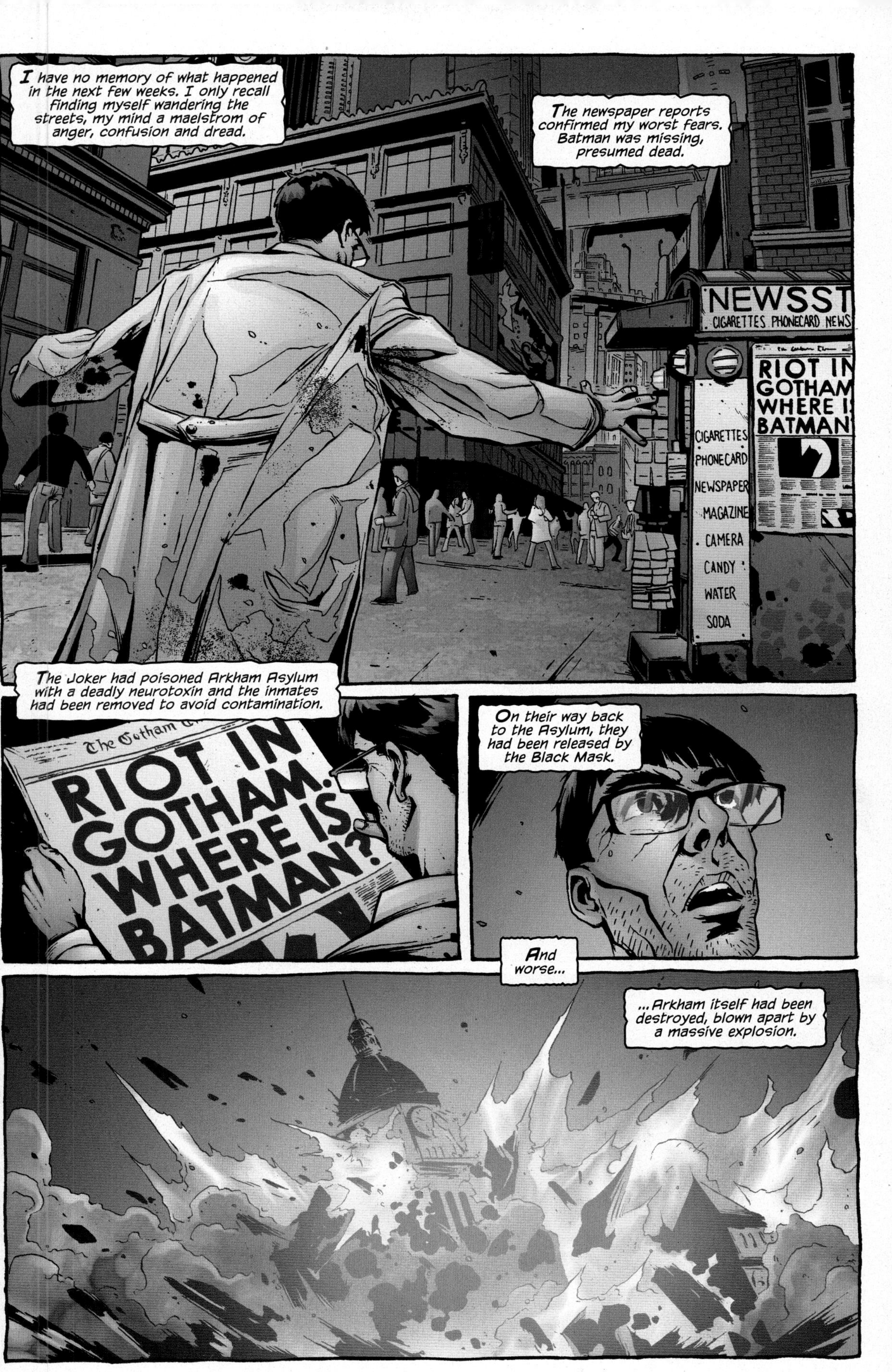
I have no memory of what happened in the next few weeks. I only recall finding myself wandering the streets, my mind a maelstrom of anger, confusion and dread.
The newspaper reports confirmed my worst fears. Batman was missing, presumed dead.
NEWSST
CIGARETTES PHONECARD NEWS
RIOT IN GOTHAM WHERE IS BATMAN
CIGARETTES
PHONECARD
NEWSPAPER
MAGAZINE
CAMERA
CANDY
WATER
SODA
The Joker had poisoned Arkham Asylum with a deadly neurotoxin and the inmates had been removed to avoid contamination.
The Gotham
RIOT IN GOTHAM. WHERE IS BATMAN?
On their way back to the Asylum, they had been released by the Black Mask.
And worse...
...Arkham itself had been destroyed, blown apart by a massive explosion.

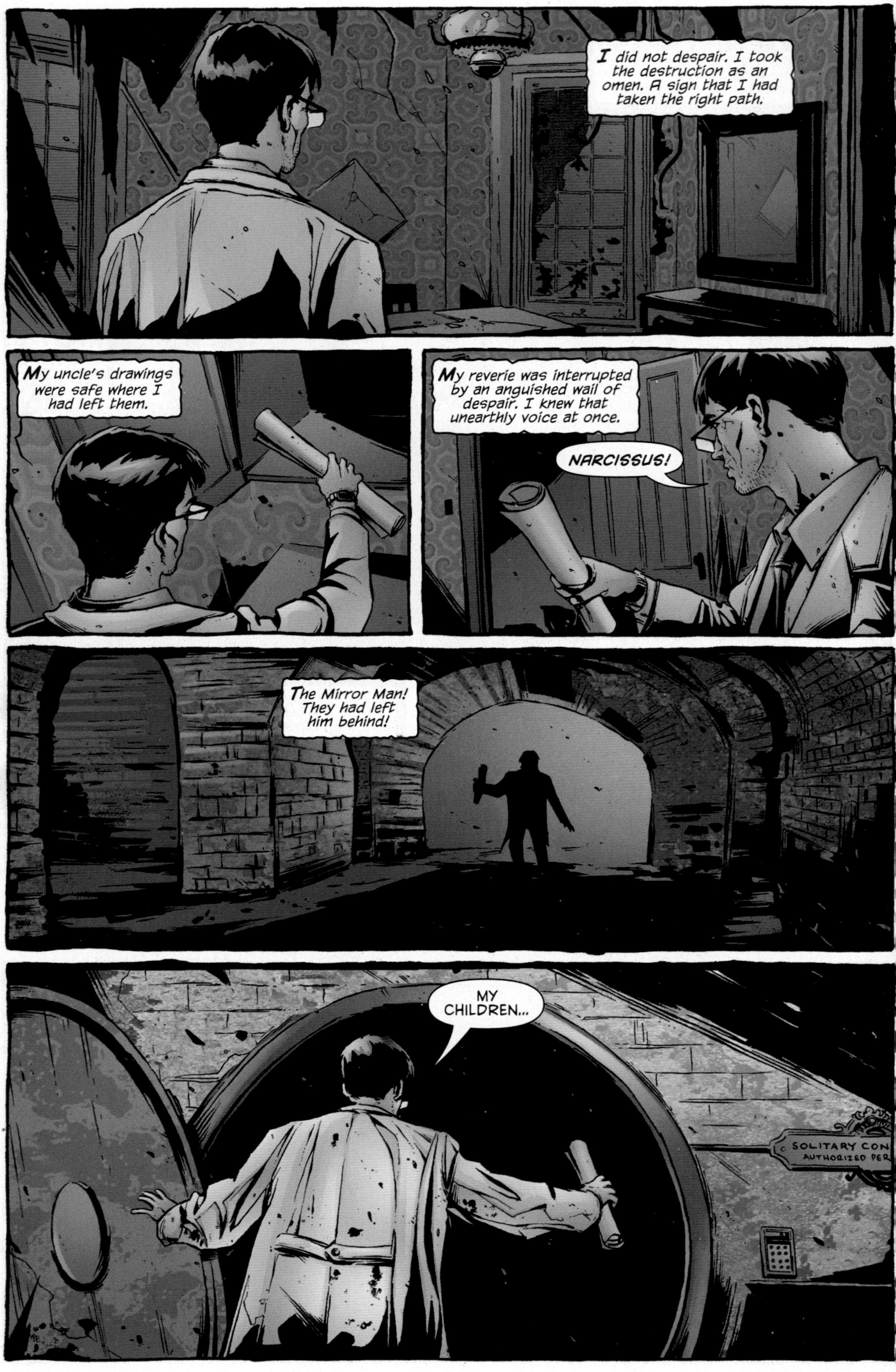
I did not despair. I took the destruction as an omen. A sign that I had taken the right path.
My uncle's drawings were safe where I had left them.
My reverie was interrupted by an anguished wail of despair. I knew that unearthly voice at once.
NARCISSUS!
The Mirror Man! They had left him behind!
MY CHILDREN...
SOLITARY CON
AUTHORIZED PER

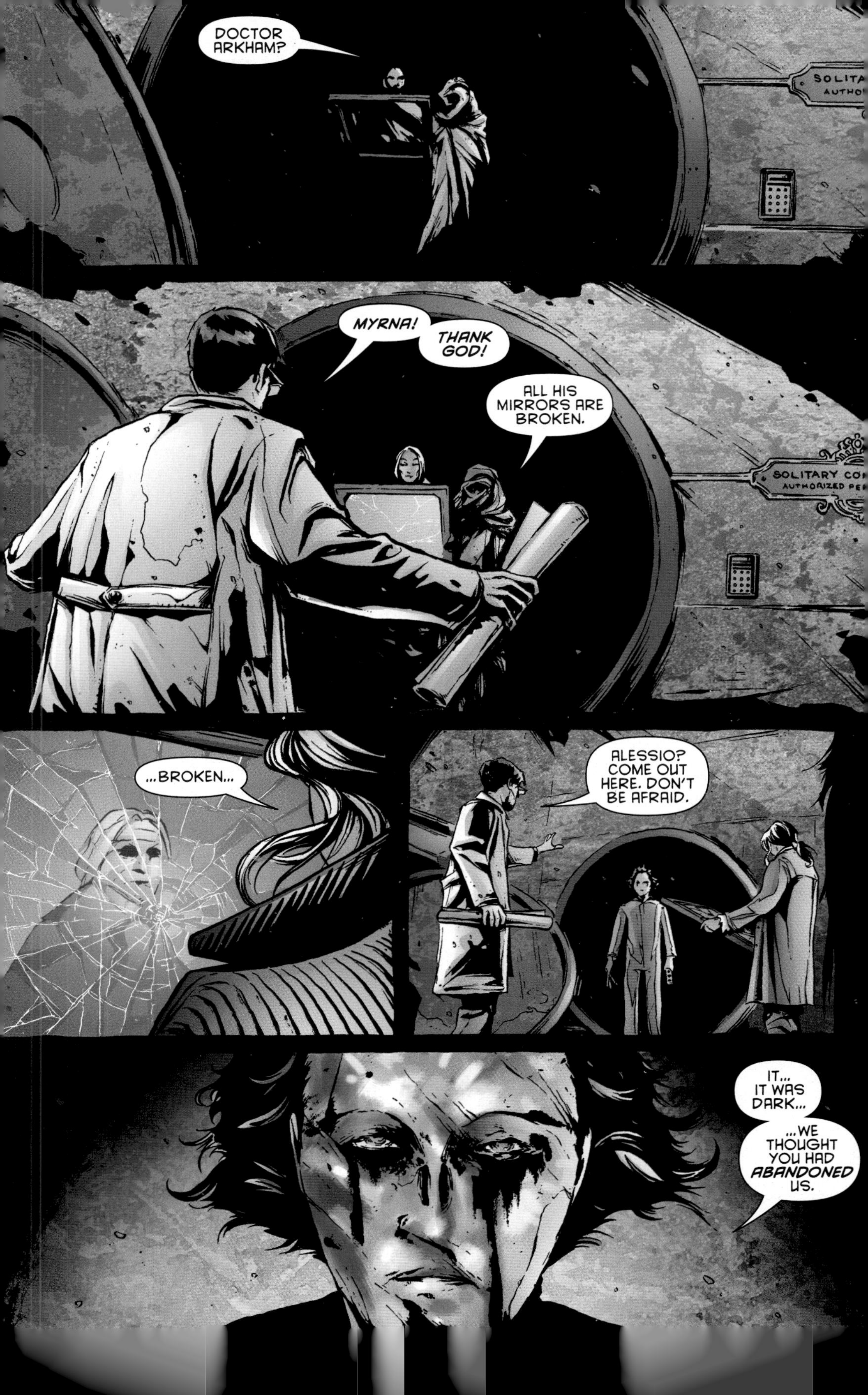
DOCTOR ARKHAM?
SOLITA AUTHO
MYRNA!
THANK GOD!
ALL HIS MIRRORS ARE BROKEN.
SOLITARY CO AUTHORIZED PE
...BROKEN...
ALESSIO? COME OUT HERE. DON'T BE AFRAID.
IT... IT WAS DARK...
...WE THOUGHT YOU HAD ABANDONED US.

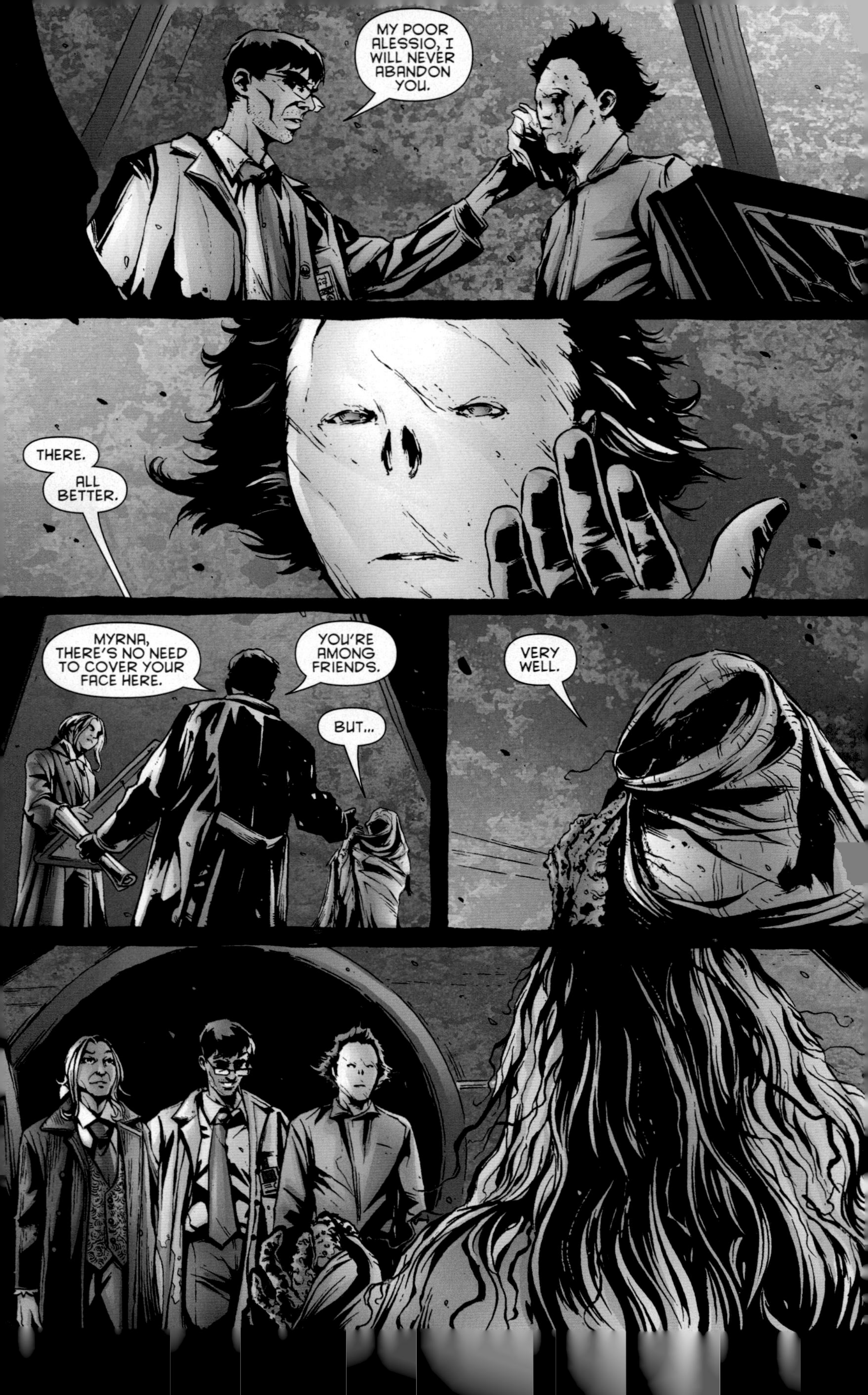
MY POOR ALESSIO, I WILL NEVER ABANDON YOU.
THERE.
ALL BETTER.
MYRNA, THERE'S NO NEED TO COVER YOUR FACE HERE.
YOU'RE AMONG FRIENDS.
BUT...
VERY WELL.

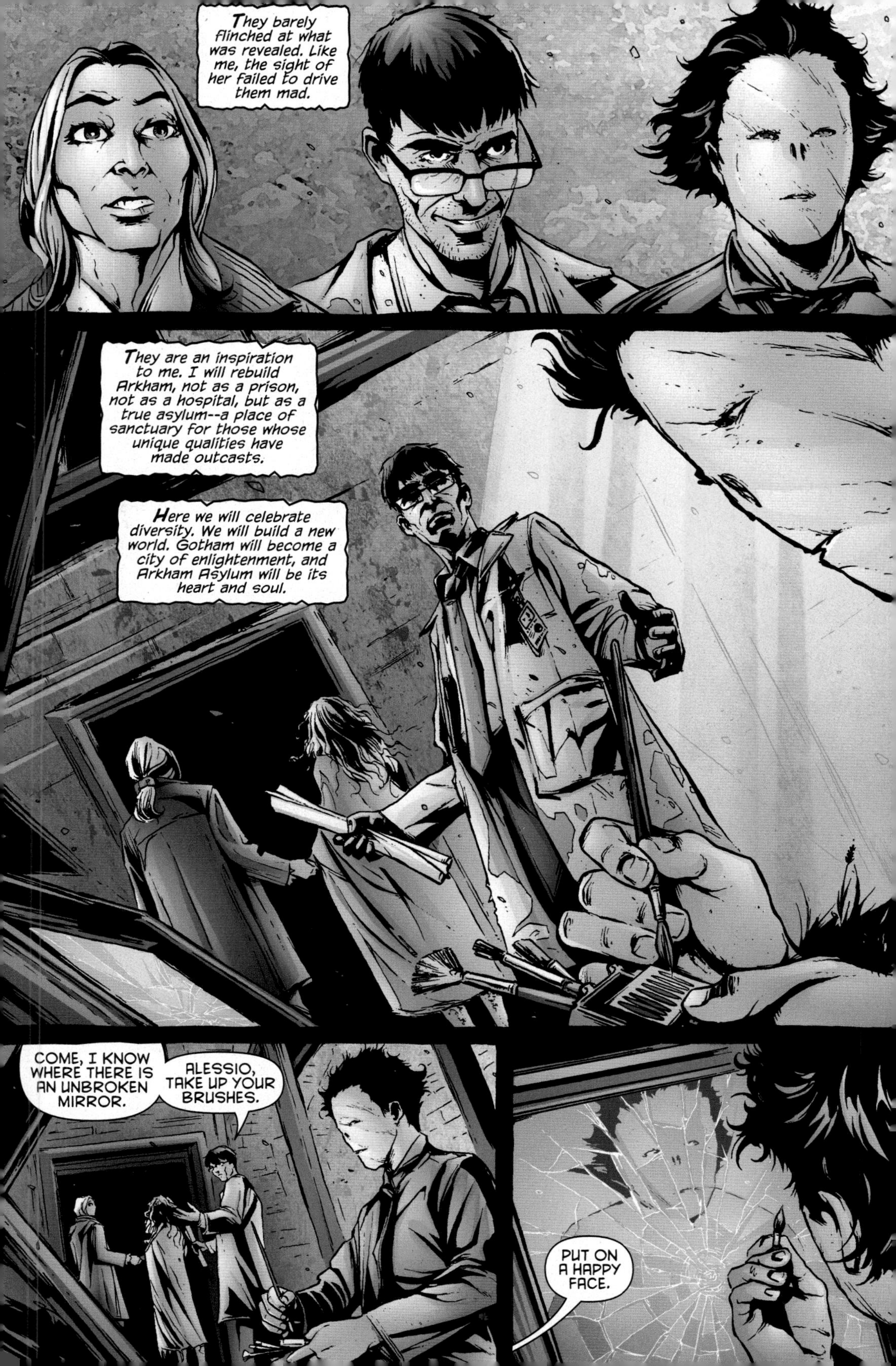
They barely flinched at what was revealed. Like me, the sight of her failed to drive them mad.
They are an inspiration to me. I will rebuild Arkham, not as a prison, not as a hospital, but as a true asylum--a place of sanctuary for those whose unique qualities have made outcasts.
Here we will celebrate diversity. We will build a new world. Gotham will become a city of enlightenment, and Arkham Asylum will be its heart and soul.
COME, I KNOW WHERE THERE IS AN UNBROKEN MIRROR.
ALESSIO, TAKE UP YOUR BRUSHES.
PUT ON A HAPPY FACE.

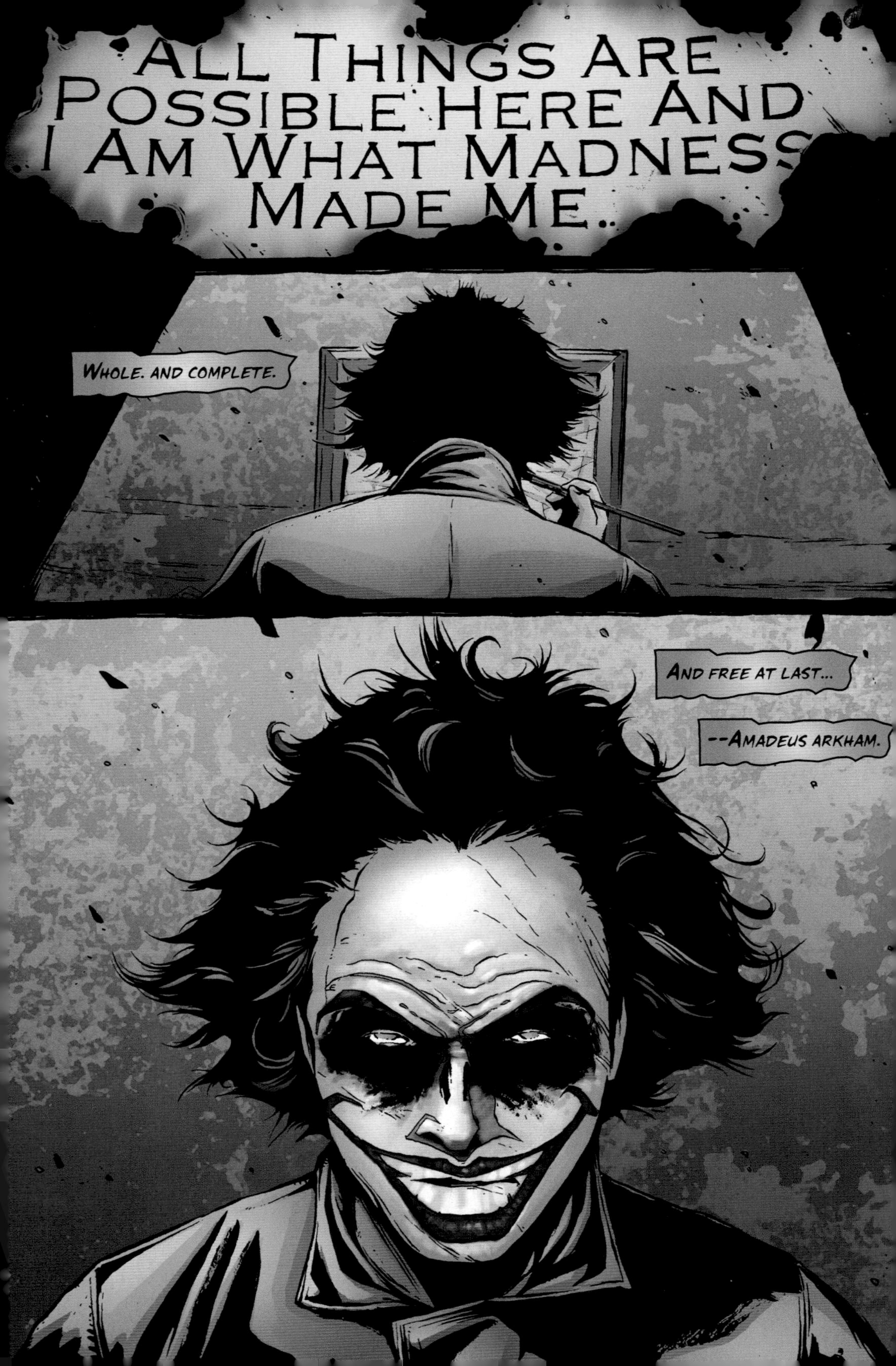
ALL THINGS ARE POSSIBLE HERE AND I AM WHAT MADNESS MADE ME..
WHOLE. AND COMPLETE.
AND FREE AT LAST...
--AMADEUS ARKHAM.

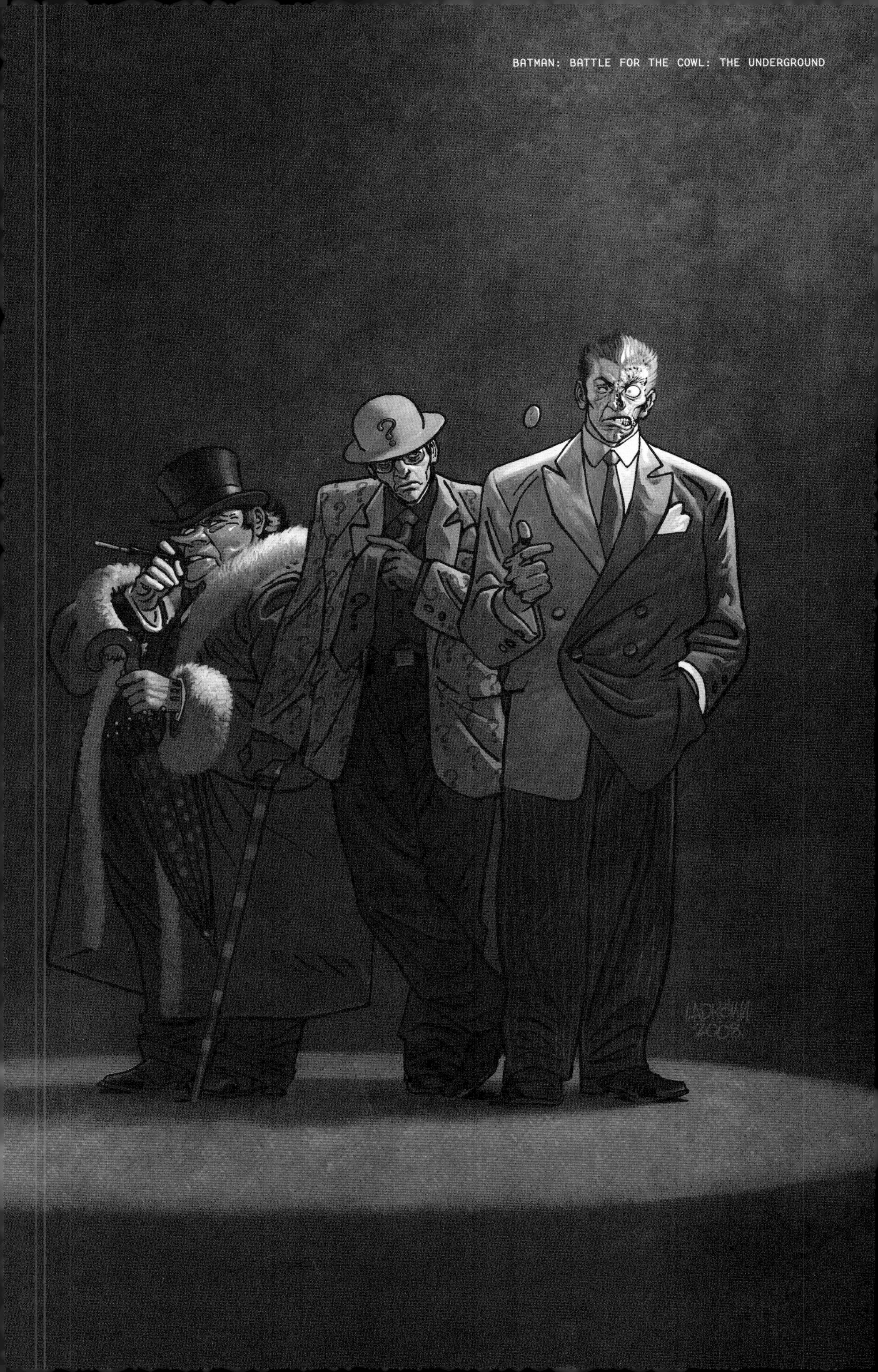

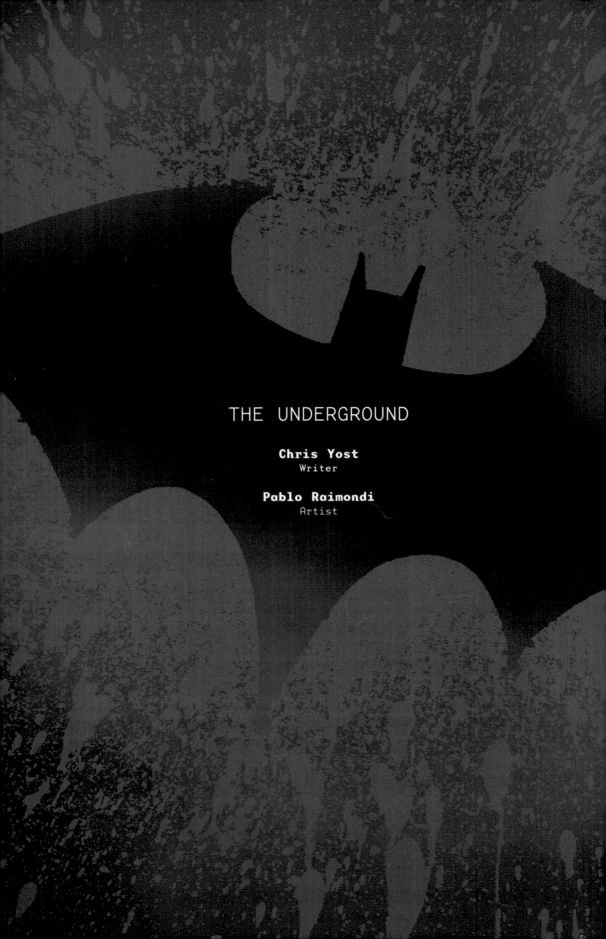

THE UNDERGROUND

Chris Yost
Writer

Pablo Raimondi
Artist

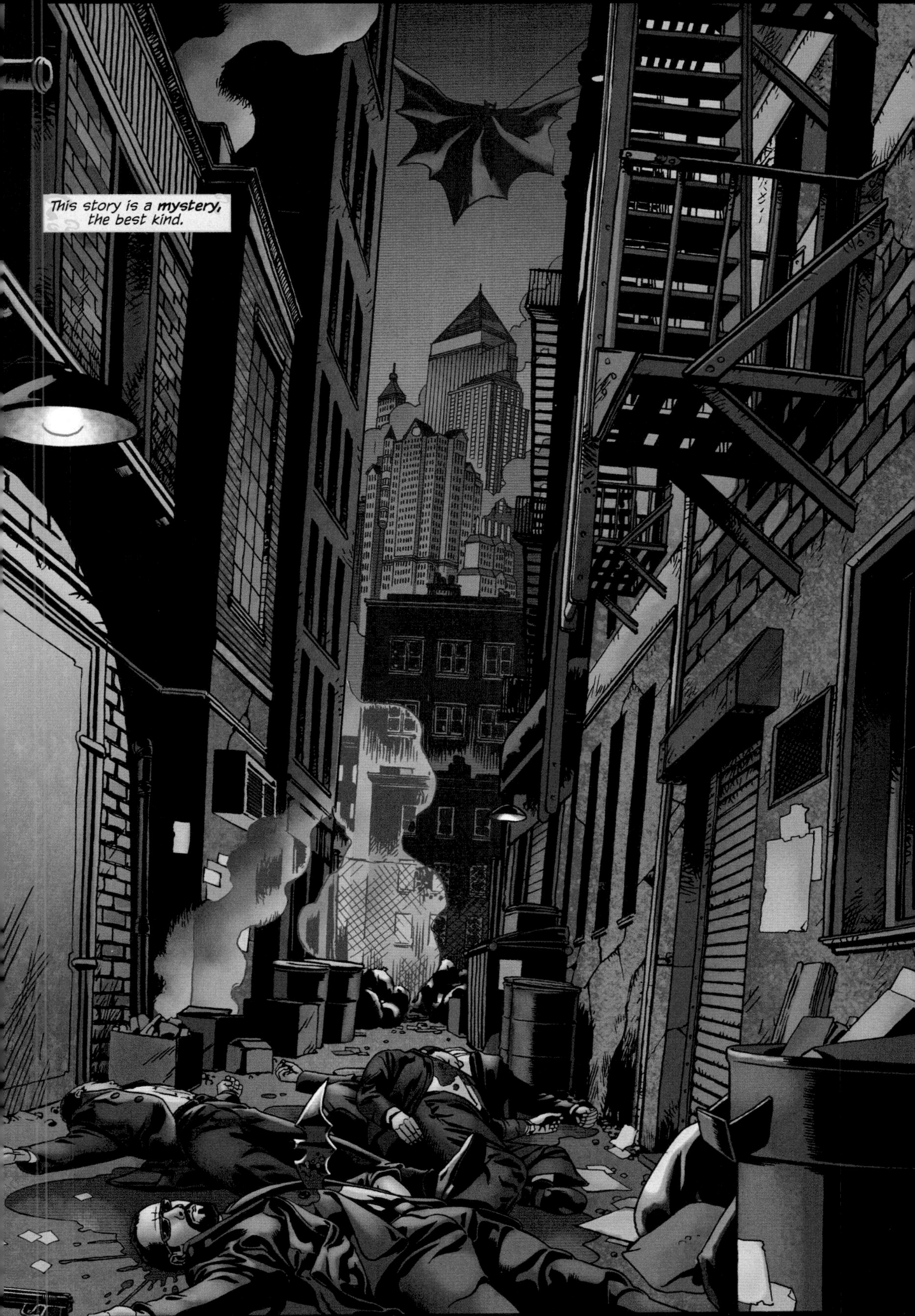
This story is a mystery, the best kind.

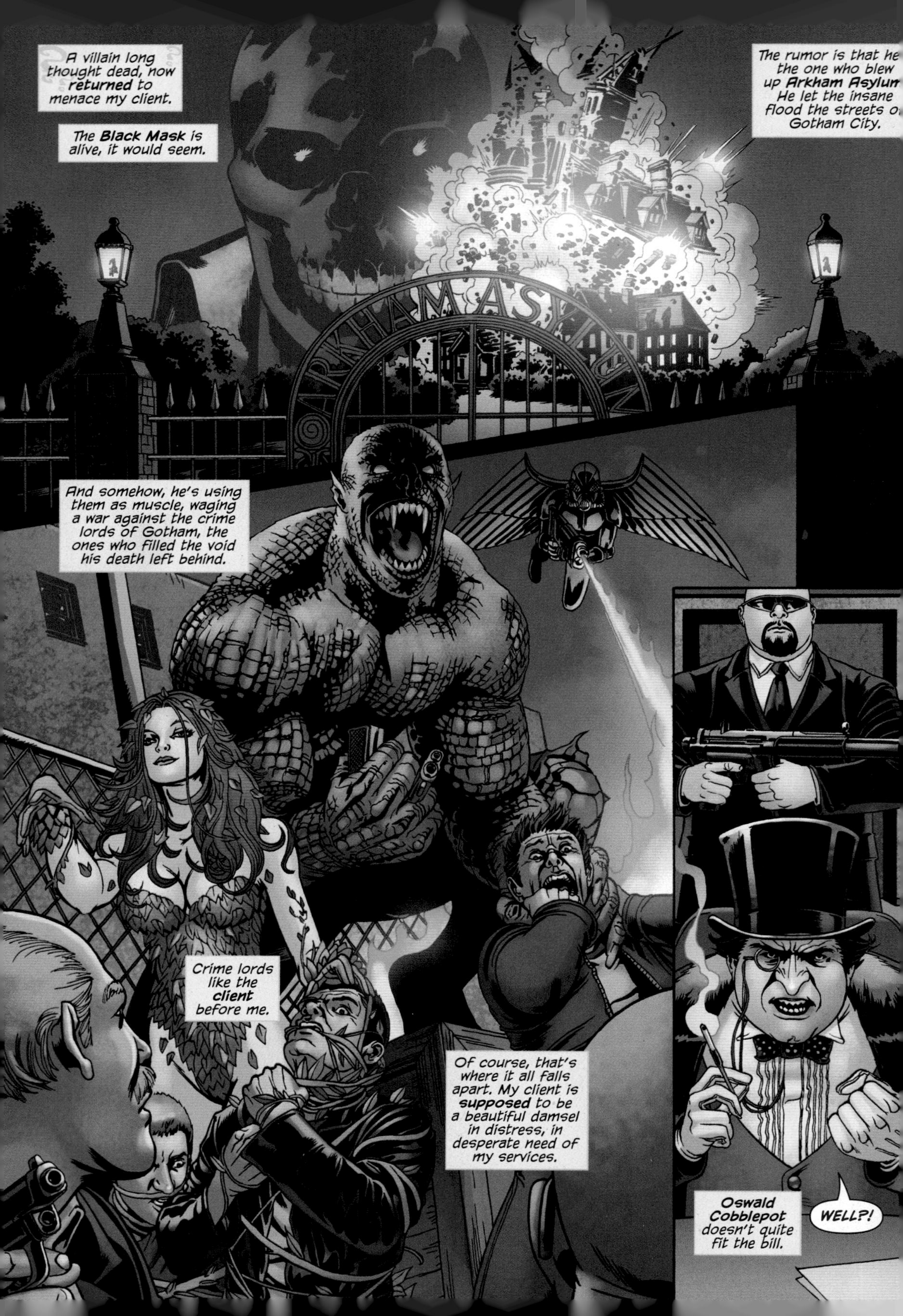
A villain long thought dead, now returned to menace my client.
The Black Mask is alive, it would seem.
The rumor is that he's the one who blew up Arkham Asylum. He let the insane flood the streets of Gotham City.
ARKHAM ASYLUM
And somehow, he's using them as muscle, waging a war against the crime lords of Gotham, the ones who filled the void his death left behind.
Crime lords like the client before me.
Of course, that's where it all falls apart. My client is supposed to be a beautiful damsel in distress, in desperate need of my services.
Oswald Cobblepot doesn't quite fit the bill.
WELL?!

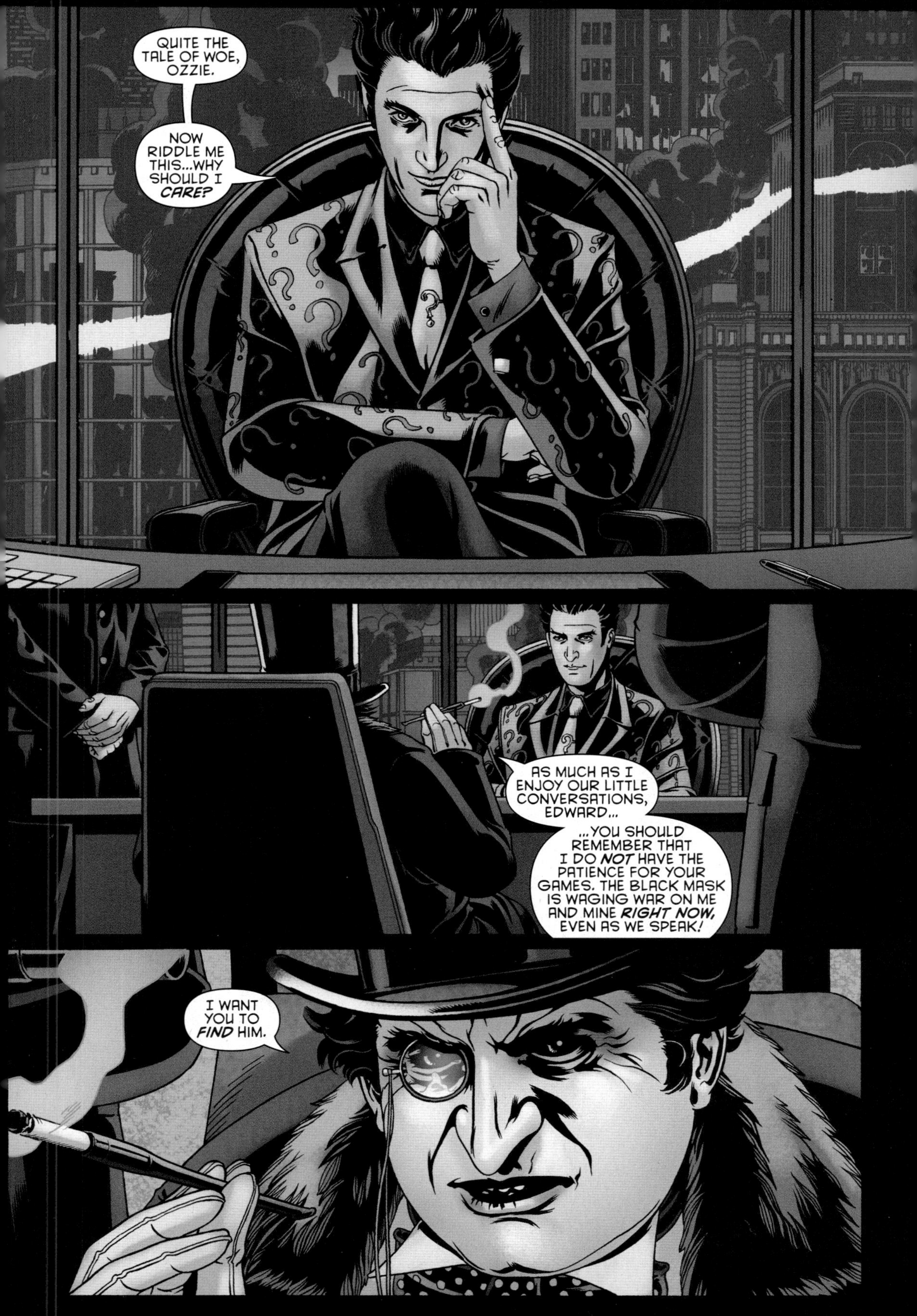
QUITE THE TALE OF WOE, OZZIE.
NOW RIDDLE ME THIS...WHY SHOULD I CARE?
AS MUCH AS I ENJOY OUR LITTLE CONVERSATIONS, EDWARD...
...YOU SHOULD REMEMBER THAT I DO NOT HAVE THE PATIENCE FOR YOUR GAMES. THE BLACK MASK IS WAGING WAR ON ME AND MINE RIGHT NOW, EVEN AS WE SPEAK!
I WANT YOU TO FIND HIM.

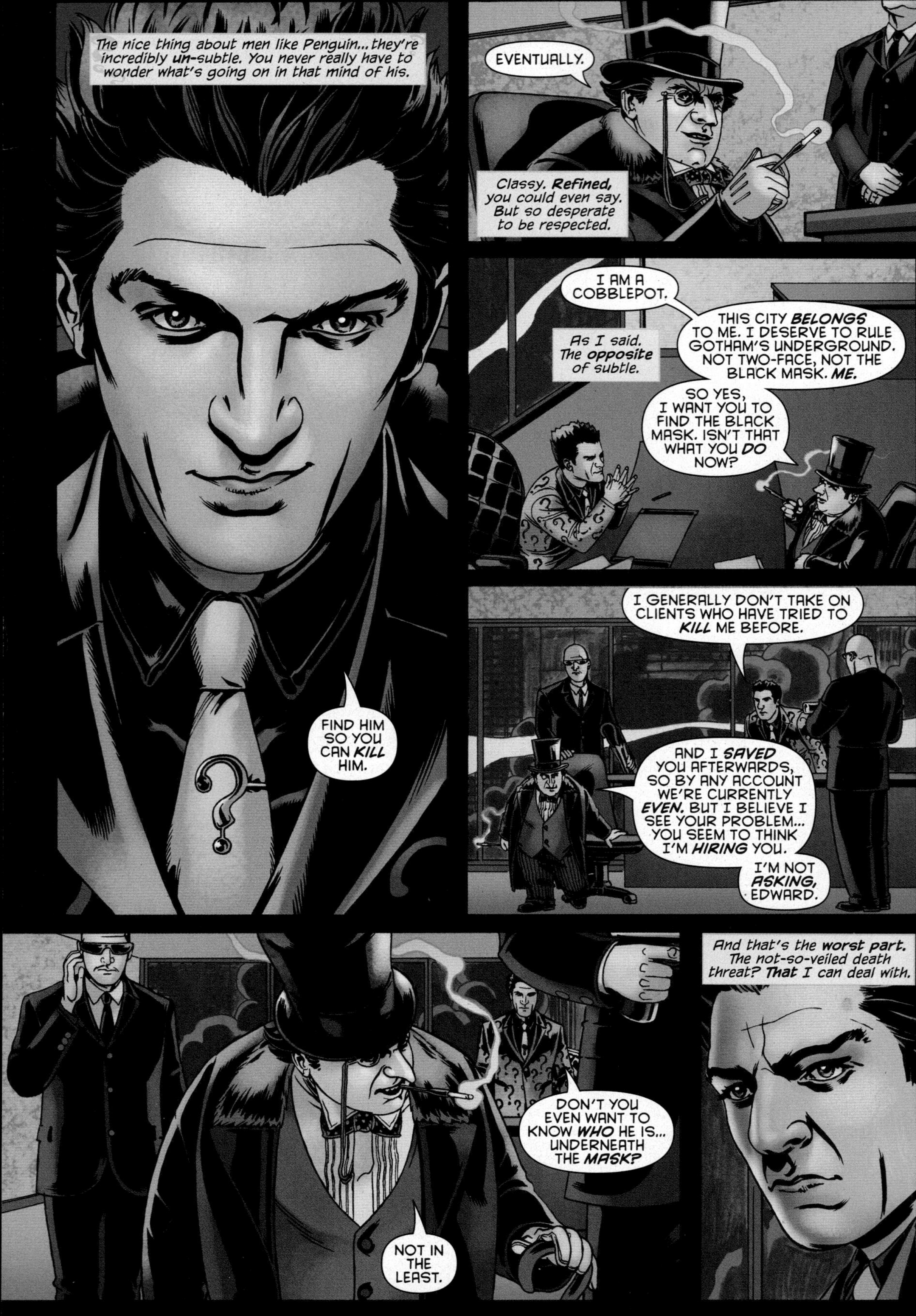
The nice thing about men like Penguin... they're incredibly un-subtle. You never really have to wonder what's going on in that mind of his.
EVENTUALLY.
Classy. Refined, you could even say. But so desperate to be respected.
FIND HIM SO YOU CAN KILL HIM.
I AM A COBBLEPOT.
As I said. The opposite of subtle.
THIS CITY BELONGS TO ME. I DESERVE TO RULE GOTHAM'S UNDERGROUND. NOT TWO-FACE, NOT THE BLACK MASK. ME.
SO YES, I WANT YOU TO FIND THE BLACK MASK. ISN'T THAT WHAT YOU DO NOW?
I GENERALLY DON'T TAKE ON CLIENTS WHO HAVE TRIED TO KILL ME BEFORE.
AND I SAVED YOU AFTERWARDS, SO BY ANY ACCOUNT WE'RE CURRENTLY EVEN. BUT I BELIEVE I SEE YOUR PROBLEM... YOU SEEM TO THINK I'M HIRING YOU.
I'M NOT ASKING, EDWARD.
DON'T YOU EVEN WANT TO KNOW WHO HE IS... UNDERNEATH THE MASK?
NOT IN THE LEAST.
And that's the worst part. The not-so-veiled death threat? That I can deal with.

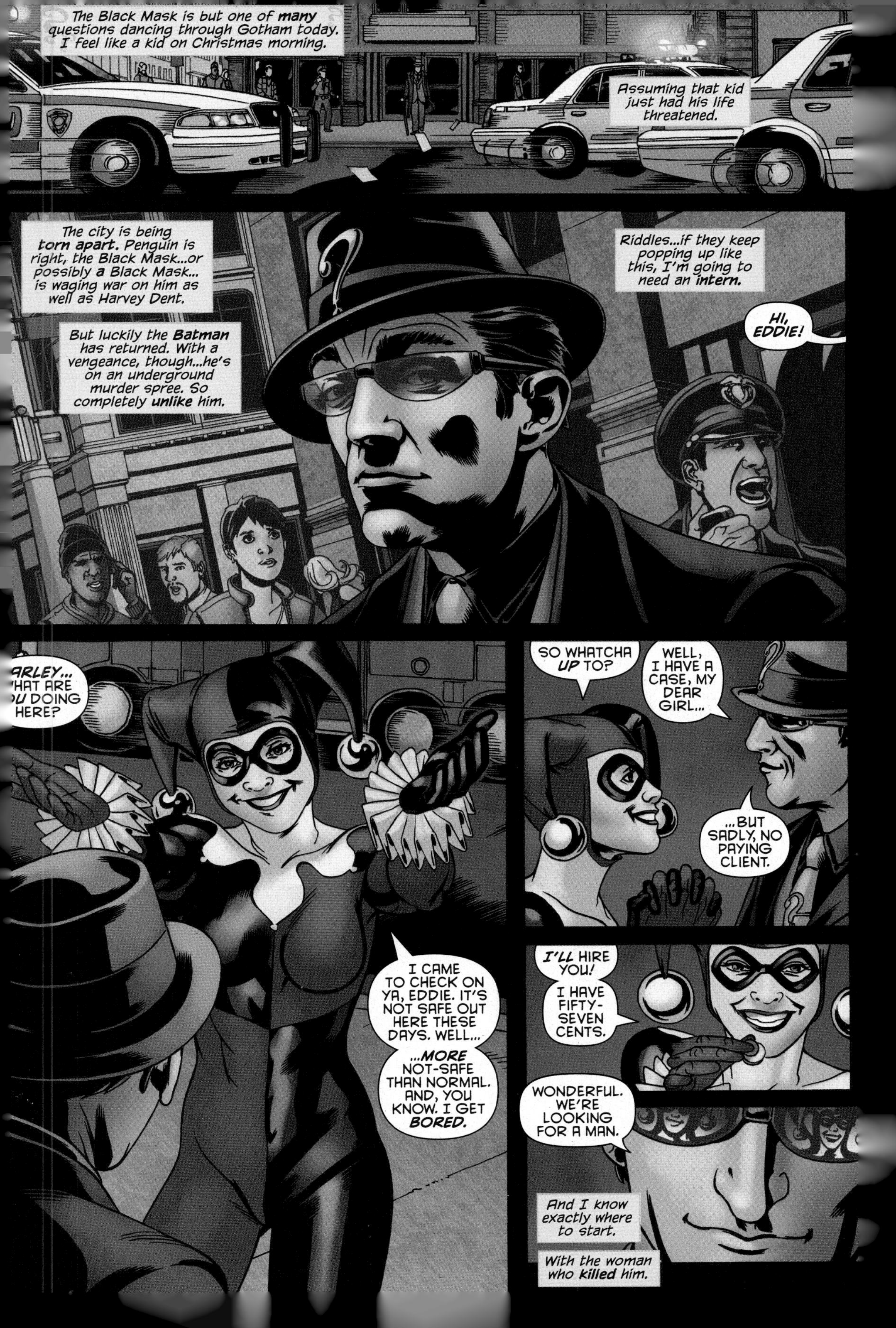
The Black Mask is but one of **many** questions dancing through Gotham today. I feel like a kid on Christmas morning.
Assuming that kid just had his life threatened.
The city is being **torn apart.** Penguin is right, the Black Mask...or possibly **a** Black Mask... is waging war on him as well as Harvey Dent.
But luckily the **Batman** has returned. With a vengeance, though...he's on an underground murder spree. So completely **unlike** him.
Riddles...if they keep popping up like this, I'm going to need an **intern.**
HI, EDDIE!
ARLEY... WHAT ARE OU DOING HERE?
I CAME TO CHECK ON YA, EDDIE. IT'S NOT SAFE OUT HERE THESE DAYS. WELL...
...**MORE** NOT-SAFE THAN NORMAL. AND, YOU KNOW. I GET **BORED.**
SO WHATCHA **UP** TO?
WELL, I HAVE A CASE, MY DEAR GIRL...
...BUT SADLY, NO PAYING CLIENT.
I'LL HIRE YOU!
I HAVE FIFTY-SEVEN CENTS.
WONDERFUL. WE'RE LOOKING FOR A MAN.
And I know exactly where to start.
With the woman who **killed** him.

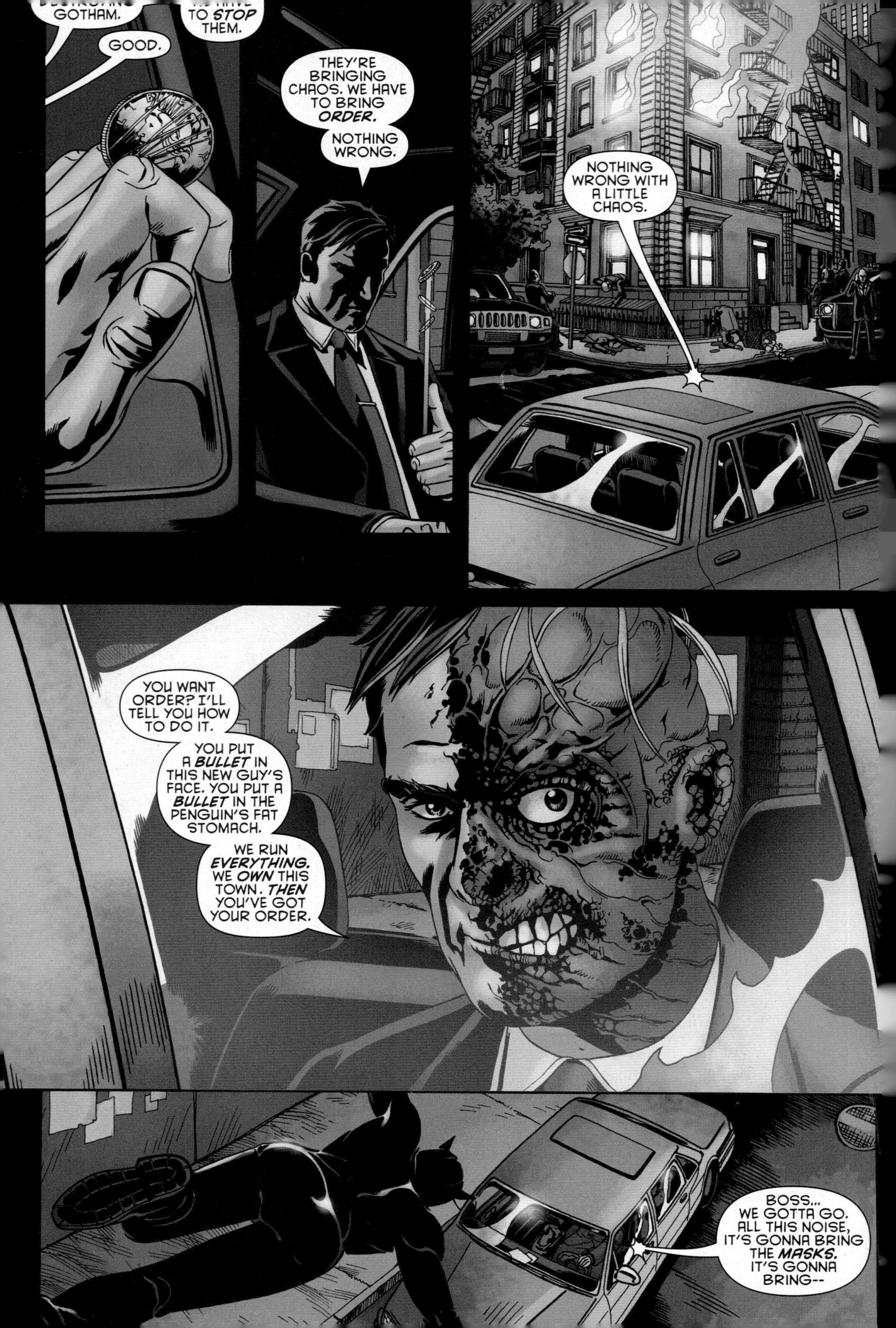
GOTHAM.
TO STOP THEM.
GOOD.
THEY'RE BRINGING CHAOS. WE HAVE TO BRING ORDER.
NOTHING WRONG.
NOTHING WRONG WITH A LITTLE CHAOS.
YOU WANT ORDER? I'LL TELL YOU HOW TO DO IT.
YOU PUT A BULLET IN THIS NEW GUY'S FACE. YOU PUT A BULLET IN THE PENGUIN'S FAT STOMACH.
WE RUN EVERYTHING. WE OWN THIS TOWN. THEN YOU'VE GOT YOUR ORDER.
BOSS... WE GOTTA GO. ALL THIS NOISE, IT'S GONNA BRING THE MASKS. IT'S GONNA BRING--

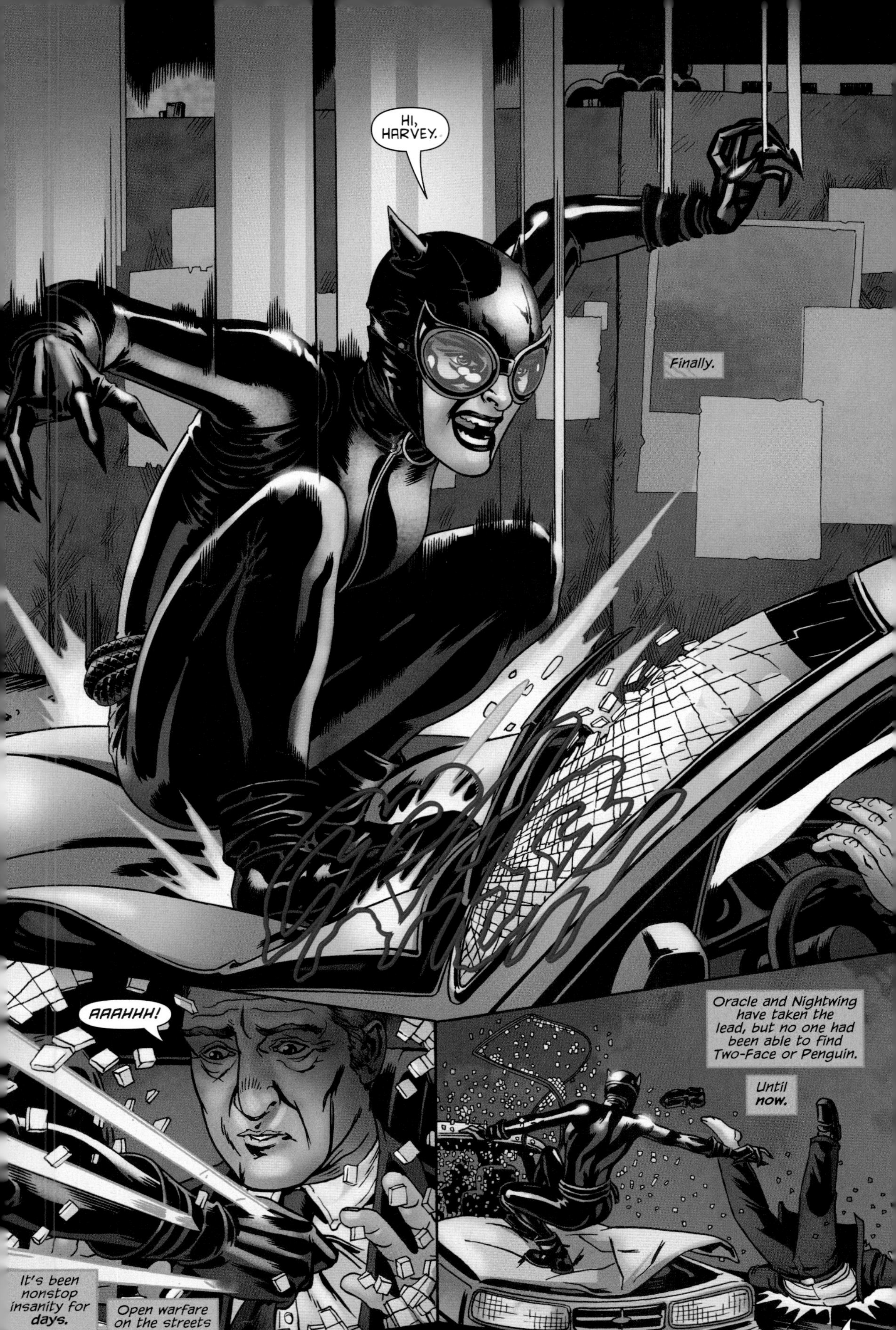
HI, HARVEY.
Finally.
AAAHHH!
It's been nonstop insanity for days.
Open warfare on the streets of Gotham.
Oracle and Nightwing have taken the lead, but no one had been able to find Two-Face or Penguin.
Until now.
UHNN!

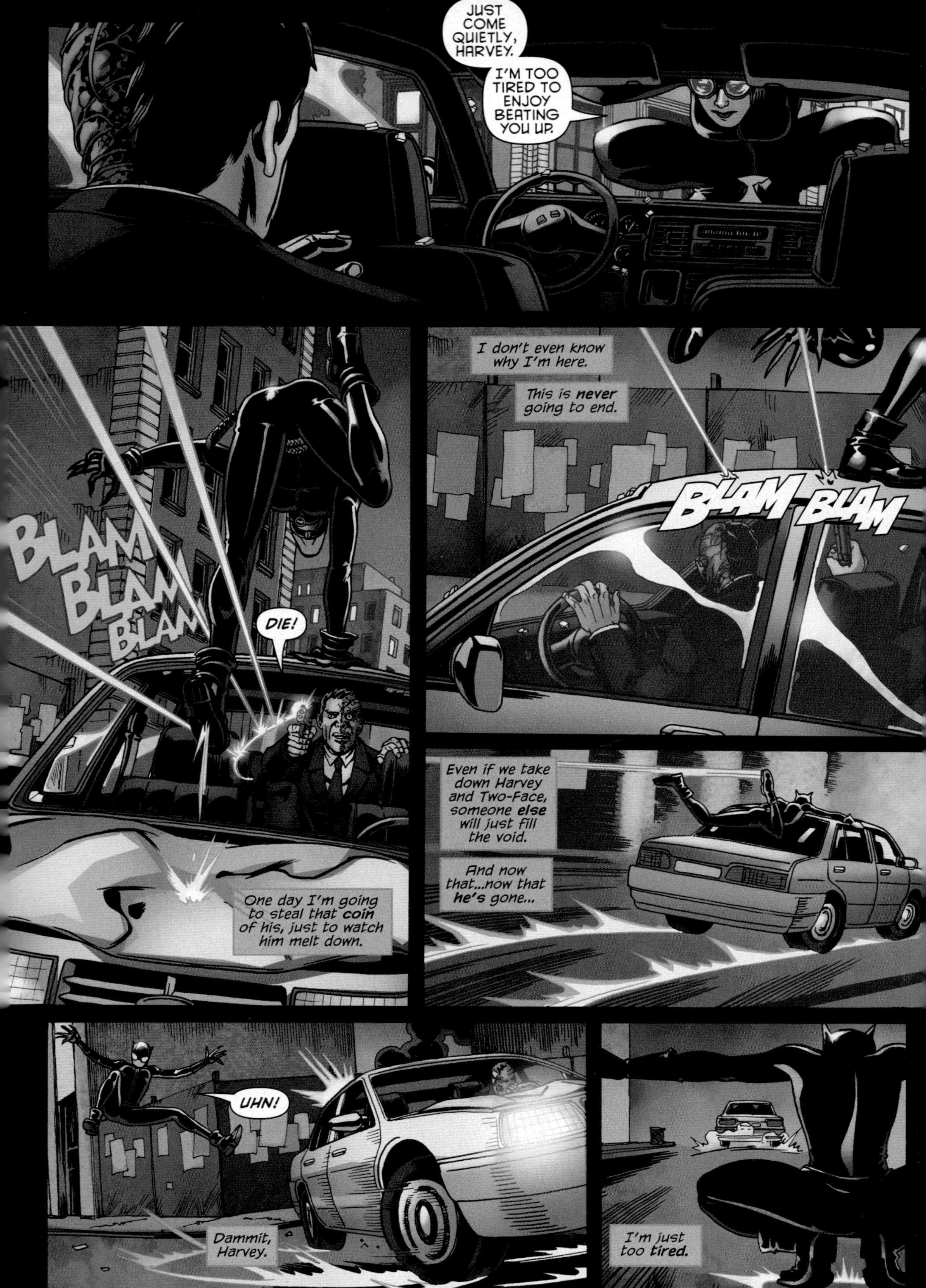
JUST COME QUIETLY, HARVEY.
I'M TOO TIRED TO ENJOY BEATING YOU UP.
BLAM BLAM BLAM
DIE!
One day I'm going to steal that **coin** of his, just to watch him melt down.
I don't even know why I'm here.
This is **never** going to end.
BLAM BLAM
Even if we take down Harvey and Two-Face, someone **else** will just fill the void.
And now that...now that **he's** gone...
UHN!
Dammit, Harvey.
I'm just too **tired**.

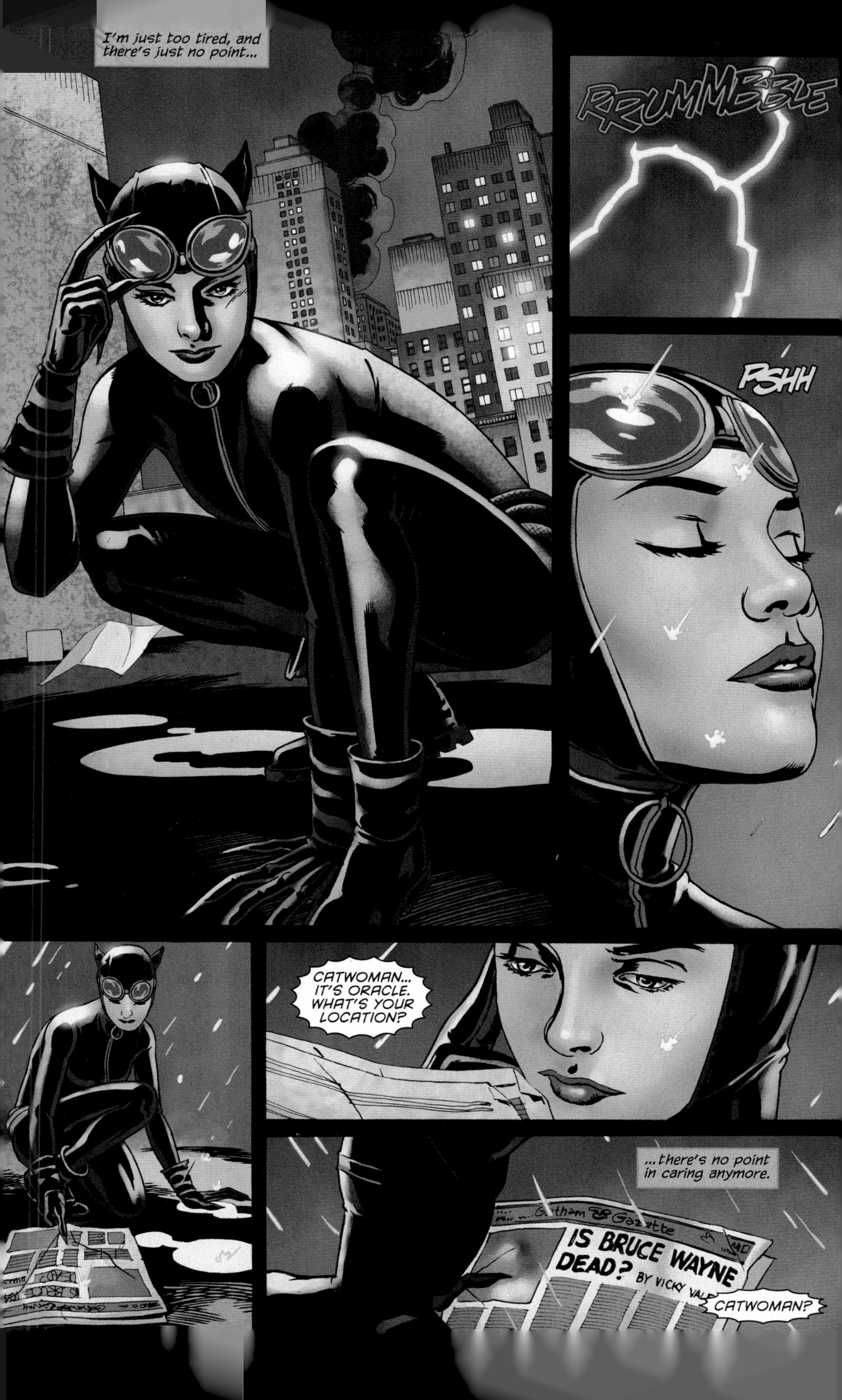

I'm just too tired, and there's just no point...
RRUMMBBLE
PSHH
CATWOMAN... IT'S ORACLE. WHAT'S YOUR LOCATION?
...there's no point in caring anymore.
Gotham Gazette
IS BRUCE WAYNE DEAD? BY VICKY VALE
CATWOMAN?

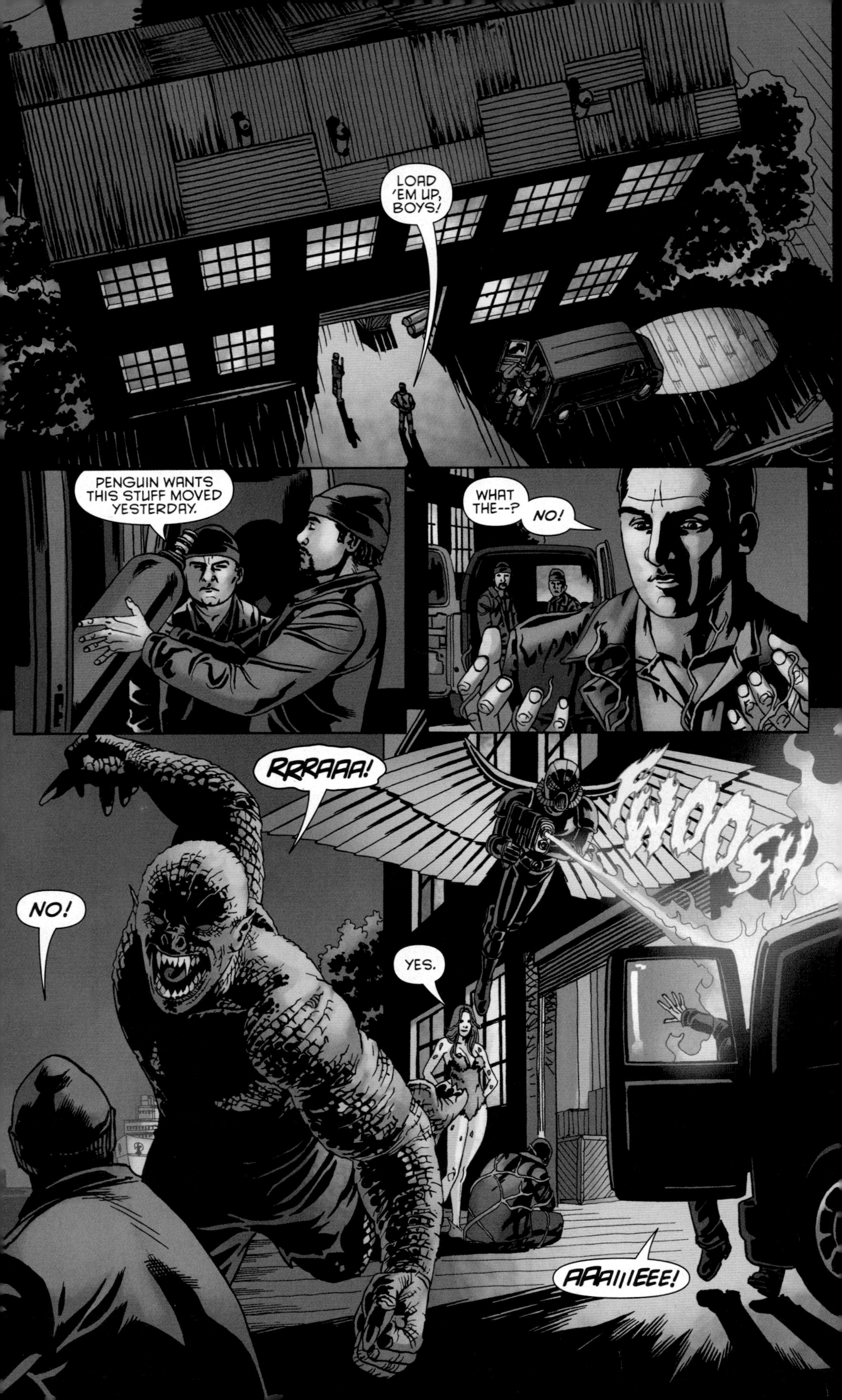
LOAD 'EM UP, BOYS!
PENGUIN WANTS THIS STUFF MOVED YESTERDAY.
WHAT THE--?
NO!
RRRAAA!
WOOSH
NO!
YES.
AAAIIIEEE!

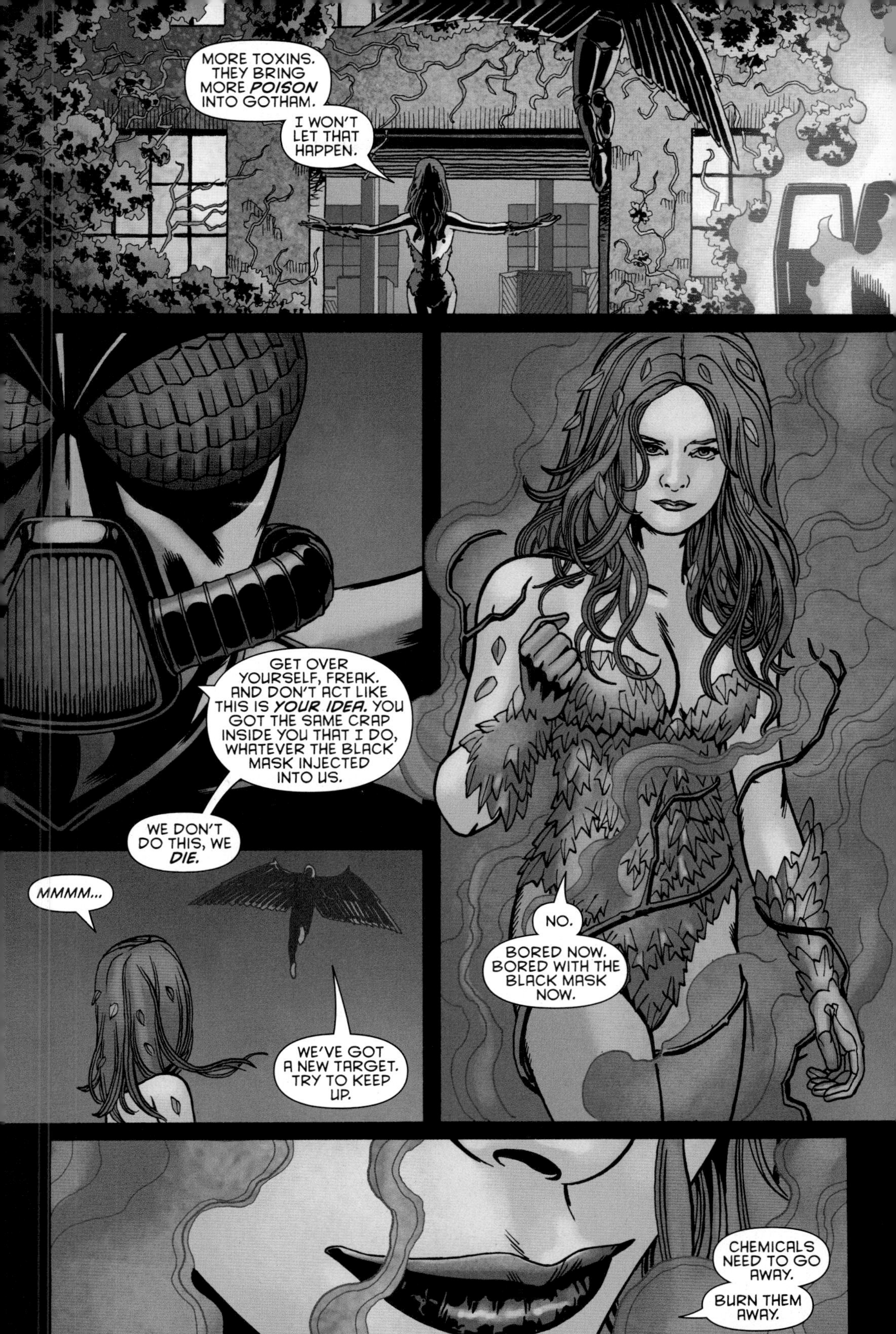
MORE TOXINS. THEY BRING MORE *POISON* INTO GOTHAM.
I WON'T LET THAT HAPPEN.
GET OVER YOURSELF, FREAK. AND DON'T ACT LIKE THIS IS *YOUR IDEA.* YOU GOT THE SAME CRAP INSIDE YOU THAT I DO, WHATEVER THE BLACK MASK INJECTED INTO US.
WE DON'T DO THIS, WE *DIE.*
NO.
BORED NOW. BORED WITH THE BLACK MASK NOW.
MMMM...
WE'VE GOT A NEW TARGET. TRY TO KEEP UP.
CHEMICALS NEED TO GO AWAY.
BURN THEM AWAY.

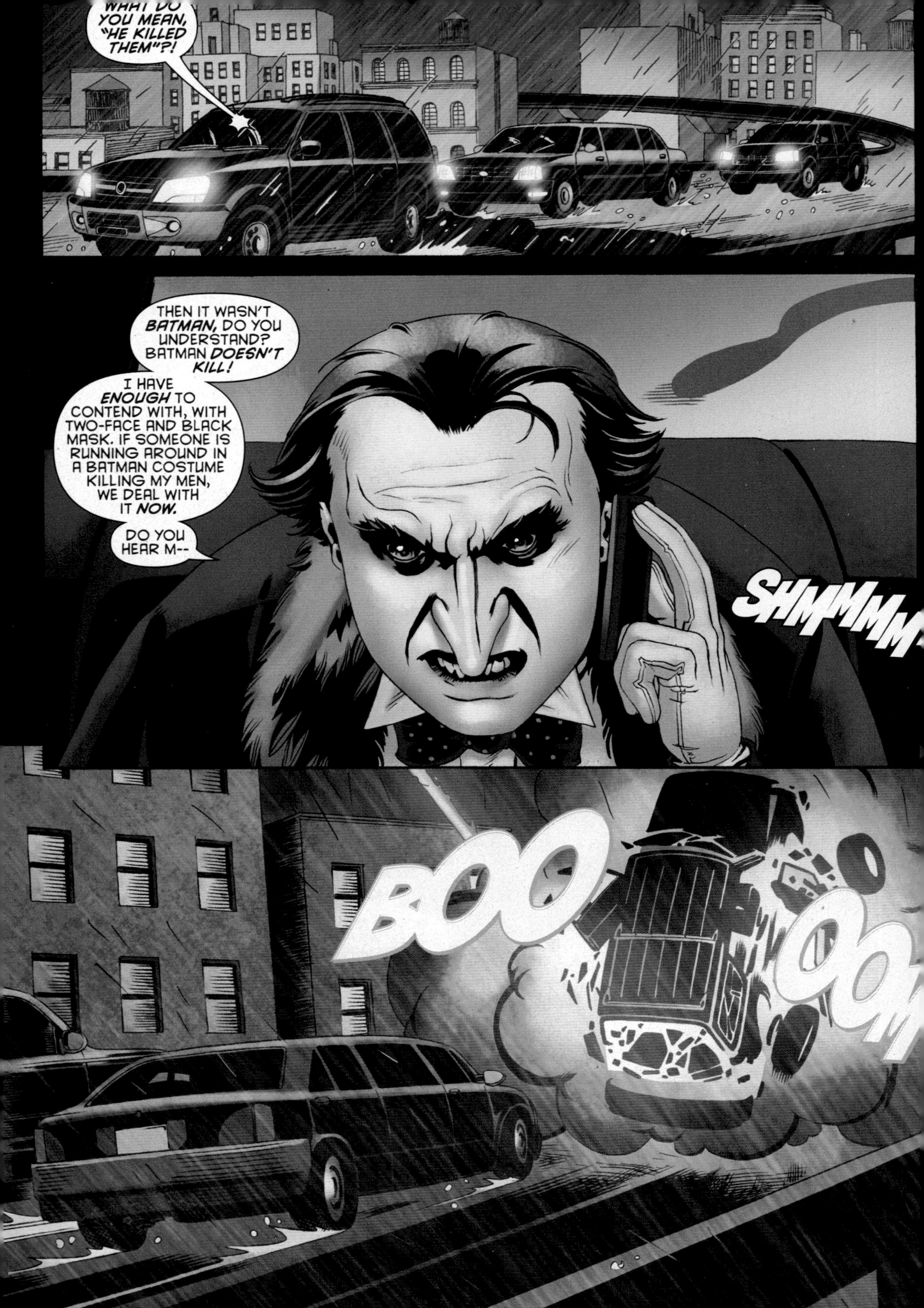
WHAT DO YOU MEAN, "HE KILLED THEM"?!
THEN IT WASN'T BATMAN, DO YOU UNDERSTAND? BATMAN DOESN'T KILL!
I HAVE ENOUGH TO CONTEND WITH, WITH TWO-FACE AND BLACK MASK. IF SOMEONE IS RUNNING AROUND IN A BATMAN COSTUME KILLING MY MEN, WE DEAL WITH IT NOW.
DO YOU HEAR M--
SHMMMM
BOOOOM

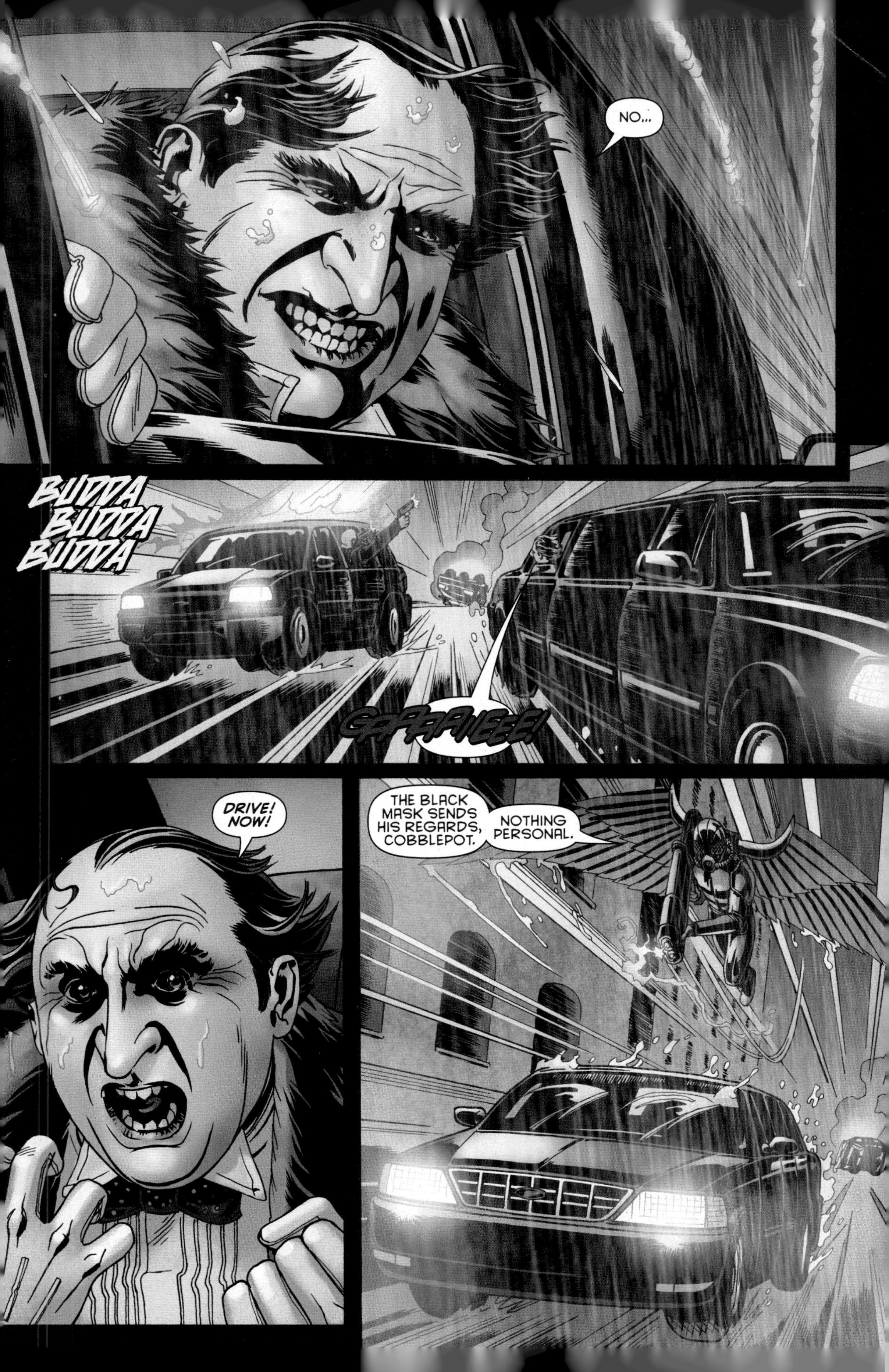
NO...
BUDDA BUDDA BUDDA
GAAAAIEEE!
DRIVE! NOW!
THE BLACK MASK SENDS HIS REGARDS, COBBLEPOT.
NOTHING PERSONAL.

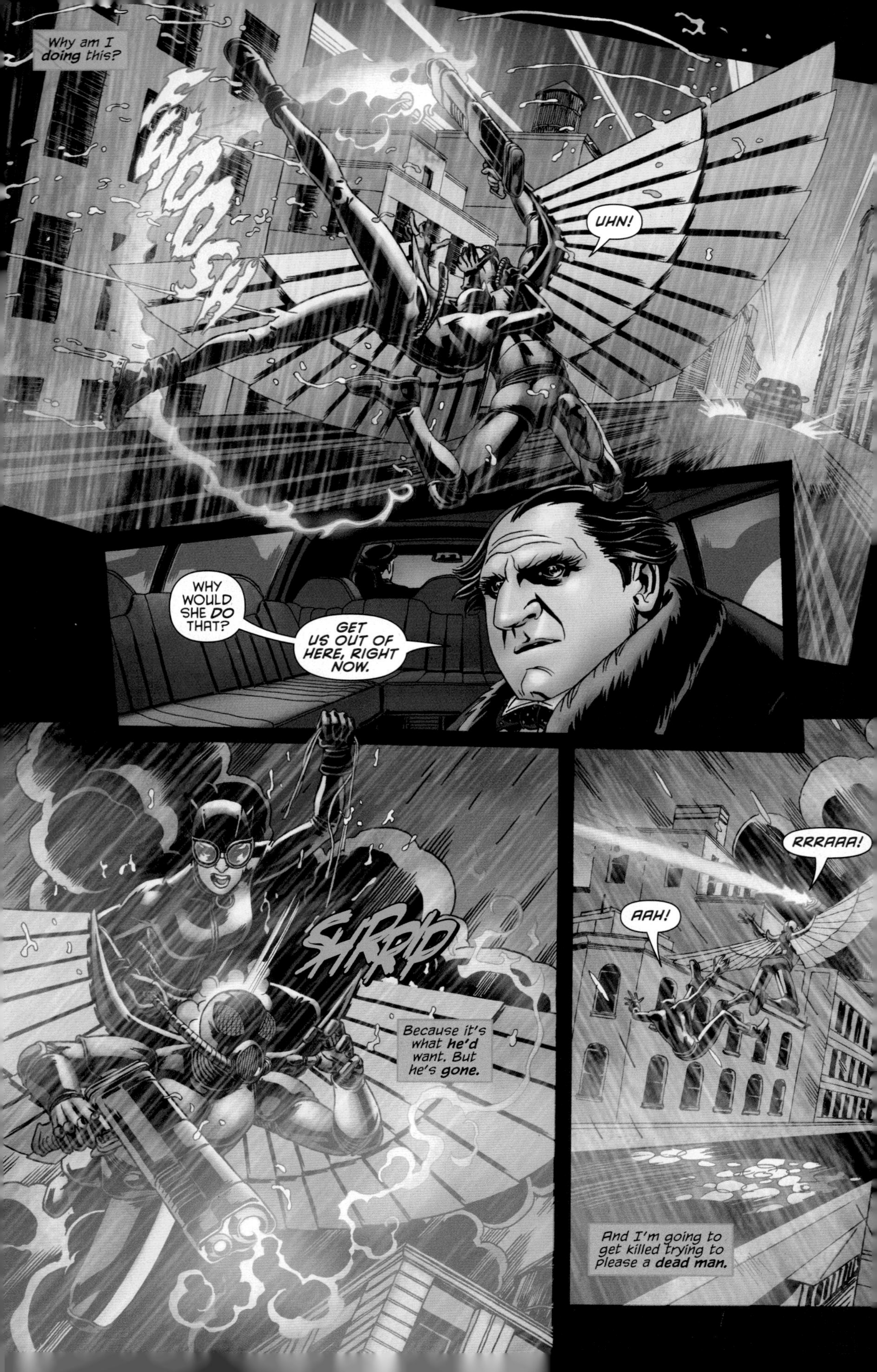
Why am I doing this?
WOOSH
UHN!
WHY WOULD SHE DO THAT?
GET US OUT OF HERE, RIGHT NOW.
SHRRIP
Because it's what he'd want. But he's gone.
RRRAAA!
AAH!
And I'm going to get killed trying to please a dead man.

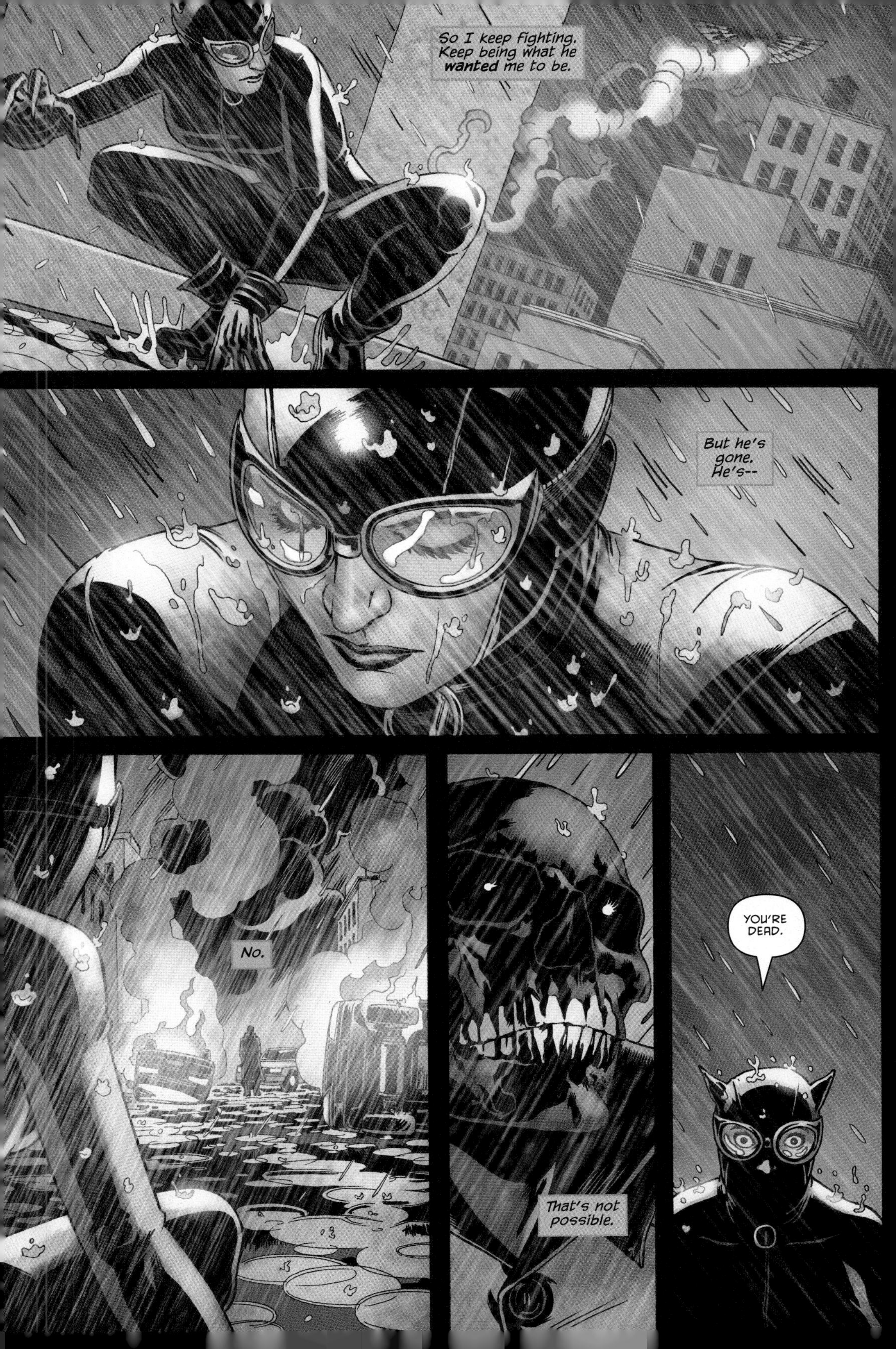
So I keep fighting. Keep being what he **wanted** me to be.
But he's gone. He's--
No.
That's not possible.
YOU'RE DEAD.

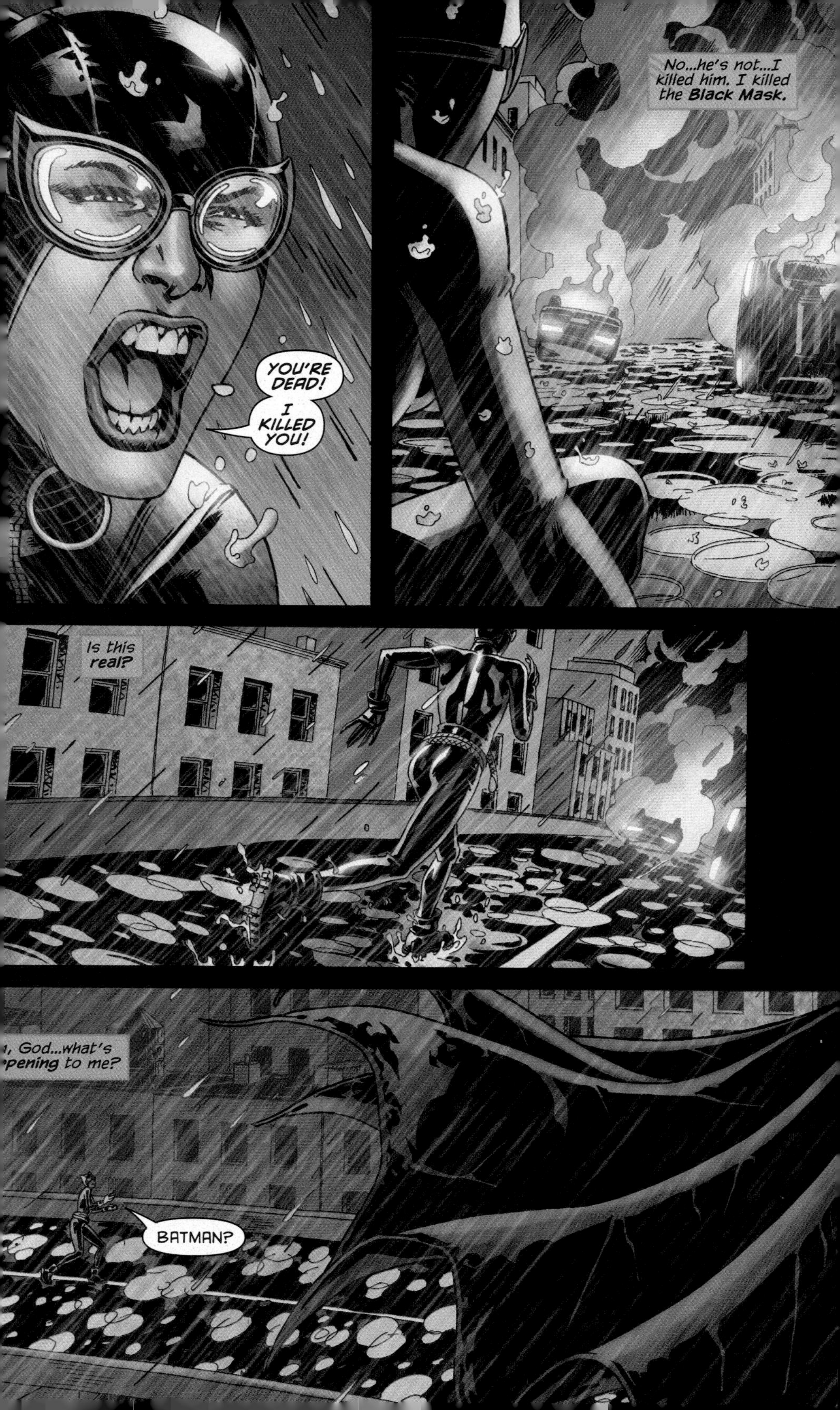
YOU'RE DEAD!
I KILLED YOU!
No...he's not...I killed him. I killed the Black Mask.
Is this real?
, God...what's
ppening to me?
BATMAN?

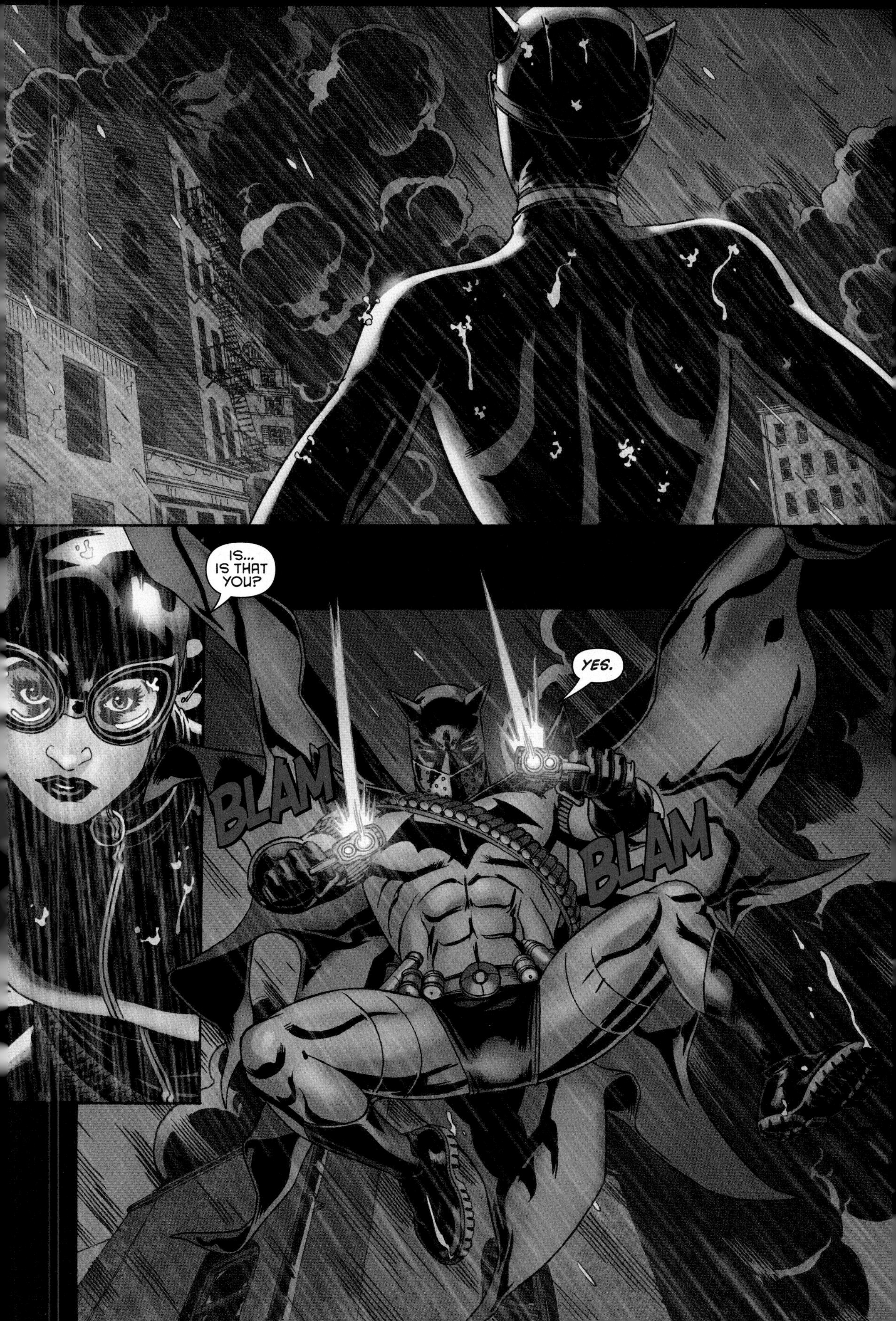
IS... IS THAT YOU?
YES.
BLAM
BLAM

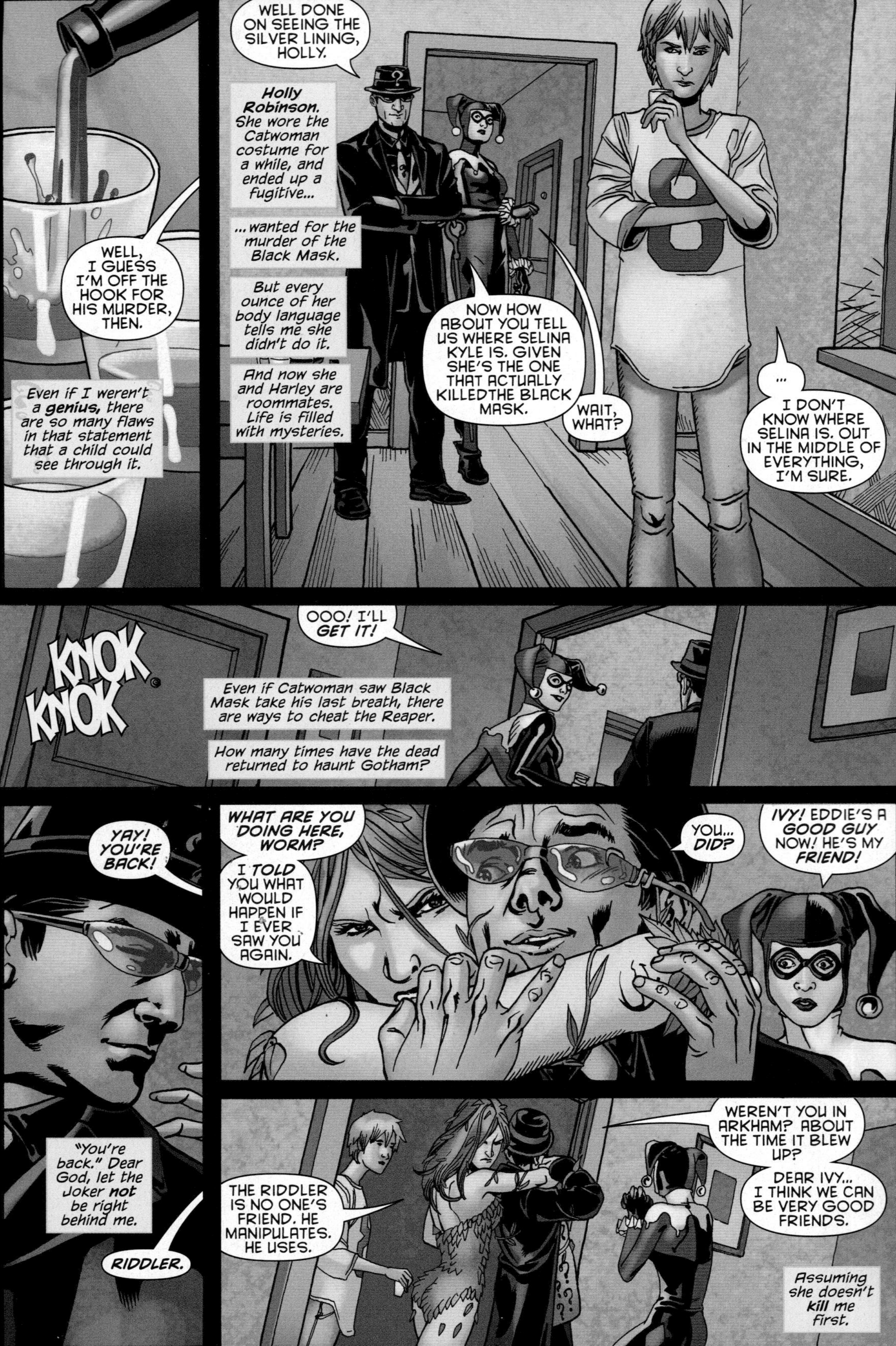
WELL, I GUESS I'M OFF THE HOOK FOR HIS MURDER, THEN.
Even if I weren't a **genius**, there are so many flaws in that statement that a child could see through it.
WELL DONE ON SEEING THE SILVER LINING, HOLLY.
Holly Robinson. She wore the Catwoman costume for a while, and ended up a fugitive...
...wanted for the murder of the Black Mask.
But every ounce of her body language tells me she didn't do it.
And now she and Harley are roommates. Life is filled with mysteries.
NOW HOW ABOUT YOU TELL US WHERE SELINA KYLE IS. GIVEN SHE'S THE ONE THAT ACTUALLY KILLEDTHE BLACK MASK.
WAIT, WHAT?
...
I DON'T KNOW WHERE SELINA IS. OUT IN THE MIDDLE OF EVERYTHING, I'M SURE.
KNOK KNOK
OOO! I'LL **GET IT!**
Even if Catwoman saw Black Mask take his last breath, there are ways to cheat the Reaper.
How many times have the dead returned to haunt Gotham?
YAY! YOU'RE BACK!
"You're back." Dear God, let the Joker **not** be right behind me.
RIDDLER.
WHAT ARE YOU DOING HERE, WORM?
I **TOLD** YOU WHAT WOULD HAPPEN IF I EVER SAW YOU AGAIN.
YOU... **DID?**
IVY! EDDIE'S A **GOOD GUY** NOW! HE'S MY **FRIEND!**
THE RIDDLER IS NO ONE'S FRIEND. HE MANIPULATES. HE USES.
WEREN'T YOU IN ARKHAM? ABOUT THE TIME IT BLEW UP?
DEAR IVY... I THINK WE CAN BE VERY GOOD FRIENDS.
Assuming she doesn't **kill** me first.

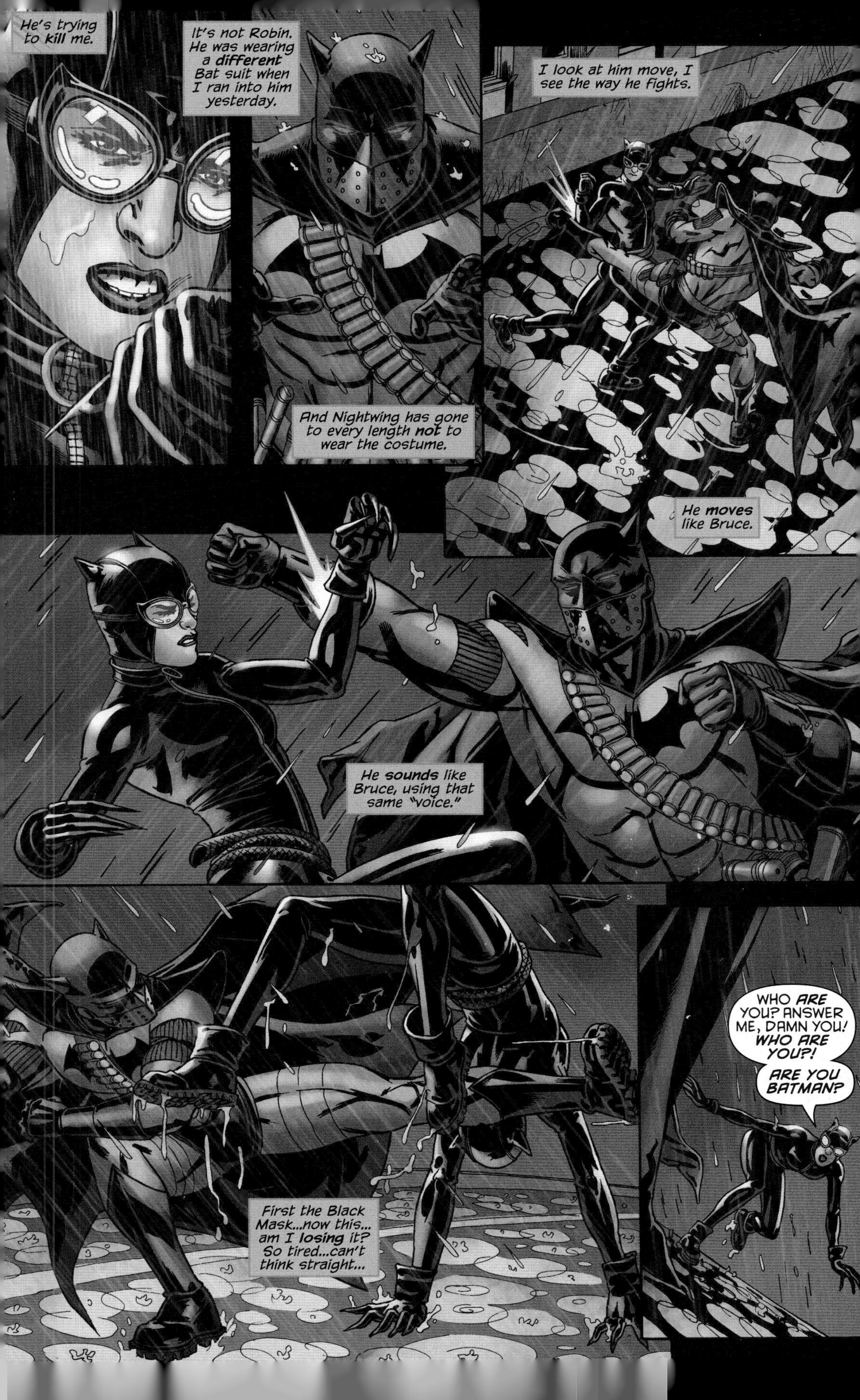
He's trying to **kill** me.
It's not Robin. He was wearing a **different** Bat suit when I ran into him yesterday.
And Nightwing has gone to every length **not** to wear the costume.
I look at him move, I see the way he fights.
He **moves** like Bruce.
He **sounds** like Bruce, using that same "voice."
First the Black Mask...now this... am I **losing** it? So tired...can't think straight...
WHO **ARE** YOU? ANSWER ME, DAMN YOU! **WHO ARE YOU?!**
ARE YOU BATMAN?

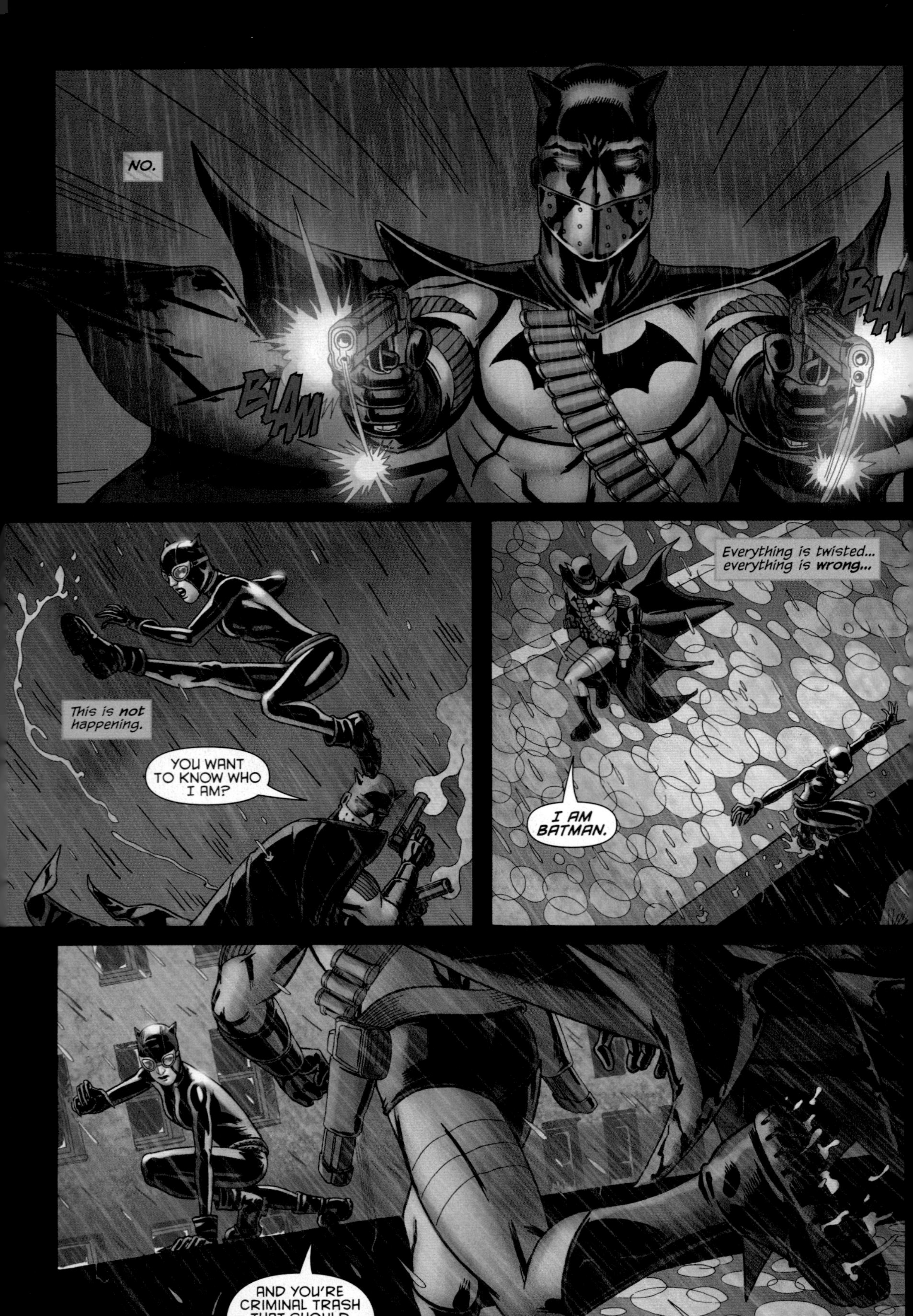
NO.
BLAM
BLAM
This is not happening.
YOU WANT TO KNOW WHO I AM?
Everything is twisted... everything is wrong...
I AM BATMAN.
AND YOU'RE CRIMINAL TRASH THAT SHOULD HAVE BEEN TAKEN OUT A LONG TIME AGO.

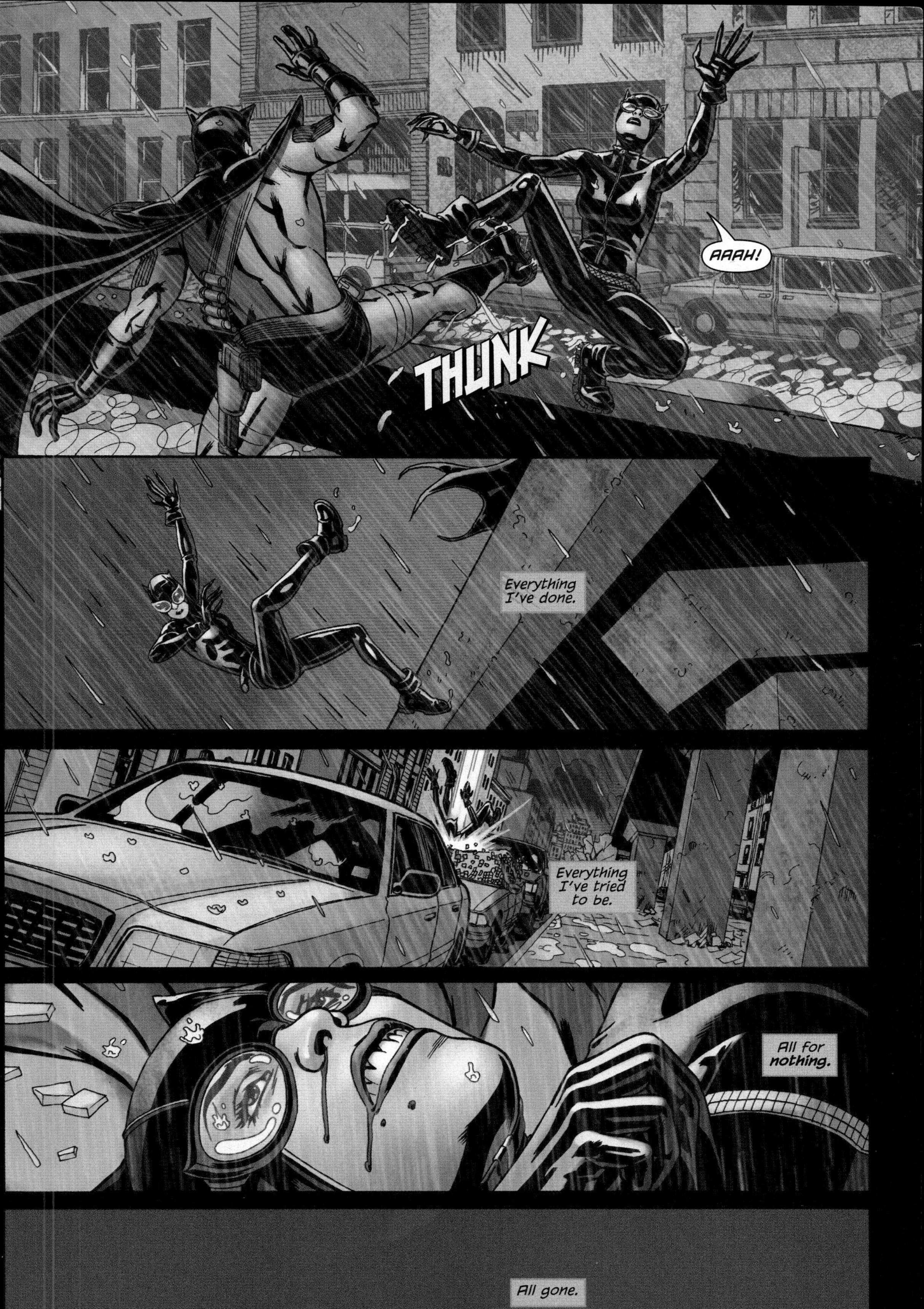
AAAH!
THUNK
Everything I've done.
Everything I've tried to be.
All for nothing.
All gone.

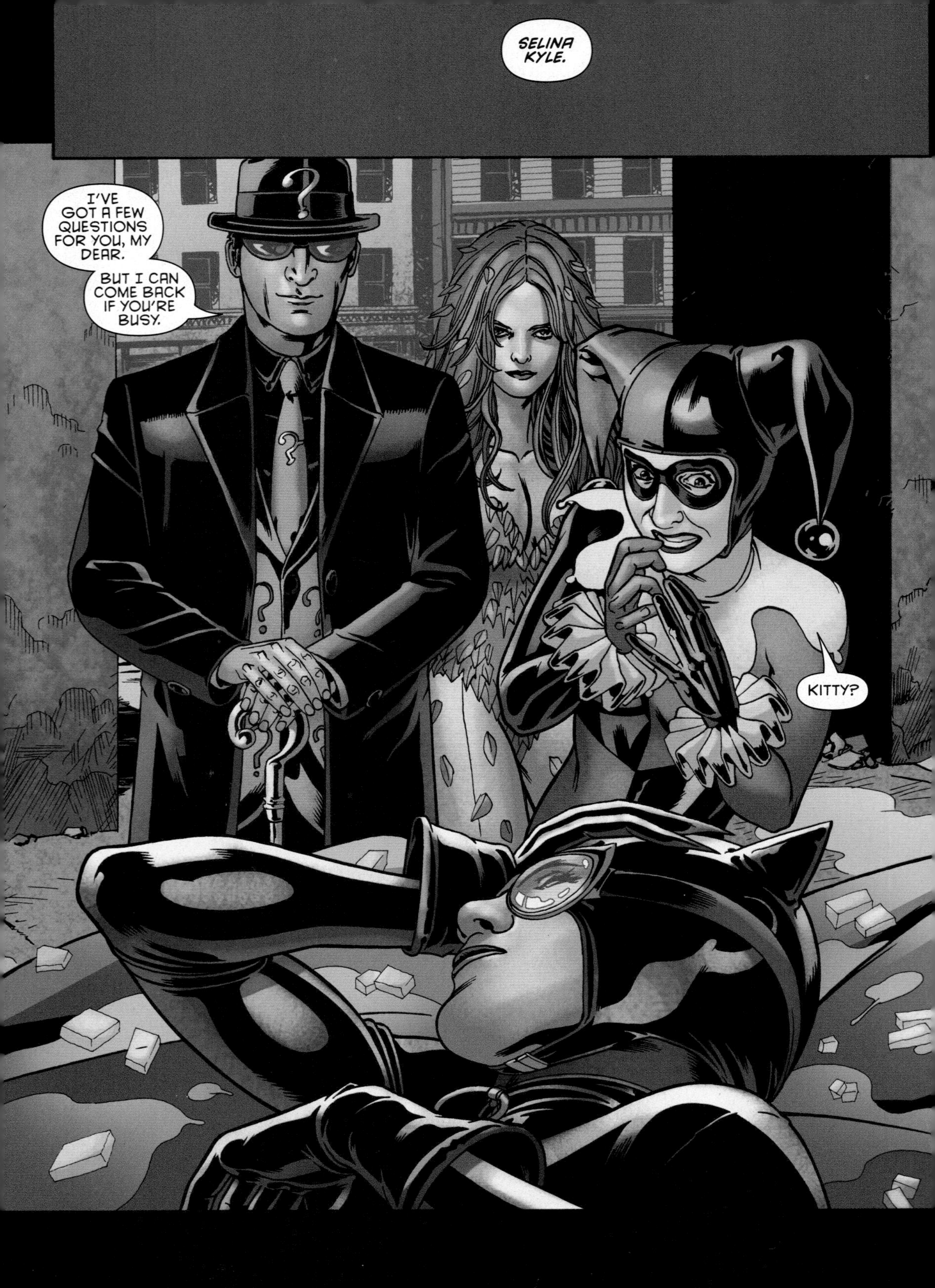
SELINA KYLE.
I'VE GOT A FEW QUESTIONS FOR YOU, MY DEAR.
BUT I CAN COME BACK IF YOU'RE BUSY.
KITTY?

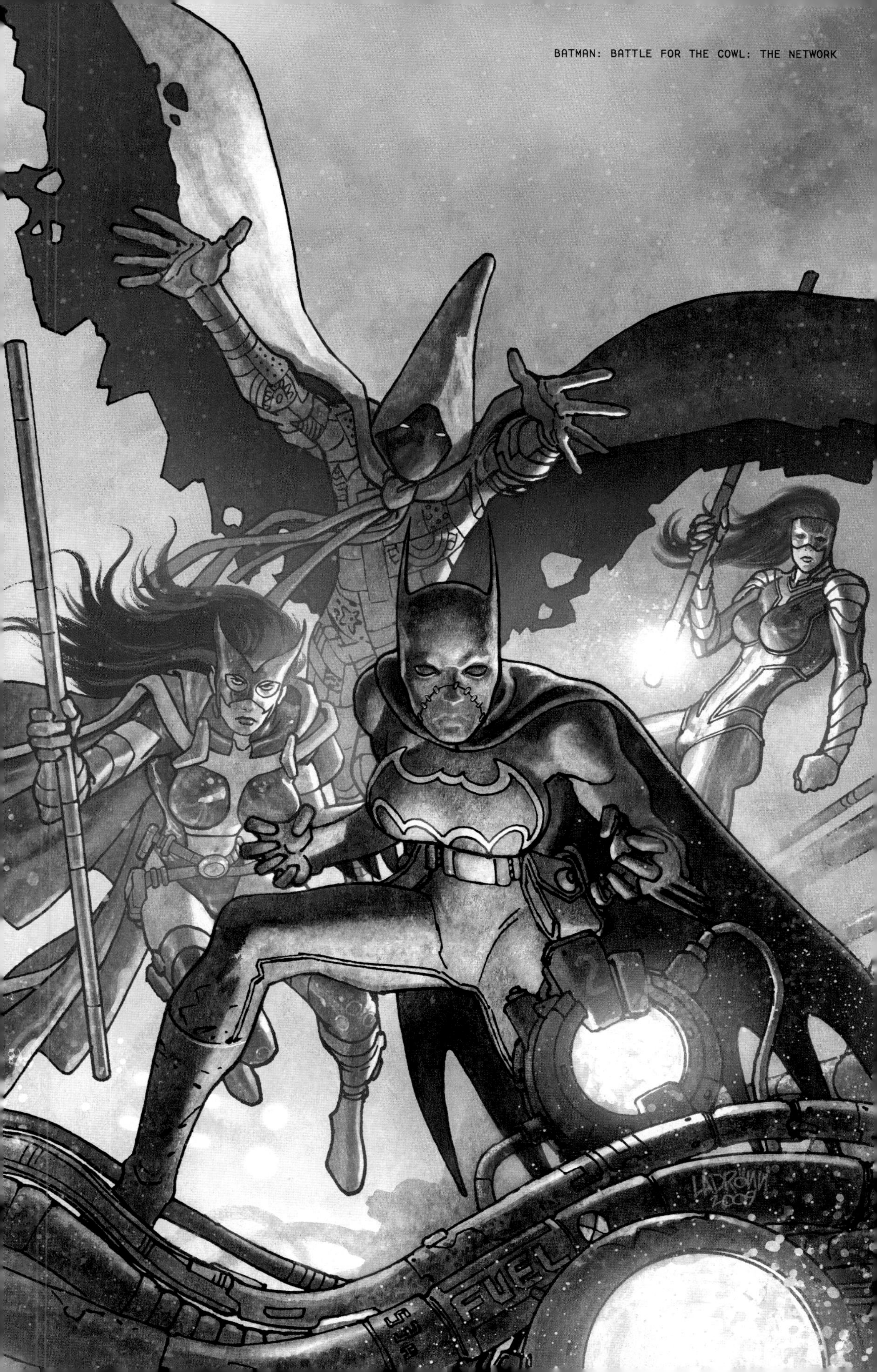
LADRONN 2009
FUEL

THE NETWORK

Fabian Nicieza
Writer

Jim Calafiore
Don Kramer
Pencillers

Mark McKenna
Inker

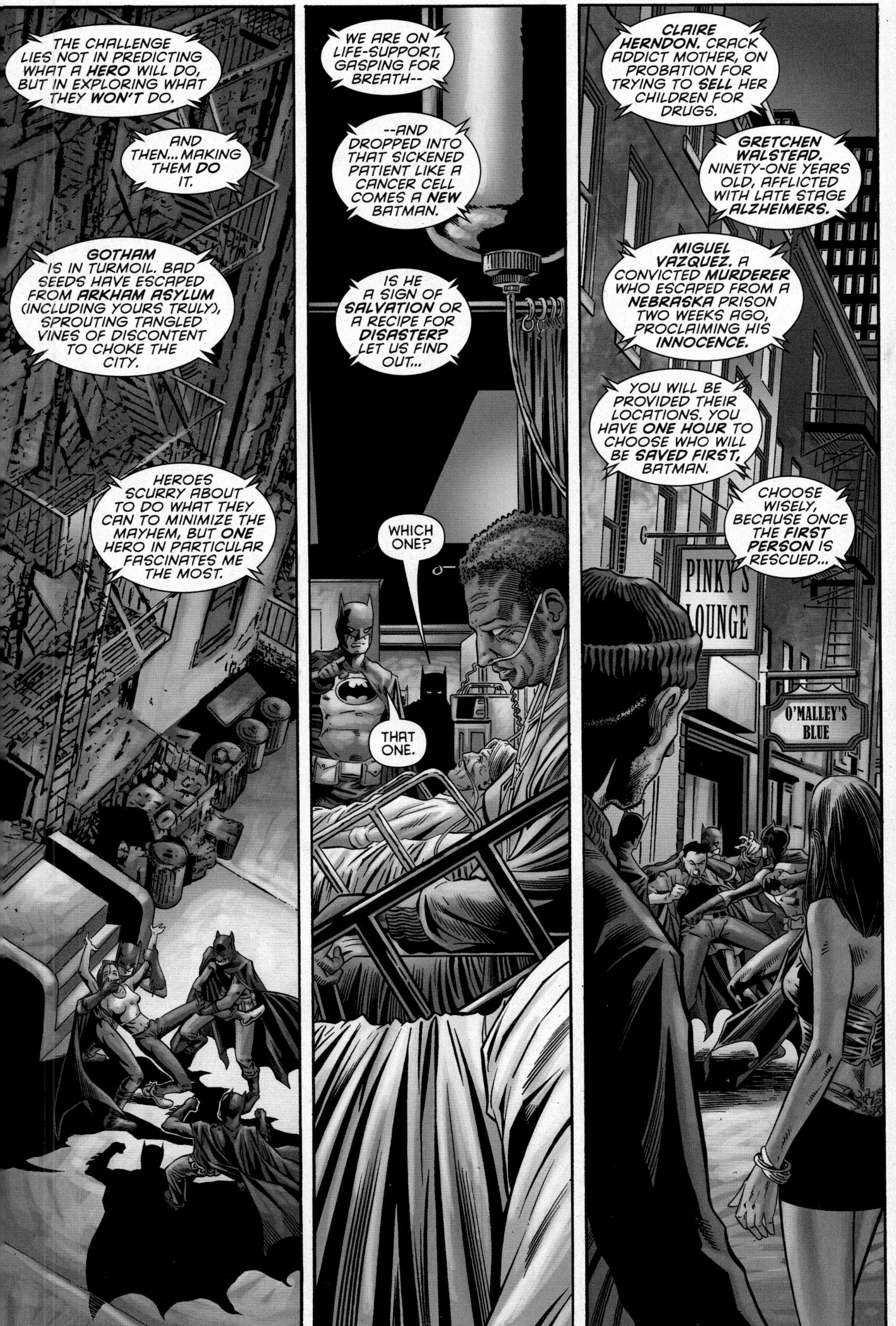
THE CHALLENGE LIES NOT IN PREDICTING WHAT A HERO WILL DO, BUT IN EXPLORING WHAT THEY WON'T DO.
AND THEN... MAKING THEM DO IT.
GOTHAM IS IN TURMOIL. BAD SEEDS HAVE ESCAPED FROM ARKHAM ASYLUM (INCLUDING YOURS TRULY), SPROUTING TANGLED VINES OF DISCONTENT TO CHOKE THE CITY.
HEROES SCURRY ABOUT TO DO WHAT THEY CAN TO MINIMIZE THE MAYHEM, BUT ONE HERO IN PARTICULAR FASCINATES ME THE MOST.
WE ARE ON LIFE-SUPPORT, GASPING FOR BREATH--
--AND DROPPED INTO THAT SICKENED PATIENT LIKE A CANCER CELL COMES A NEW BATMAN.
IS HE A SIGN OF SALVATION OR A RECIPE FOR DISASTER? LET US FIND OUT...
WHICH ONE?
THAT ONE.
CLAIRE HERNDON. CRACK ADDICT MOTHER, ON PROBATION FOR TRYING TO SELL HER CHILDREN FOR DRUGS.
GRETCHEN WALSTEAD. NINETY-ONE YEARS OLD, AFFLICTED WITH LATE STAGE ALZHEIMERS.
MIGUEL VAZQUEZ. A CONVICTED MURDERER WHO ESCAPED FROM A NEBRASKA PRISON TWO WEEKS AGO, PROCLAIMING HIS INNOCENCE.
YOU WILL BE PROVIDED THEIR LOCATIONS. YOU HAVE ONE HOUR TO CHOOSE WHO WILL BE SAVED FIRST, BATMAN.
CHOOSE WISELY, BECAUSE ONCE THE FIRST PERSON IS RESCUED...
PINKY'S LOUNGE
O'MALLEY'S BLUE

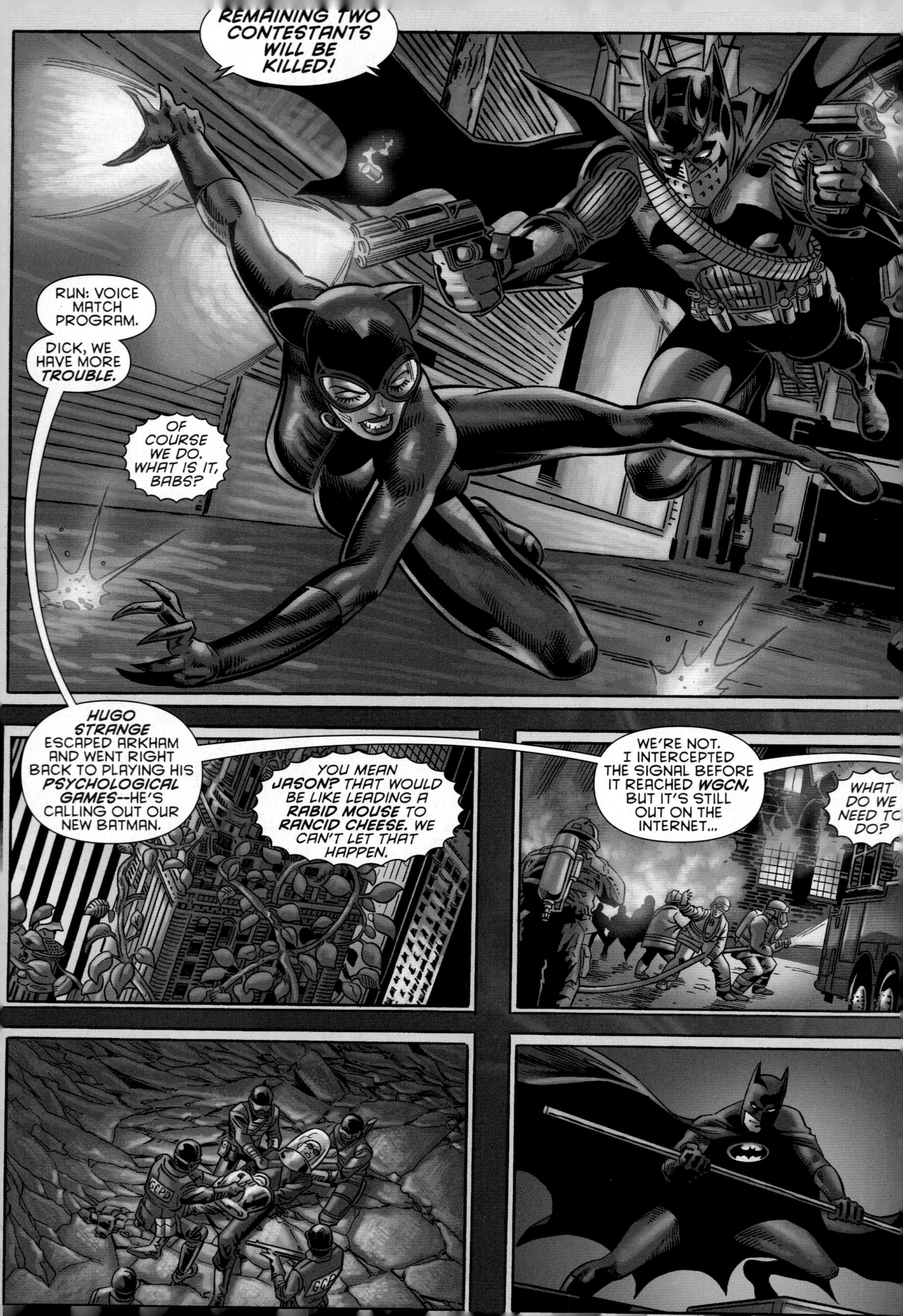
REMAINING TWO CONTESTANTS WILL BE KILLED!
RUN: VOICE MATCH PROGRAM.
DICK, WE HAVE MORE TROUBLE.
OF COURSE WE DO. WHAT IS IT, BABS?
HUGO STRANGE ESCAPED ARKHAM AND WENT RIGHT BACK TO PLAYING HIS PSYCHOLOGICAL GAMES--HE'S CALLING OUT OUR NEW BATMAN.
YOU MEAN JASON? THAT WOULD BE LIKE LEADING A RABID MOUSE TO RANCID CHEESE. WE CAN'T LET THAT HAPPEN.
WE'RE NOT. I INTERCEPTED THE SIGNAL BEFORE IT REACHED WGCN, BUT IT'S STILL OUT ON THE INTERNET...
WHAT DO WE NEED TO DO?
GCPD

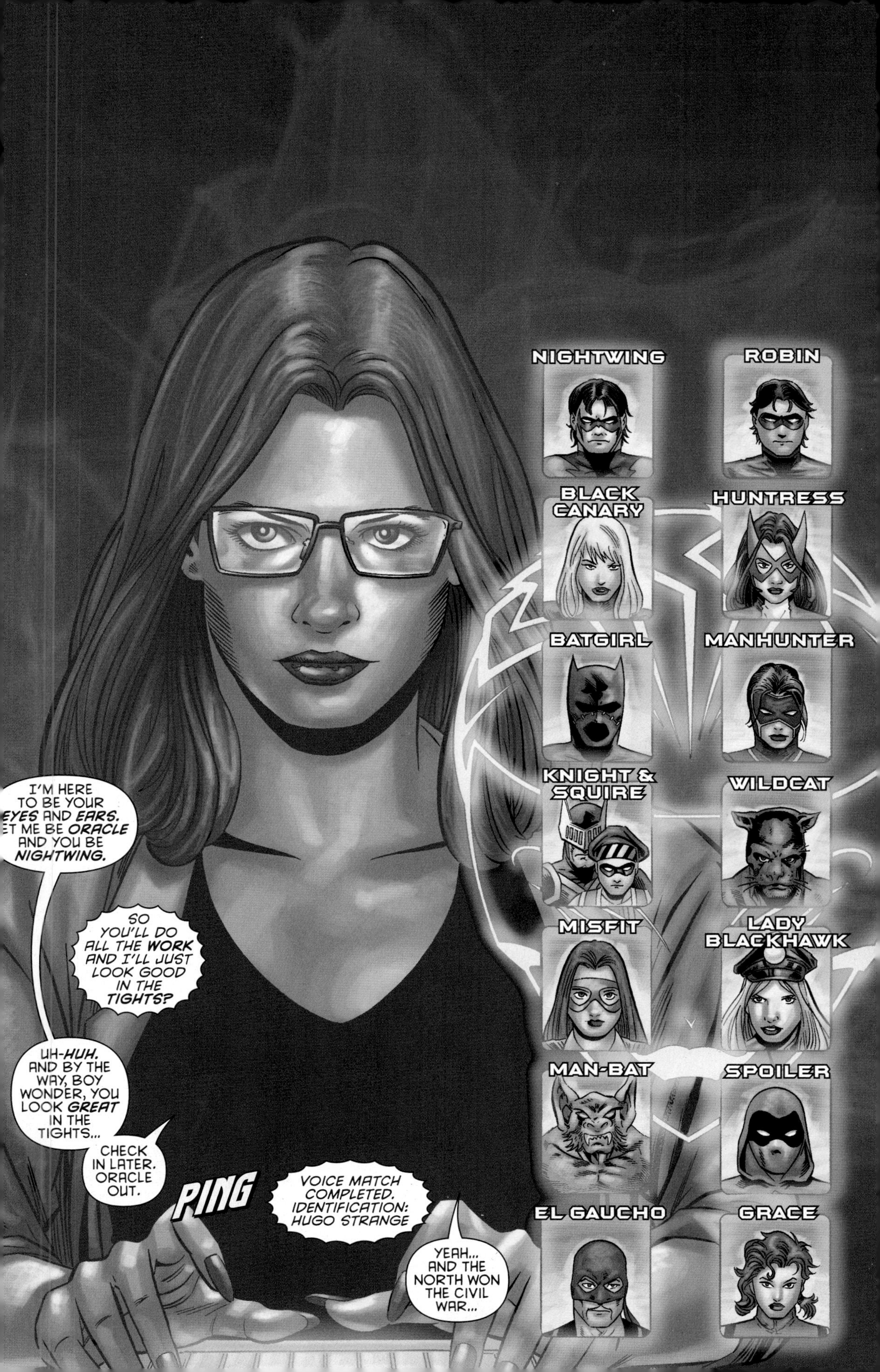

NIGHTWING
ROBIN
BLACK CANARY
HUNTRESS
BATGIRL
MANHUNTER
KNIGHT & SQUIRE
WILDCAT
MISFIT
LADY BLACKHAWK
MAN-BAT
SPOILER
EL GAUCHO
GRACE
I'M HERE TO BE YOUR EYES AND EARS. ET ME BE ORACLE AND YOU BE NIGHTWING.
SO YOU'LL DO ALL THE WORK AND I'LL JUST LOOK GOOD IN THE TIGHTS?
UH-HUH. AND BY THE WAY, BOY WONDER, YOU LOOK GREAT IN THE TIGHTS...
CHECK IN LATER. ORACLE OUT.
PING
VOICE MATCH COMPLETED. IDENTIFICATION: HUGO STRANGE
YEAH... AND THE NORTH WON THE CIVIL WAR...

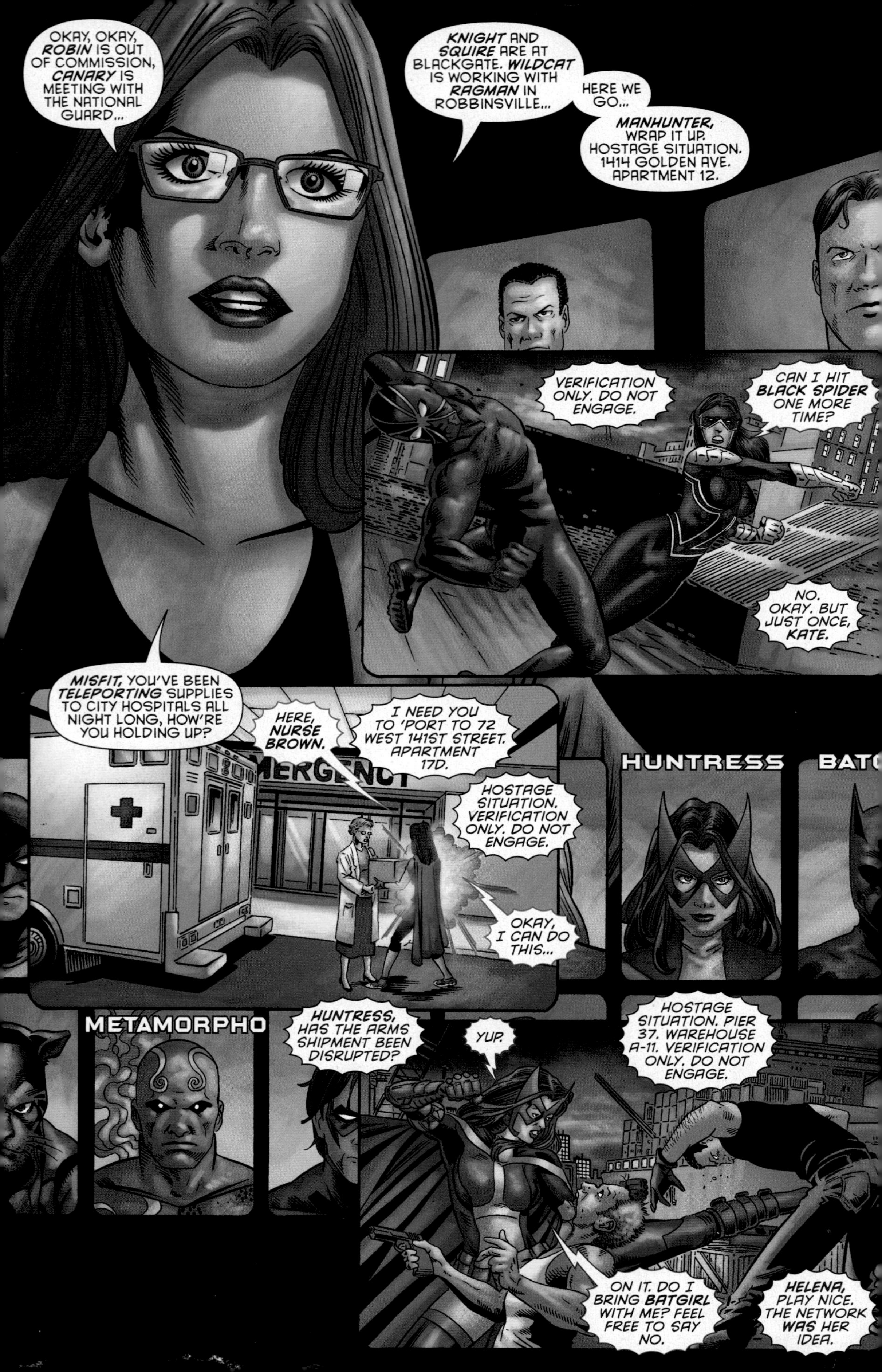

OKAY, OKAY, ROBIN IS OUT OF COMMISSION, CANARY IS MEETING WITH THE NATIONAL GUARD...
KNIGHT AND SQUIRE ARE AT BLACKGATE. WILDCAT IS WORKING WITH RAGMAN IN ROBBINSVILLE...
HERE WE GO...
MANHUNTER, WRAP IT UP. HOSTAGE SITUATION. 1414 GOLDEN AVE. APARTMENT 12.
VERIFICATION ONLY. DO NOT ENGAGE.
CAN I HIT BLACK SPIDER ONE MORE TIME?
NO. OKAY. BUT JUST ONCE, KATE.
MISFIT, YOU'VE BEEN TELEPORTING SUPPLIES TO CITY HOSPITALS ALL NIGHT LONG, HOW'RE YOU HOLDING UP?
HERE, NURSE BROWN.
I NEED YOU TO 'PORT TO 72 WEST 141ST STREET. APARTMENT 17D.
HOSTAGE SITUATION. VERIFICATION ONLY. DO NOT ENGAGE.
OKAY, I CAN DO THIS...
HUNTRESS
METAMORPHO
HUNTRESS, HAS THE ARMS SHIPMENT BEEN DISRUPTED?
YUP.
HOSTAGE SITUATION. PIER 37. WAREHOUSE A-11. VERIFICATION ONLY. DO NOT ENGAGE.
ON IT. DO I BRING BATGIRL WITH ME? FEEL FREE TO SAY NO.
HELENA, PLAY NICE. THE NETWORK WAS HER IDEA.

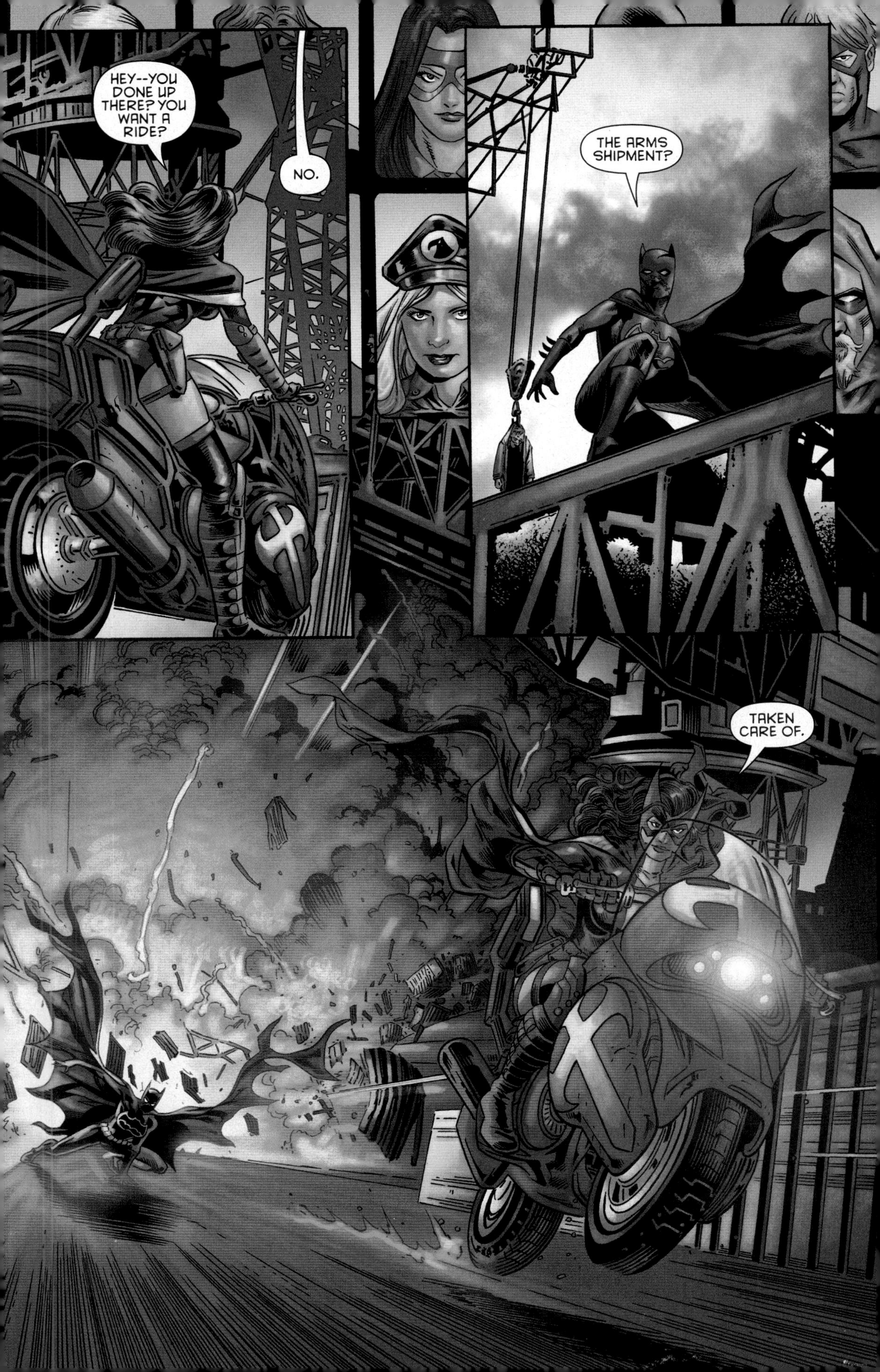
HEY--YOU DONE UP THERE? YOU WANT A RIDE?
NO.
THE ARMS SHIPMENT?
TAKEN CARE OF.

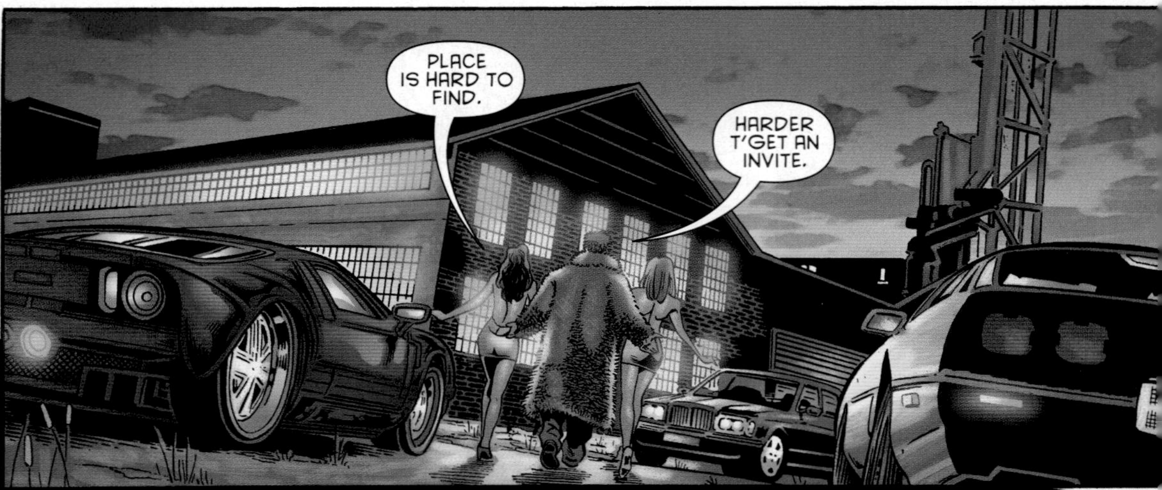
PLACE IS HARD TO FIND.
HARDER T'GET AN INVITE.

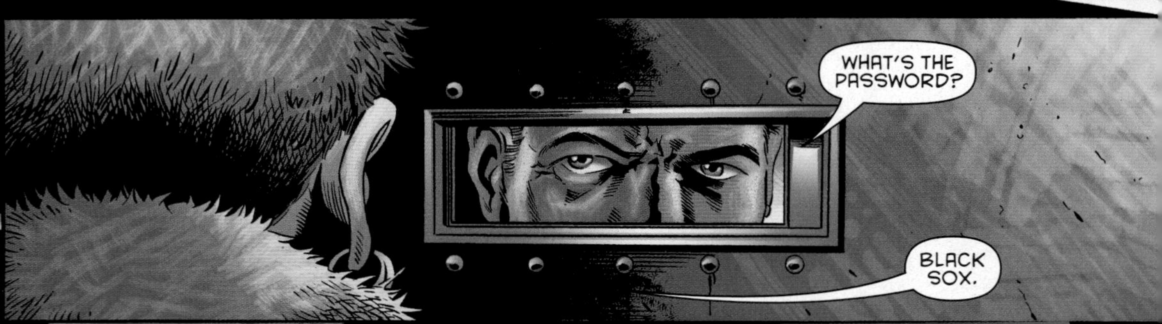
WHAT'S THE PASSWORD?
BLACK SOX.

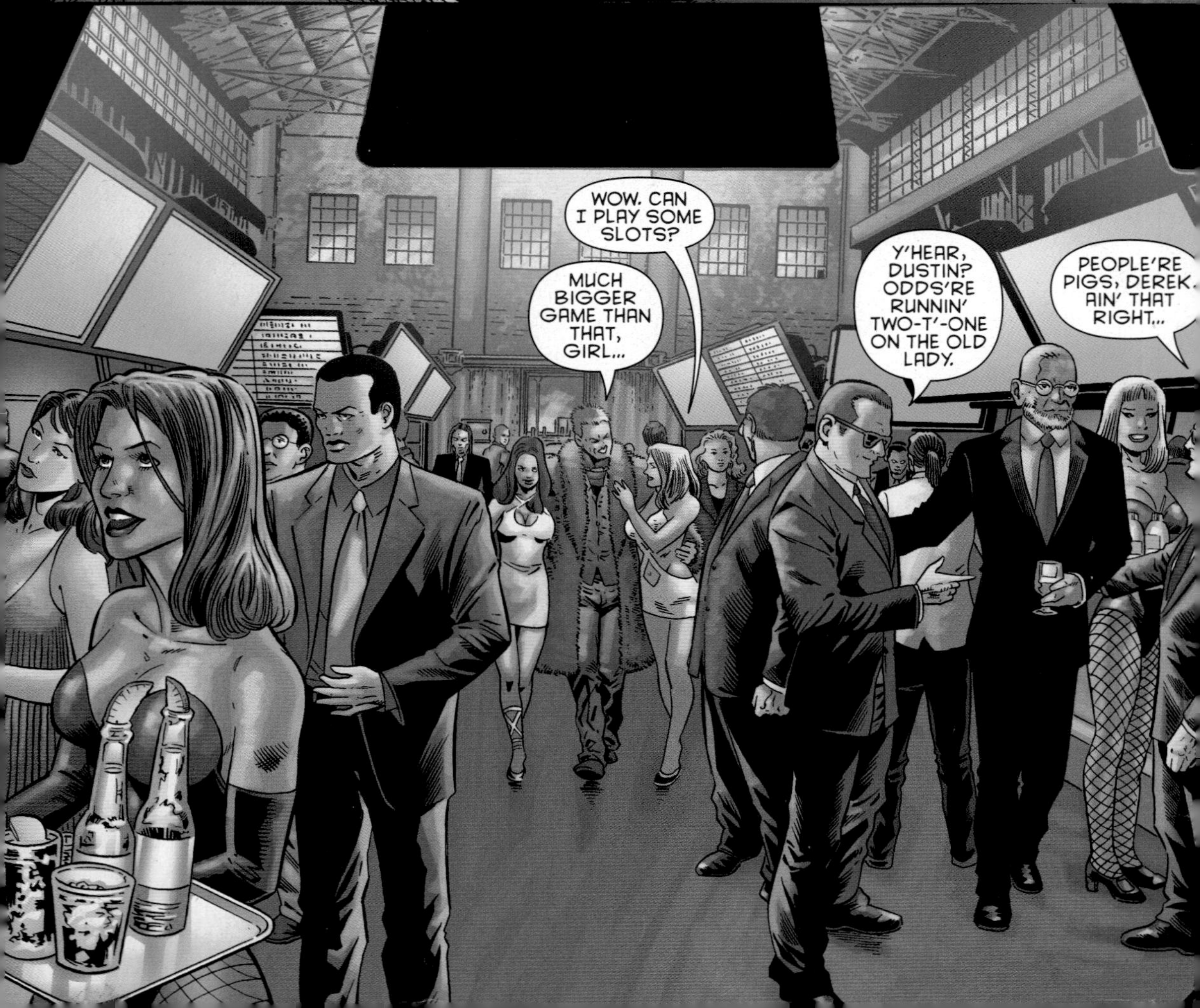
WOW. CAN I PLAY SOME SLOTS?
MUCH BIGGER GAME THAN THAT, GIRL...
Y'HEAR, DUSTIN? ODDS'RE RUNNIN' TWO-T'-ONE ON THE OLD LADY.
PEOPLE'RE PIGS, DEREK. AIN' THAT RIGHT...

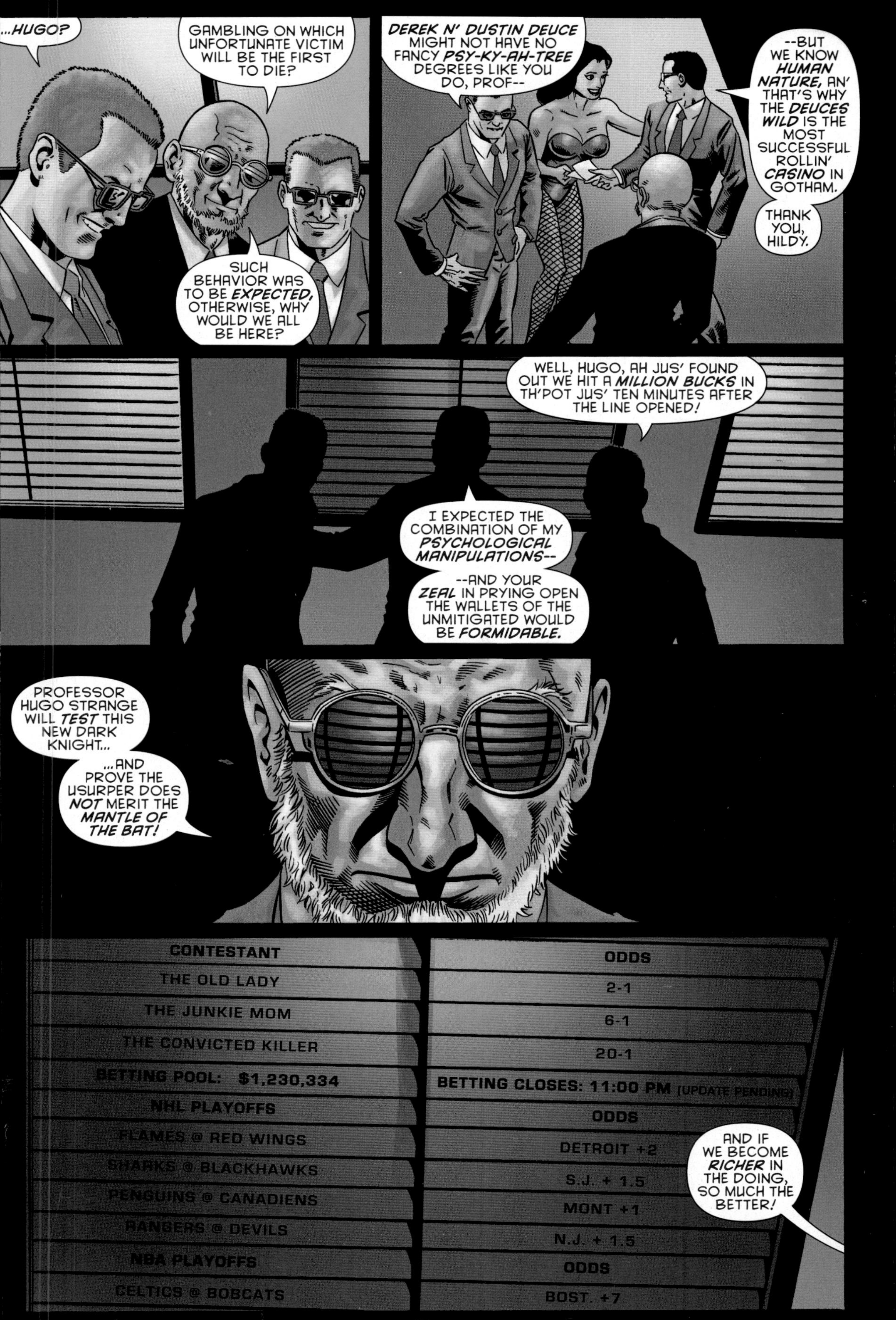
...HUGO?
GAMBLING ON WHICH UNFORTUNATE VICTIM WILL BE THE FIRST TO DIE?
SUCH BEHAVIOR WAS TO BE EXPECTED, OTHERWISE, WHY WOULD WE ALL BE HERE?
DEREK N' DUSTIN DEUCE MIGHT NOT HAVE NO FANCY PSY-KY-AH-TREE DEGREES LIKE YOU DO, PROF--
--BUT WE KNOW HUMAN NATURE, AN' THAT'S WHY THE DEUCES WILD IS THE MOST SUCCESSFUL ROLLIN' CASINO IN GOTHAM.
THANK YOU, HILDY.
WELL, HUGO, AH JUS' FOUND OUT WE HIT A MILLION BUCKS IN TH'POT JUS' TEN MINUTES AFTER THE LINE OPENED!
I EXPECTED THE COMBINATION OF MY PSYCHOLOGICAL MANIPULATIONS--
--AND YOUR ZEAL IN PRYING OPEN THE WALLETS OF THE UNMITIGATED WOULD BE FORMIDABLE.
PROFESSOR HUGO STRANGE WILL TEST THIS NEW DARK KNIGHT...
...AND PROVE THE USURPER DOES NOT MERIT THE MANTLE OF THE BAT!
CONTESTANT
THE OLD LADY
THE JUNKIE MOM
THE CONVICTED KILLER
BETTING POOL: $1,230,334
NHL PLAYOFFS
FLAMES @ RED WINGS
SHARKS @ BLACKHAWKS
PENGUINS @ CANADIENS
RANGERS @ DEVILS
NBA PLAYOFFS
CELTICS @ BOBCATS
ODDS
2-1
6-1
20-1
BETTING CLOSES: 11:00 PM (UPDATE PENDING)
ODDS
DETROIT +2
S.J. + 1.5
MONT +1
N.J. + 1.5
ODDS
BOST. +7
AND IF WE BECOME RICHER IN THE DOING, SO MUCH THE BETTER!

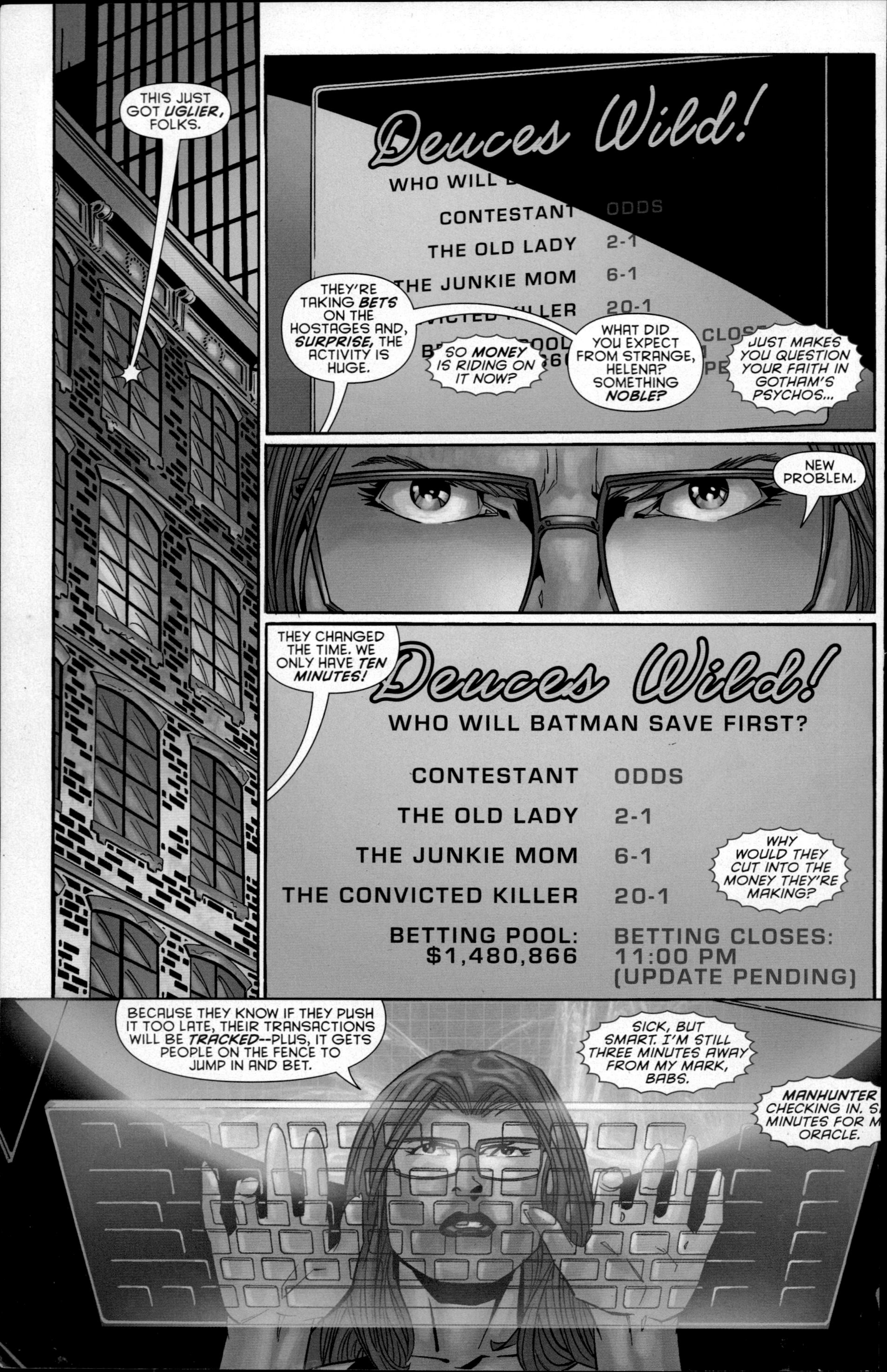
THIS JUST GOT UGLIER, FOLKS.
Deuces Wild!
WHO WILL B
CONTESTANT ODDS
THE OLD LADY 2-1
THE JUNKIE MOM 6-1
20-1
THEY'RE TAKING BETS ON THE HOSTAGES AND, SURPRISE, THE ACTIVITY IS HUGE.
SO MONEY IS RIDING ON IT NOW?
WHAT DID YOU EXPECT FROM STRANGE, HELENA? SOMETHING NOBLE?
JUST MAKES YOU QUESTION YOUR FAITH IN GOTHAM'S PSYCHOS...
NEW PROBLEM.
THEY CHANGED THE TIME. WE ONLY HAVE TEN MINUTES!
Deuces Wild!
WHO WILL BATMAN SAVE FIRST?
CONTESTANT ODDS
THE OLD LADY 2-1
THE JUNKIE MOM 6-1
THE CONVICTED KILLER 20-1
BETTING POOL: $1,480,866
BETTING CLOSES: 11:00 PM (UPDATE PENDING)
WHY WOULD THEY CUT INTO THE MONEY THEY'RE MAKING?
BECAUSE THEY KNOW IF THEY PUSH IT TOO LATE, THEIR TRANSACTIONS WILL BE TRACKED--PLUS, IT GETS PEOPLE ON THE FENCE TO JUMP IN AND BET.
SICK, BUT SMART. I'M STILL THREE MINUTES AWAY FROM MY MARK, BABS.
MANHUNTER CHECKING IN.
ORACLE.

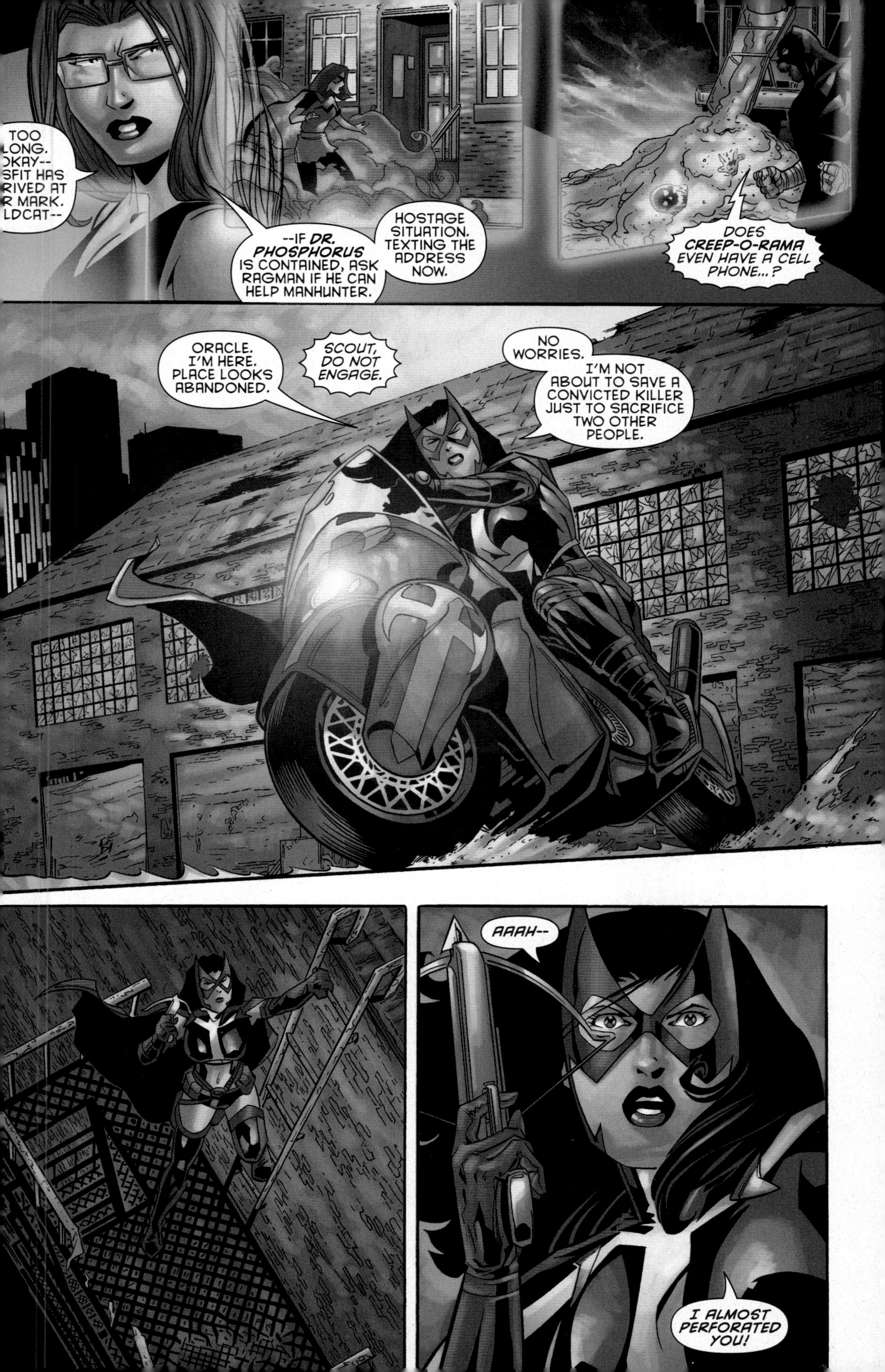

TOO LONG. OKAY-- SFIT HAS RIVED AT R MARK. LDCAT--
--IF DR. PHOSPHORUS IS CONTAINED, ASK RAGMAN IF HE CAN HELP MANHUNTER.
HOSTAGE SITUATION. TEXTING THE ADDRESS NOW.
DOES CREEP-O-RAMA EVEN HAVE A CELL PHONE...?
ORACLE. I'M HERE. PLACE LOOKS ABANDONED.
SCOUT, DO NOT ENGAGE.
NO WORRIES.
I'M NOT ABOUT TO SAVE A CONVICTED KILLER JUST TO SACRIFICE TWO OTHER PEOPLE.
AAAH--
I ALMOST PERFORATED YOU!

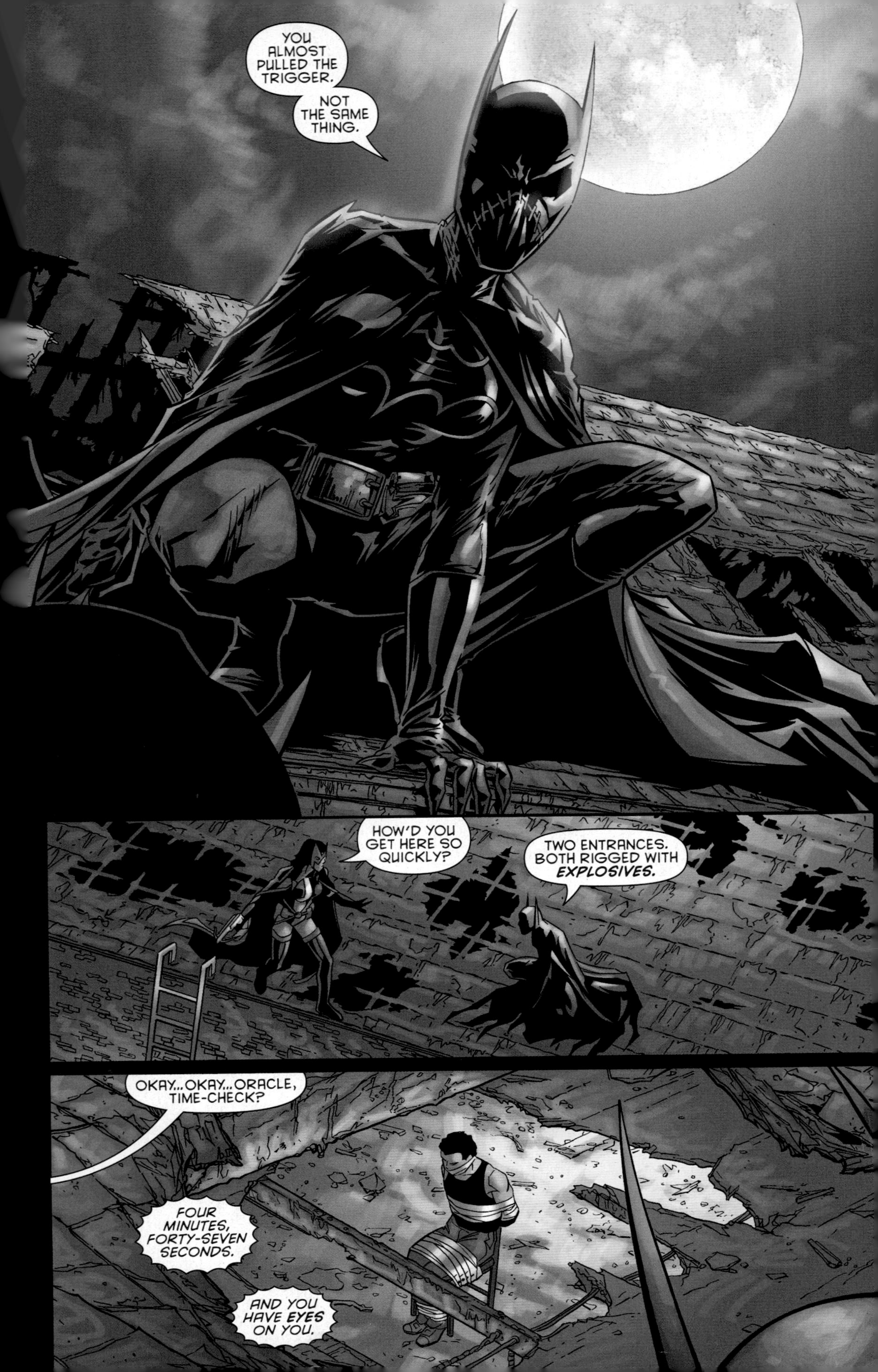
YOU ALMOST PULLED THE TRIGGER.
NOT THE SAME THING.
HOW'D YOU GET HERE SO QUICKLY?
TWO ENTRANCES. BOTH RIGGED WITH EXPLOSIVES.
OKAY...OKAY...ORACLE, TIME-CHECK?
FOUR MINUTES, FORTY-SEVEN SECONDS.
AND YOU HAVE EYES ON YOU.

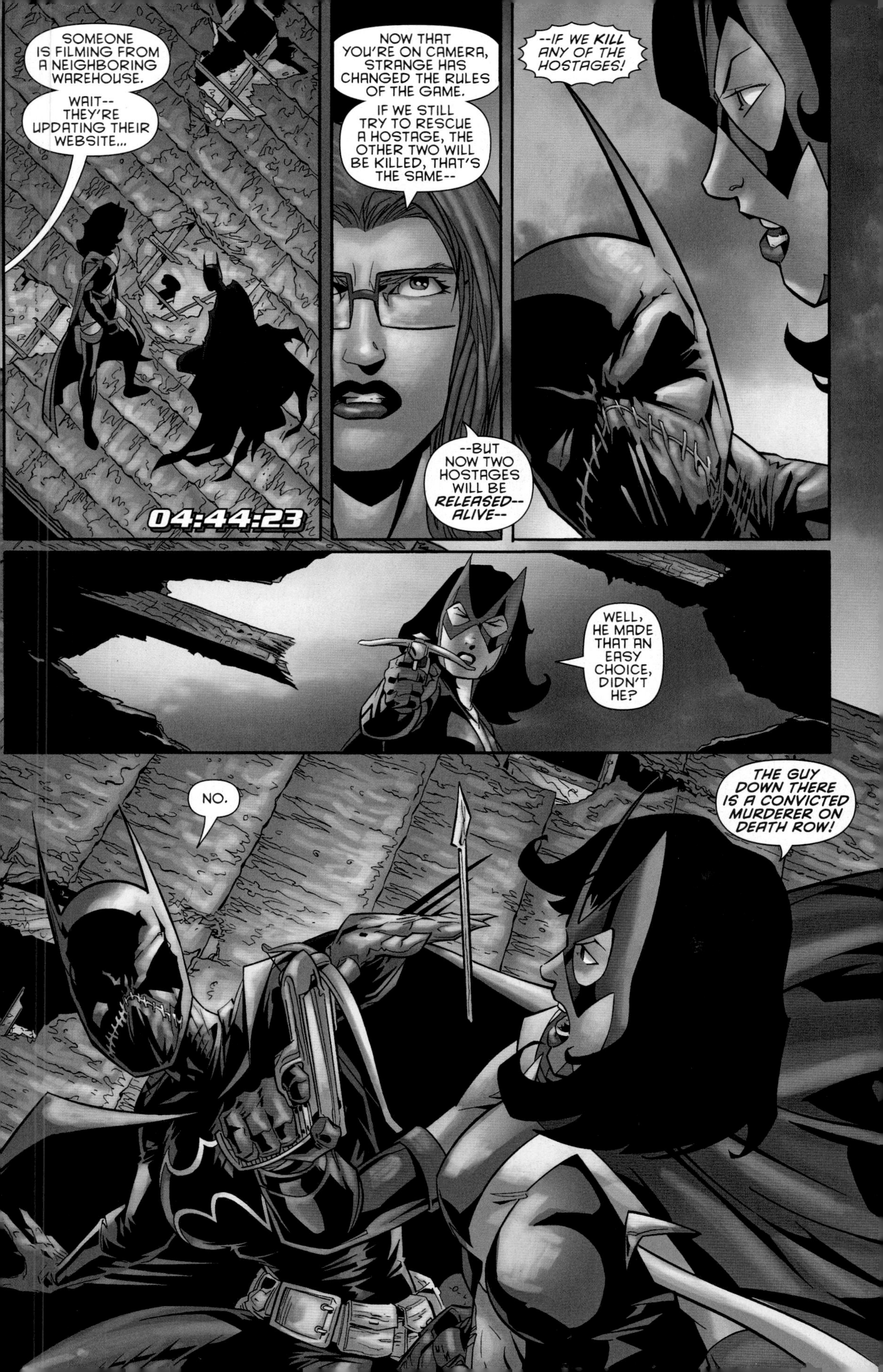
SOMEONE IS FILMING FROM A NEIGHBORING WAREHOUSE.
WAIT-- THEY'RE UPDATING THEIR WEBSITE...
04:44:23
NOW THAT YOU'RE ON CAMERA, STRANGE HAS CHANGED THE RULES OF THE GAME.
IF WE STILL TRY TO RESCUE A HOSTAGE, THE OTHER TWO WILL BE KILLED, THAT'S THE SAME--
--BUT NOW TWO HOSTAGES WILL BE RELEASED-- ALIVE--
--IF WE KILL ANY OF THE HOSTAGES!
WELL, HE MADE THAT AN EASY CHOICE, DIDN'T HE?
NO.
THE GUY DOWN THERE IS A CONVICTED MURDERER ON DEATH ROW!

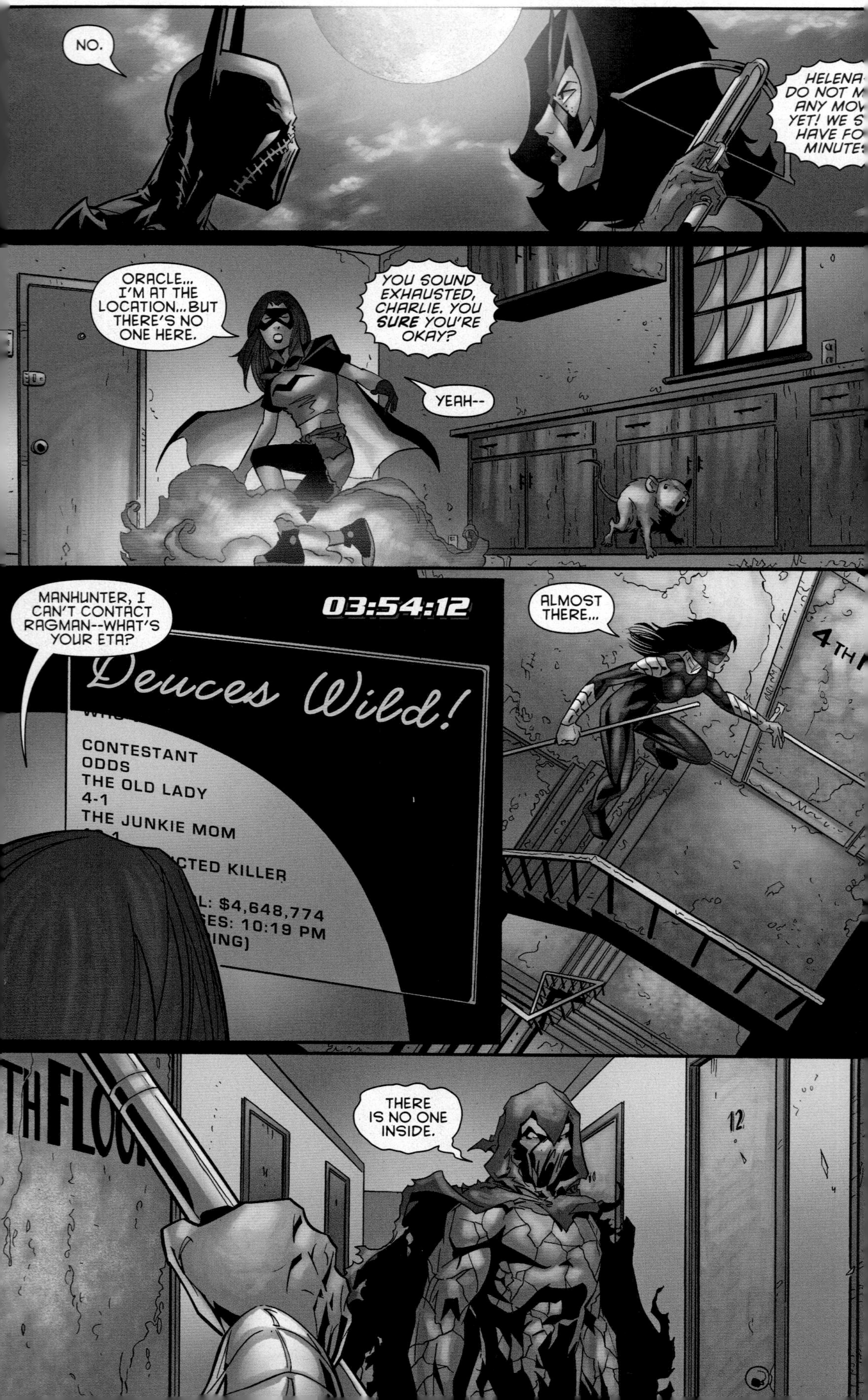
NO.
HELENA-- DO NOT M ANY MOV YET! WE S HAVE FO MINUTE
ORACLE... I'M AT THE LOCATION...BUT THERE'S NO ONE HERE.
YOU SOUND EXHAUSTED, CHARLIE. YOU SURE YOU'RE OKAY?
YEAH--
MANHUNTER, I CAN'T CONTACT RAGMAN--WHAT'S YOUR ETA?
03:54:12
Deuces Wild!
CONTESTANT
ODDS
THE OLD LADY
4-1
THE JUNKIE MOM
CTED KILLER
L: $4,648,774
SES: 10:19 PM
ING)
ALMOST THERE...
4TH
TH FLOO
THERE IS NO ONE INSIDE.
12

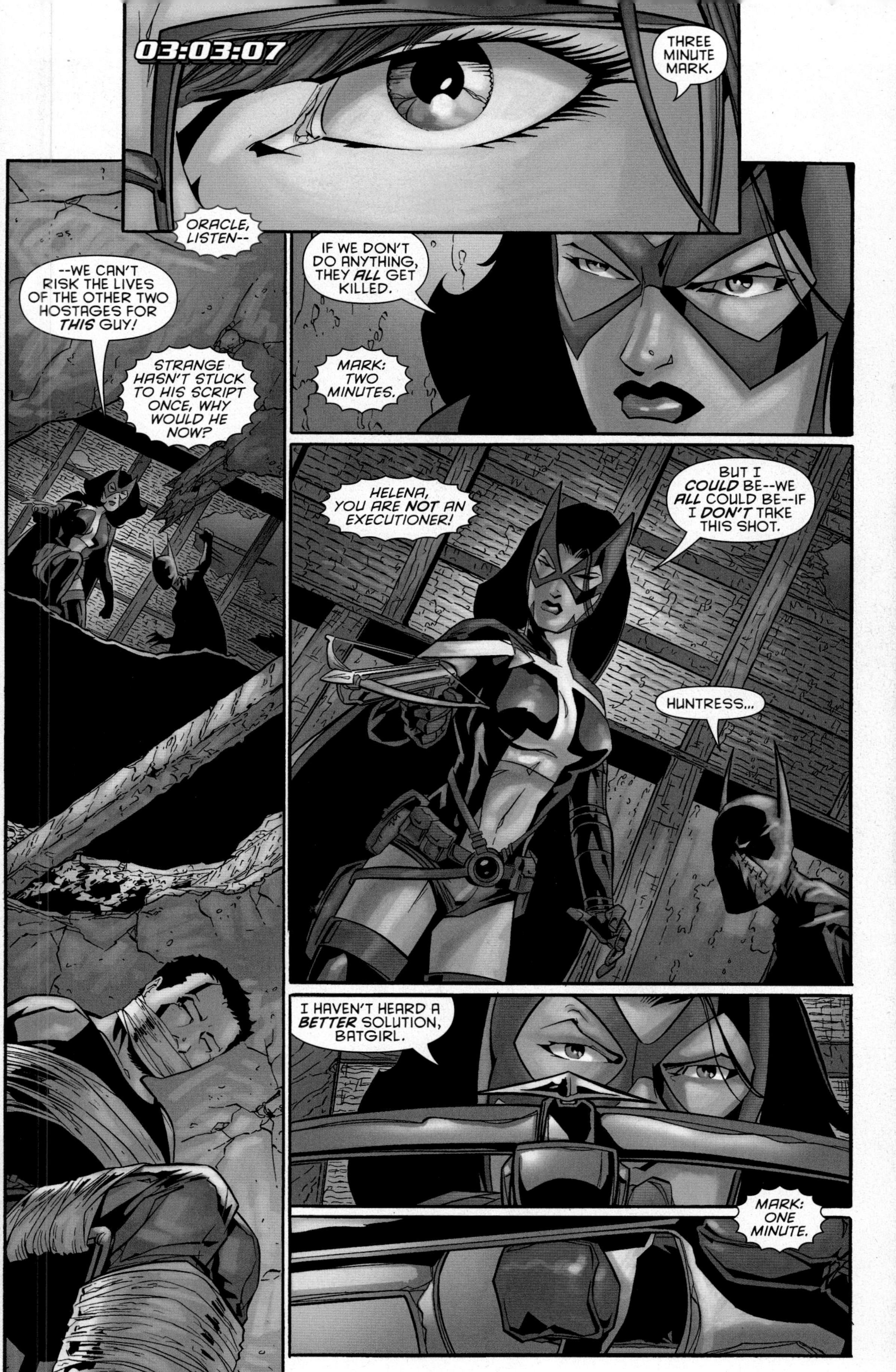
03:03:07
THREE MINUTE MARK.
ORACLE, LISTEN--
--WE CAN'T RISK THE LIVES OF THE OTHER TWO HOSTAGES FOR THIS GUY!
STRANGE HASN'T STUCK TO HIS SCRIPT ONCE, WHY WOULD HE NOW?
IF WE DON'T DO ANYTHING, THEY ALL GET KILLED.
MARK: TWO MINUTES.
HELENA, YOU ARE NOT AN EXECUTIONER!
BUT I COULD BE--WE ALL COULD BE--IF I DON'T TAKE THIS SHOT.
HUNTRESS...
I HAVEN'T HEARD A BETTER SOLUTION, BATGIRL.
MARK: ONE MINUTE.

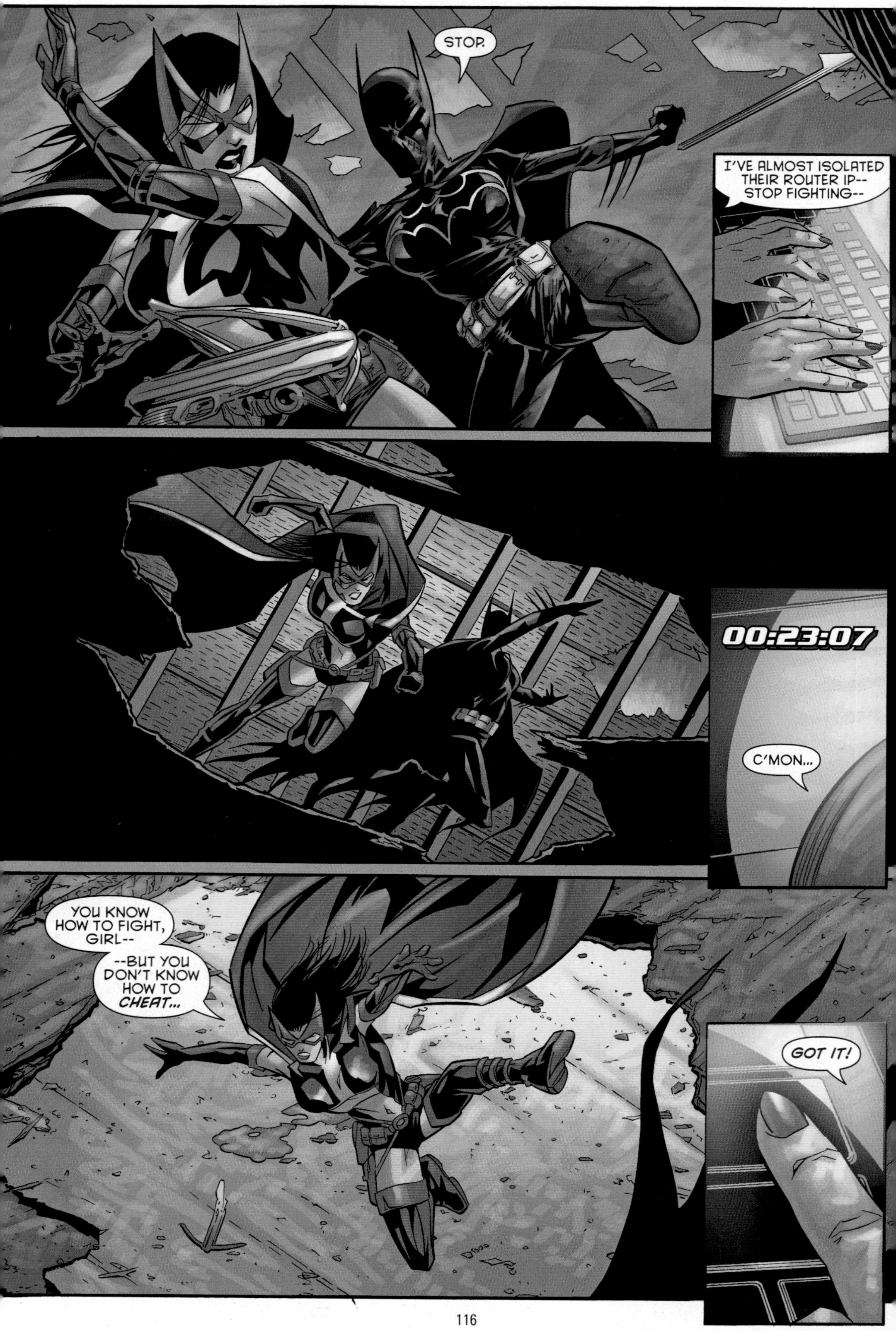
STOP.
I'VE ALMOST ISOLATED THEIR ROUTER IP-- STOP FIGHTING--
00:23:07
C'MON...
YOU KNOW HOW TO FIGHT, GIRL--
--BUT YOU DON'T KNOW HOW TO *CHEAT*...
GOT IT!

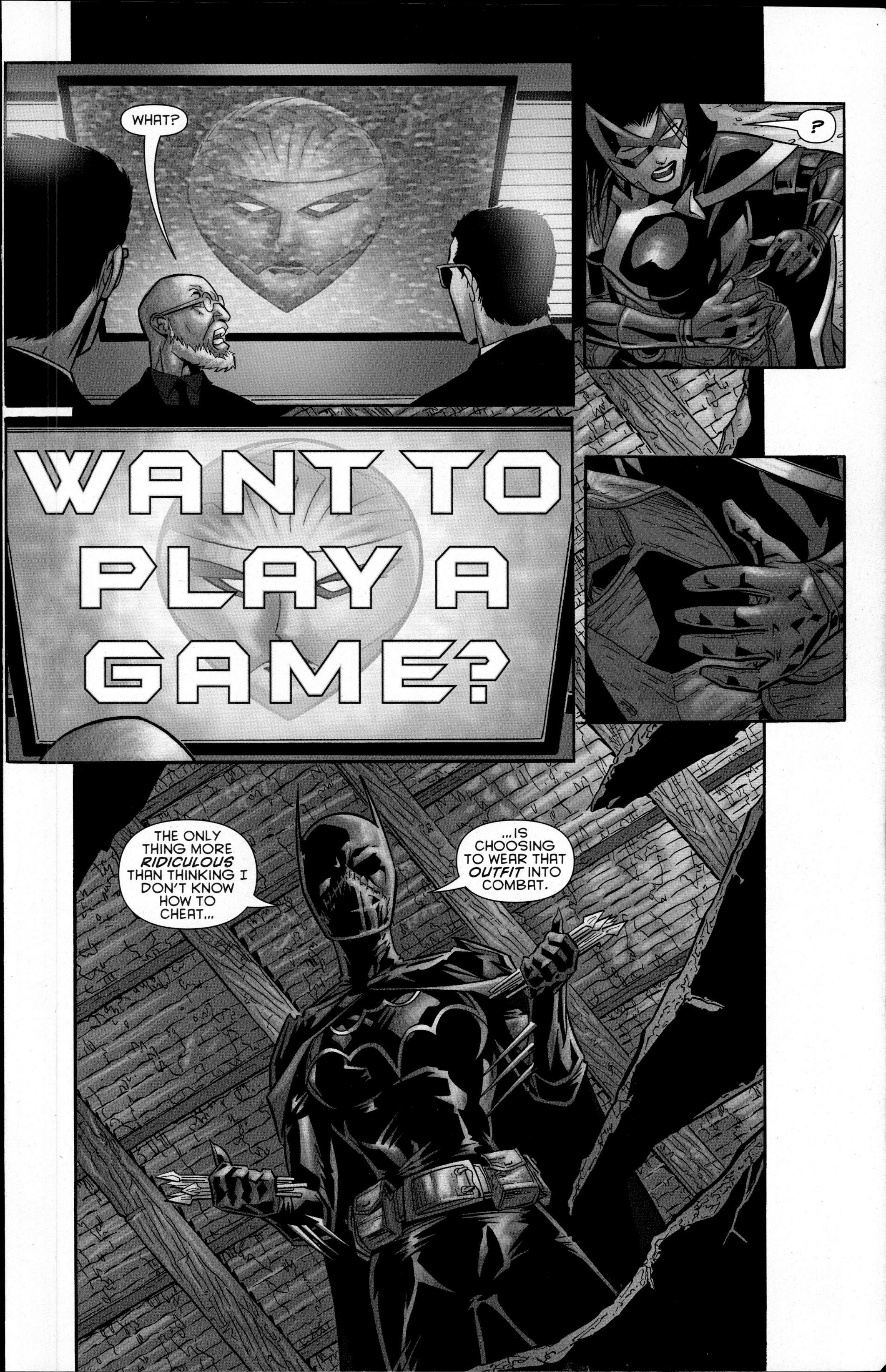
WHAT?
?
WANT TO PLAY A GAME?
THE ONLY THING MORE RIDICULOUS THAN THINKING I DON'T KNOW HOW TO CHEAT...
...IS CHOOSING TO WEAR THAT OUTFIT INTO COMBAT.

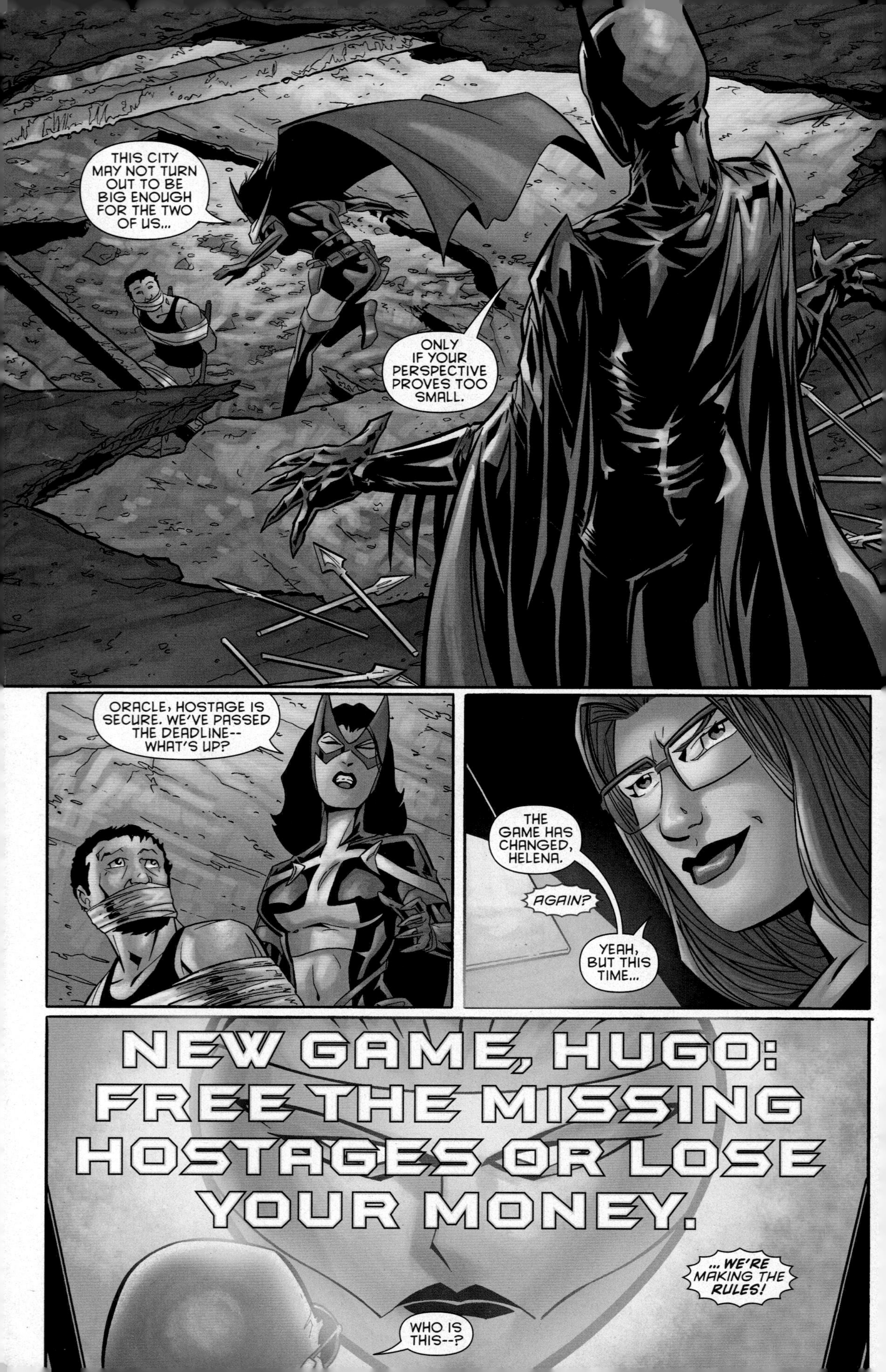
THIS CITY MAY NOT TURN OUT TO BE BIG ENOUGH FOR THE TWO OF US...
ONLY IF YOUR PERSPECTIVE PROVES TOO SMALL.
ORACLE, HOSTAGE IS SECURE. WE'VE PASSED THE DEADLINE-- WHAT'S UP?
THE GAME HAS CHANGED, HELENA.
AGAIN?
YEAH, BUT THIS TIME...
NEW GAME, HUGO: FREE THE MISSING HOSTAGES OR LOSE YOUR MONEY.
...WE'RE MAKING THE RULES!
WHO IS THIS--?

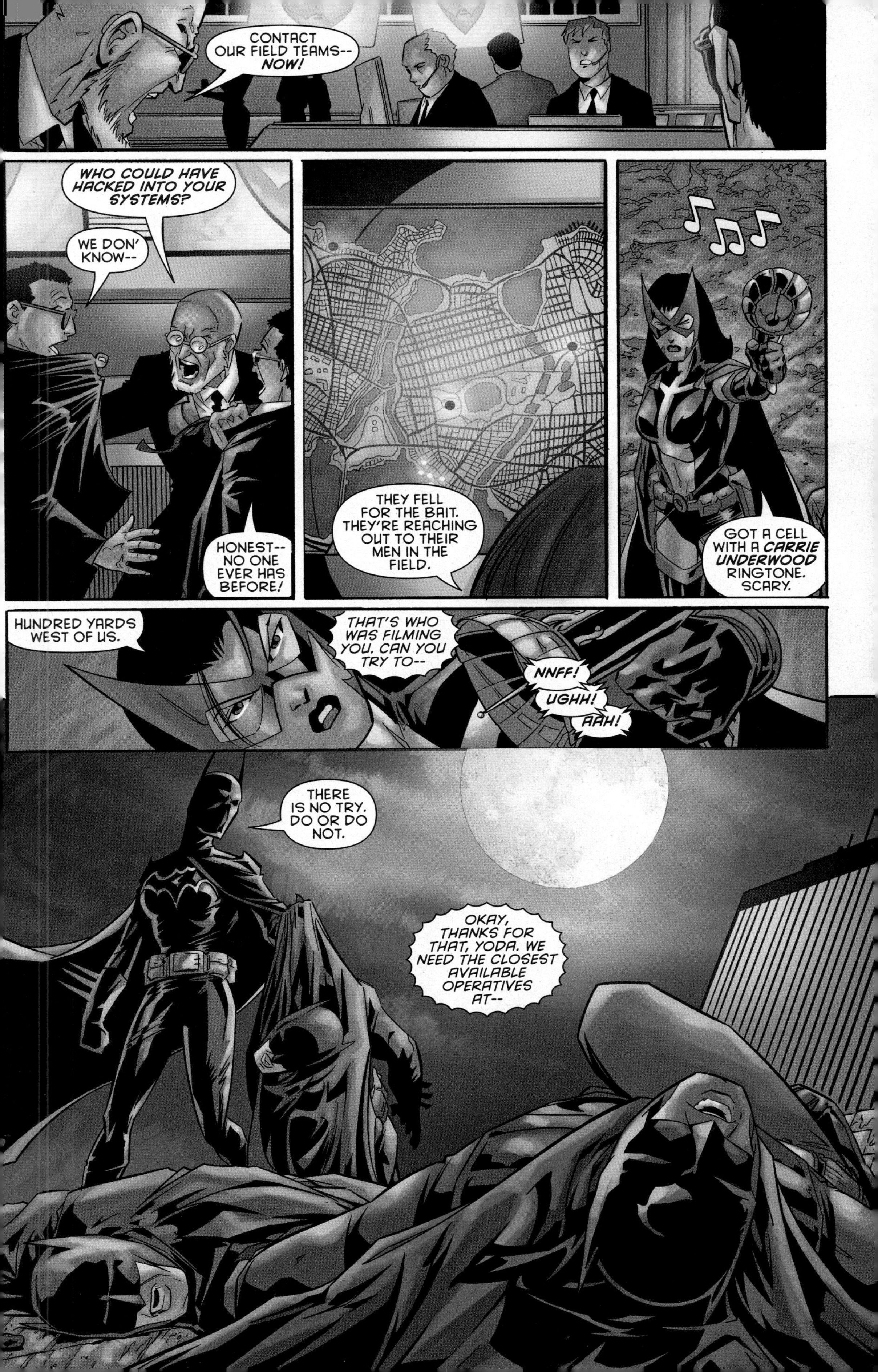
CONTACT OUR FIELD TEAMS-- NOW!
WHO COULD HAVE HACKED INTO YOUR SYSTEMS?
WE DON' KNOW--
HONEST-- NO ONE EVER HAS BEFORE!
THEY FELL FOR THE BAIT. THEY'RE REACHING OUT TO THEIR MEN IN THE FIELD.
GOT A CELL WITH A CARRIE UNDERWOOD RINGTONE. SCARY.
HUNDRED YARDS WEST OF US.
THAT'S WHO WAS FILMING YOU. CAN YOU TRY TO--
NNFF!
UGHH!
AAH!
THERE IS NO TRY. DO OR DO NOT.
OKAY, THANKS FOR THAT, YODA. WE NEED THE CLOSEST AVAILABLE OPERATIVES AT--

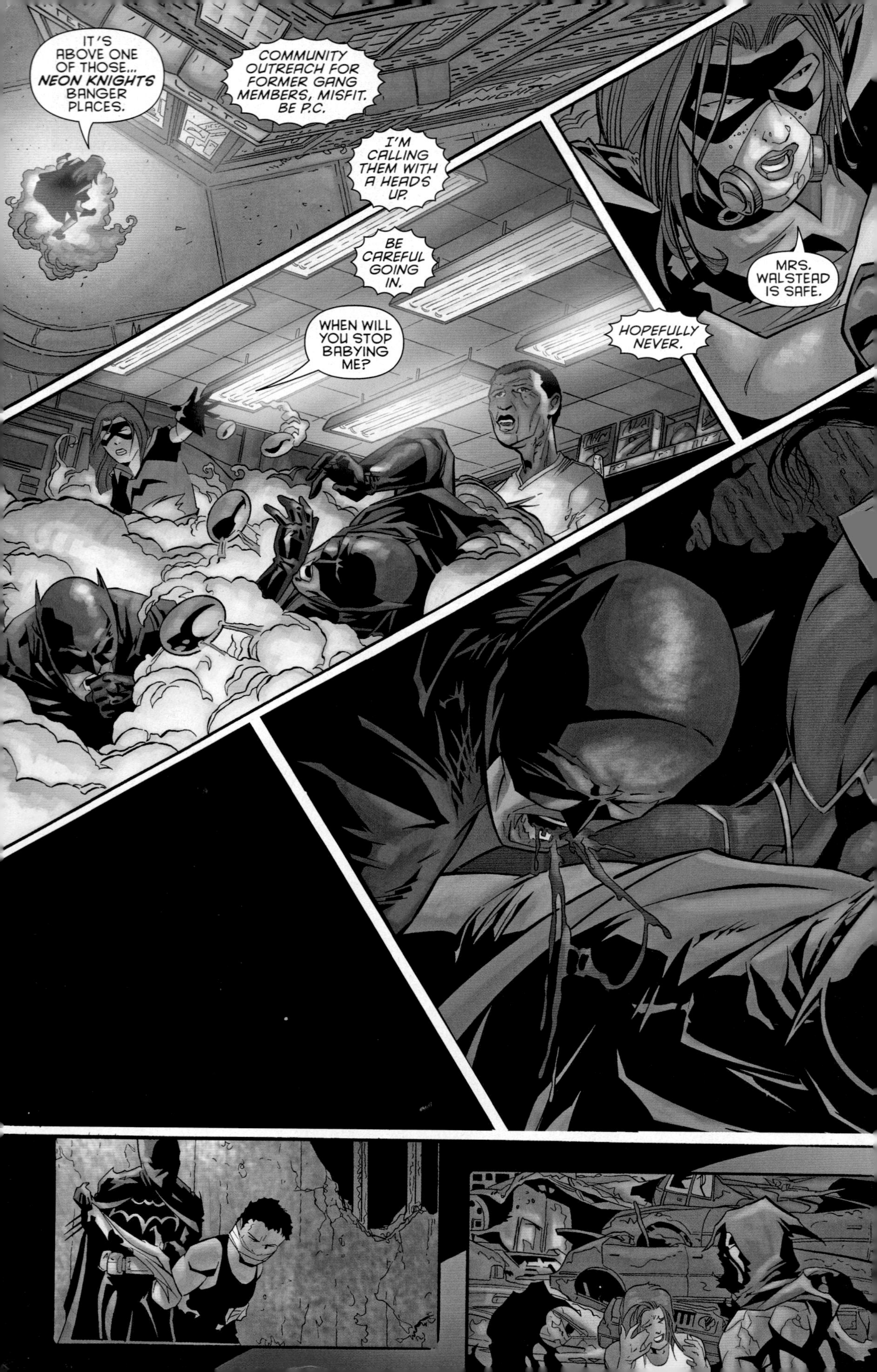

IT'S ABOVE ONE OF THOSE... NEON KNIGHTS BANGER PLACES.
COMMUNITY OUTREACH FOR FORMER GANG MEMBERS, MISFIT. BE P.C.
I'M CALLING THEM WITH A HEADS UP.
BE CAREFUL GOING IN.
WHEN WILL YOU STOP BABYING ME?
HOPEFULLY NEVER.
MRS. WALSTEAD IS SAFE.

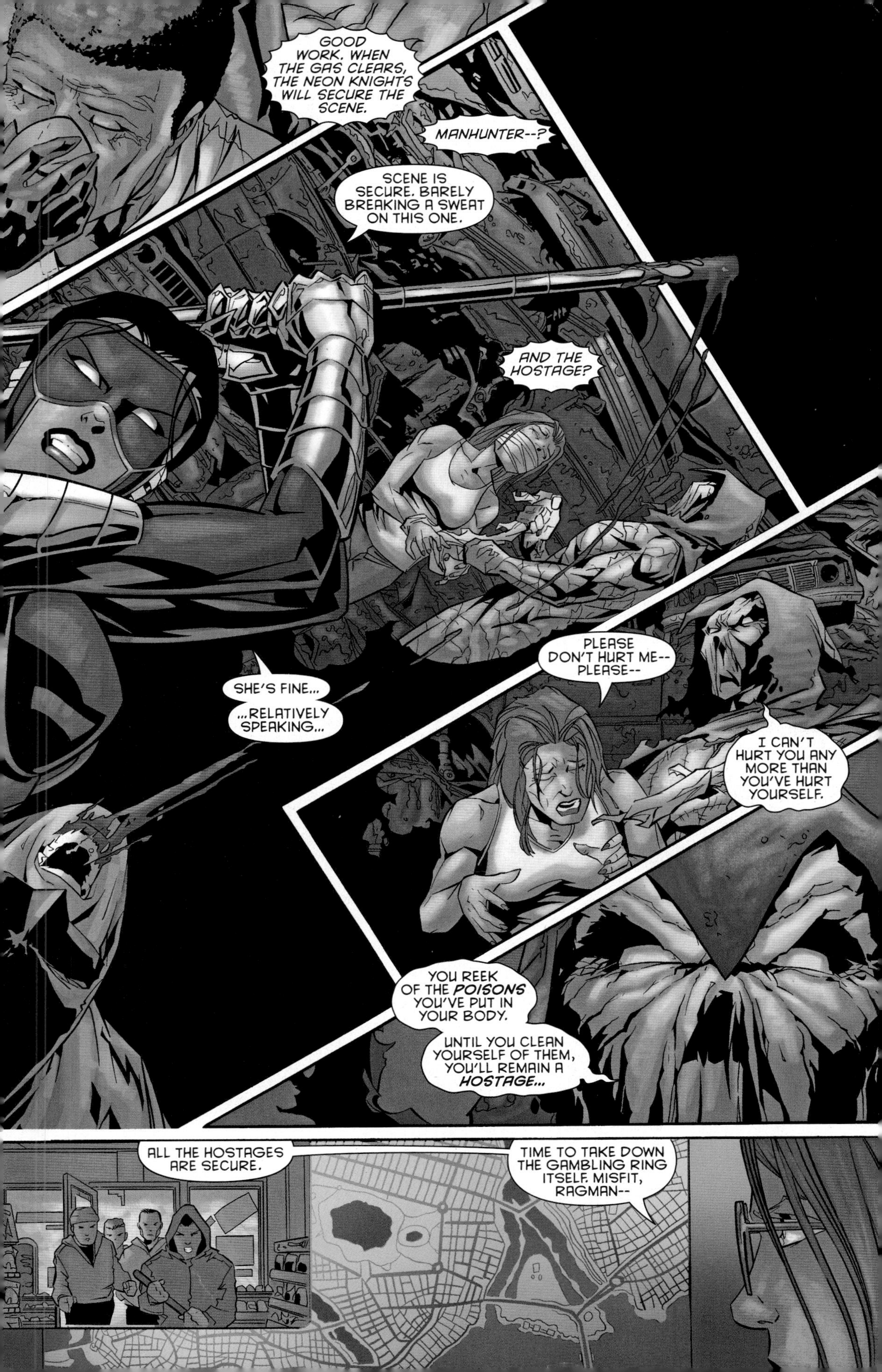

GOOD WORK. WHEN THE GAS CLEARS, THE NEON KNIGHTS WILL SECURE THE SCENE.
MANHUNTER--?
SCENE IS SECURE. BARELY BREAKING A SWEAT ON THIS ONE.
AND THE HOSTAGE?
SHE'S FINE...
...RELATIVELY SPEAKING...
PLEASE DON'T HURT ME-- PLEASE--
I CAN'T HURT YOU ANY MORE THAN YOU'VE HURT YOURSELF.
YOU REEK OF THE **POISONS** YOU'VE PUT IN YOUR BODY.
UNTIL YOU CLEAN YOURSELF OF THEM, YOU'LL REMAIN A **HOSTAGE...**
ALL THE HOSTAGES ARE SECURE.
TIME TO TAKE DOWN THE GAMBLING RING ITSELF. MISFIT, RAGMAN--

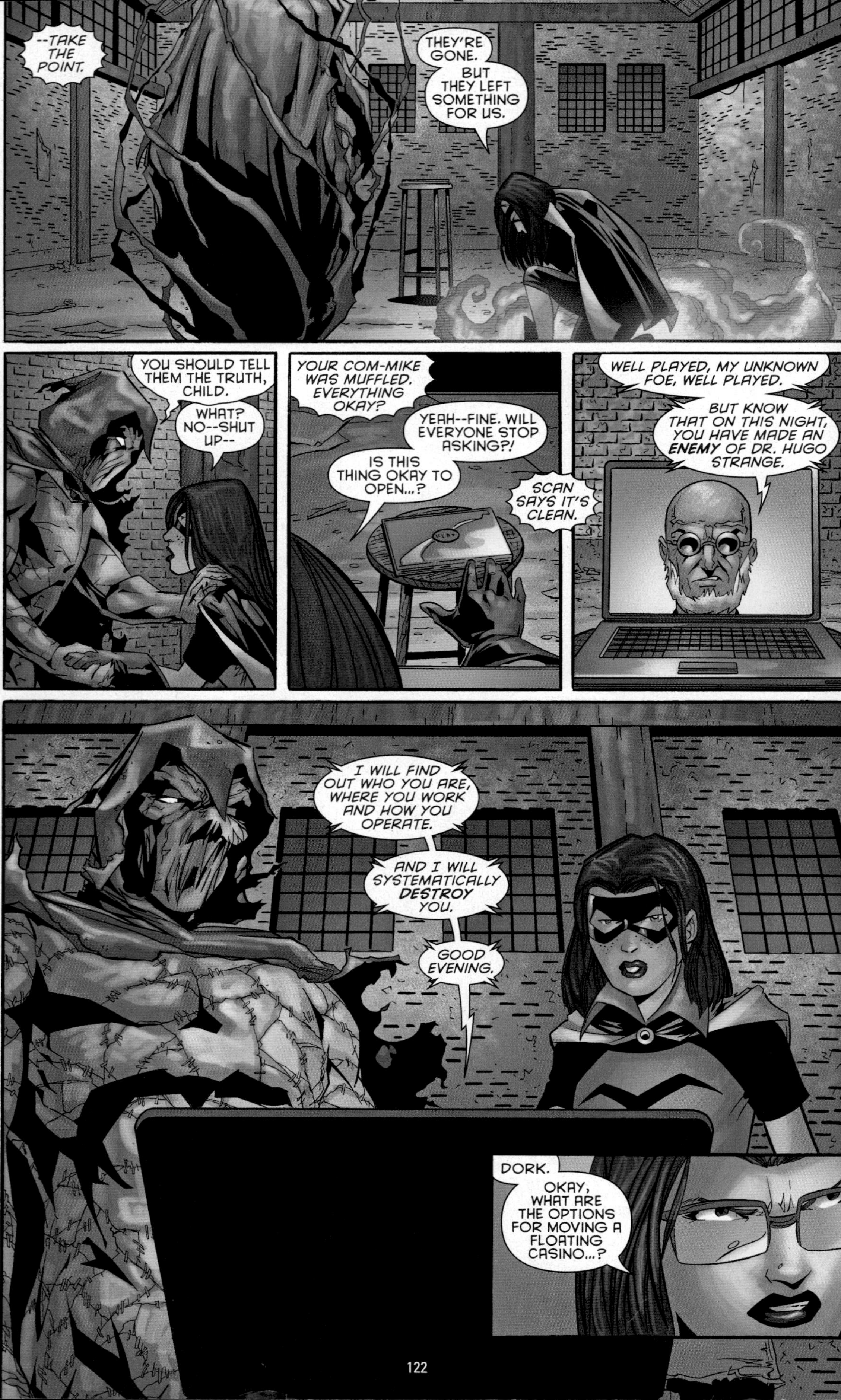

--TAKE THE POINT.
THEY'RE GONE. BUT THEY LEFT SOMETHING FOR US.
YOU SHOULD TELL THEM THE TRUTH, CHILD.
WHAT? NO--SHUT UP--
YOUR COM-MIKE WAS MUFFLED. EVERYTHING OKAY?
YEAH--FINE. WILL EVERYONE STOP ASKING?!
IS THIS THING OKAY TO OPEN...?
SCAN SAYS IT'S CLEAN.
WELL PLAYED, MY UNKNOWN FOE, WELL PLAYED.
BUT KNOW THAT ON THIS NIGHT, YOU HAVE MADE AN ENEMY OF DR. HUGO STRANGE.
I WILL FIND OUT WHO YOU ARE, WHERE YOU WORK AND HOW YOU OPERATE.
AND I WILL SYSTEMATICALLY DESTROY YOU.
GOOD EVENING.
DORK.
OKAY, WHAT ARE THE OPTIONS FOR MOVING A FLOATING CASINO...?

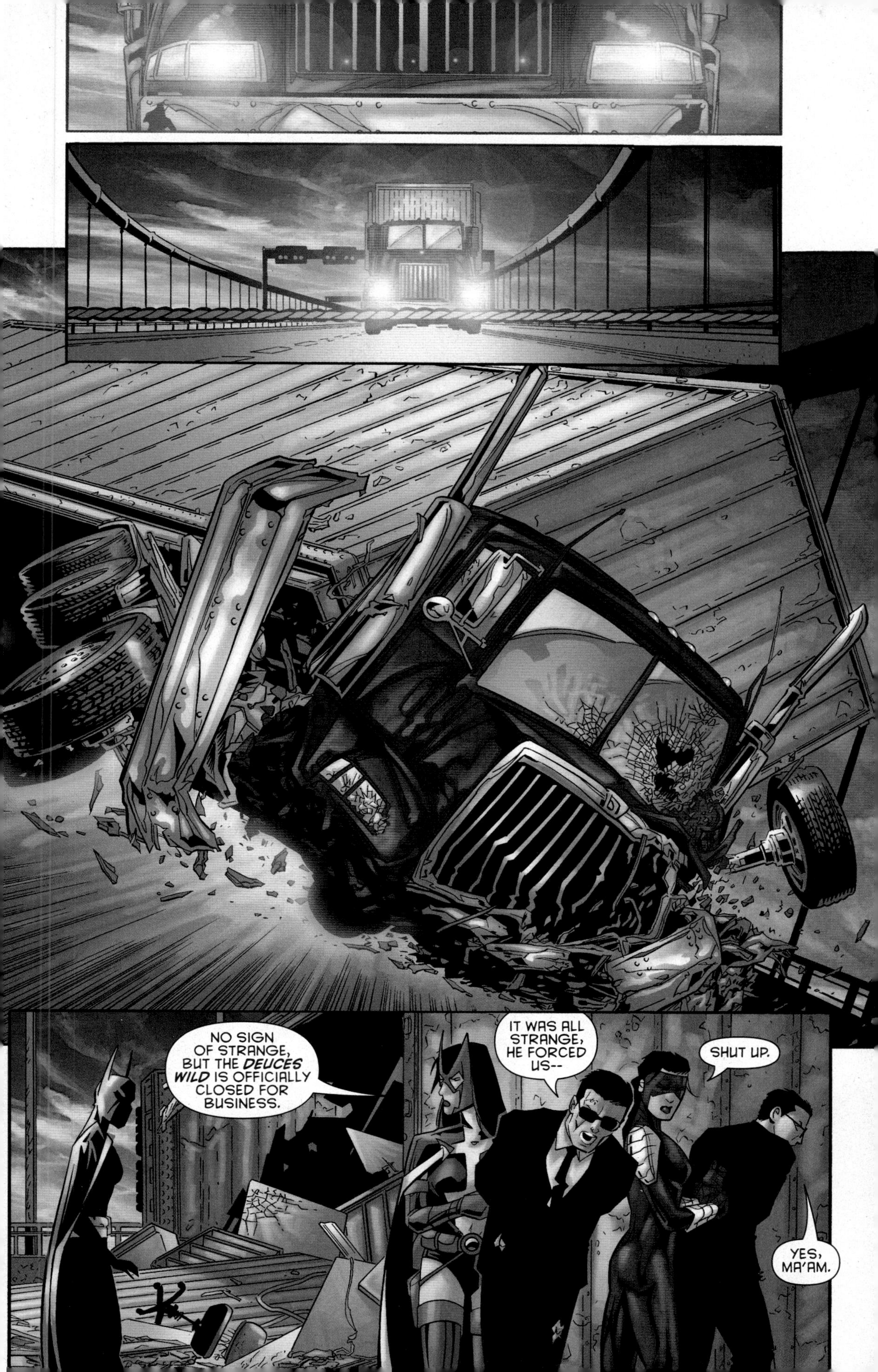
NO SIGN OF STRANGE, BUT THE DEUCES WILD IS OFFICIALLY CLOSED FOR BUSINESS.
IT WAS ALL STRANGE, HE FORCED US--
SHUT UP.
YES, MA'AM.

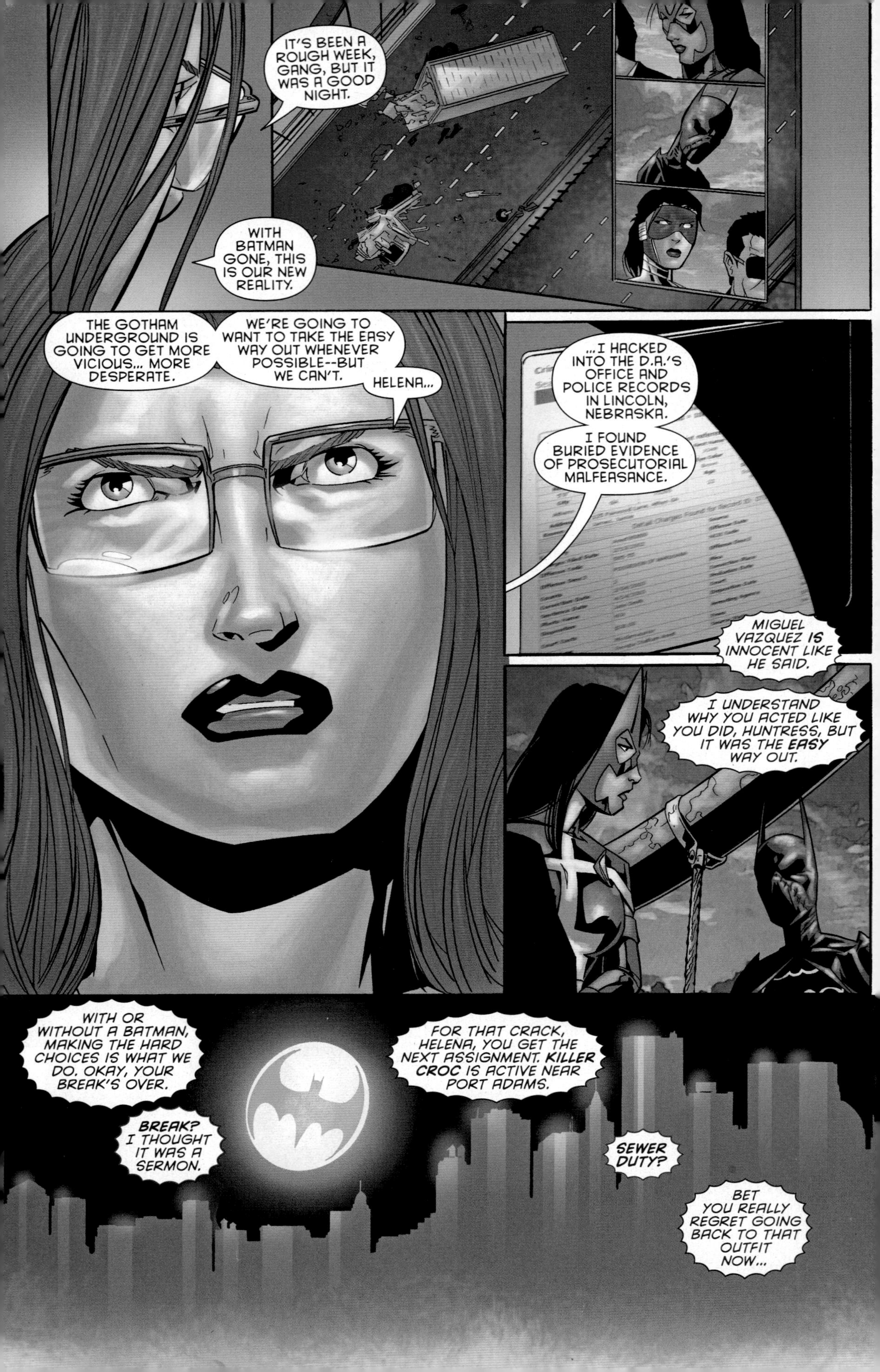
IT'S BEEN A ROUGH WEEK, GANG, BUT IT WAS A GOOD NIGHT.
WITH BATMAN GONE, THIS IS OUR NEW REALITY.
THE GOTHAM UNDERGROUND IS GOING TO GET MORE VICIOUS... MORE DESPERATE.
WE'RE GOING TO WANT TO TAKE THE EASY WAY OUT WHENEVER POSSIBLE--BUT WE CAN'T.
HELENA...
...I HACKED INTO THE D.A.'S OFFICE AND POLICE RECORDS IN LINCOLN, NEBRASKA.
I FOUND BURIED EVIDENCE OF PROSECUTORIAL MALFEASANCE.
MIGUEL VAZQUEZ **IS** INNOCENT LIKE HE SAID.
I UNDERSTAND WHY YOU ACTED LIKE YOU DID, HUNTRESS, BUT IT WAS THE **EASY** WAY OUT.
WITH OR WITHOUT A BATMAN, MAKING THE HARD CHOICES IS WHAT WE DO. OKAY, YOUR BREAK'S OVER.
BREAK? I THOUGHT IT WAS A SERMON.
FOR THAT CRACK, HELENA, YOU GET THE NEXT ASSIGNMENT. **KILLER CROC** IS ACTIVE NEAR PORT ADAMS.
SEWER DUTY?
BET YOU REALLY REGRET GOING BACK TO THAT OUTFIT NOW...

MORE CLASSIC TALES OF THE DARK KNIGHT

BATMAN: HUSH
VOLUME ONE

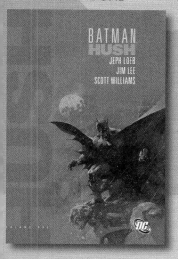

BATMAN
HUSH
JEPH LOEB
JIM LEE
SCOTT WILLIAMS

JEPH LOEB
JIM LEE

BATMAN: HUSH
VOLUME TWO

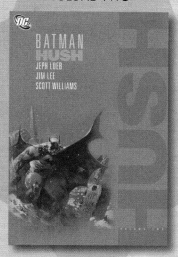

BATMAN
HUSH
JEPH LOEB
JIM LEE
SCOTT WILLIAMS

JEPH LOEB
JIM LEE

BATMAN:
THE LONG HALLOWEEN

JEPH LOEB TIM SALE
BATMAN
THE LONG HALLOWEEN

JEPH LOEB
TIM SALE

BATMAN:
DARK VICTORY

JEPH LOEB TIM SALE
BATMAN
Dark Victory

JEPH LOEB
TIM SALE

BATMAN:
HAUNTED KNIGHT

JEPH LOEB TIM SALE
BATMAN
HAUNTED KNIGHT

JEPH LOEB
TIM SALE

BATMAN:
YEAR 100

Batman
Year
100
by PAUL POPE
with JOSE VILLARRUBIA

PAUL POPE

SEARCH THE GRAPHIC NOVELS SECTION OF
DCCOMICS.COM
FOR ART AND INFORMATION ON ALL OF OUR BOOKS!

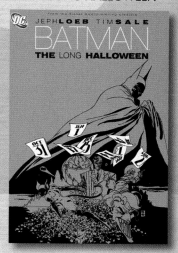

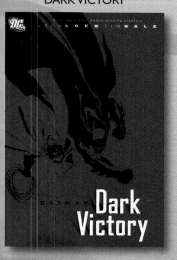

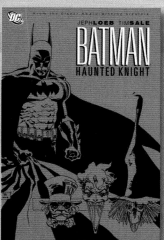

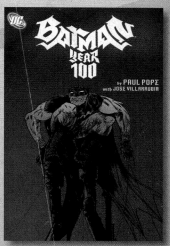

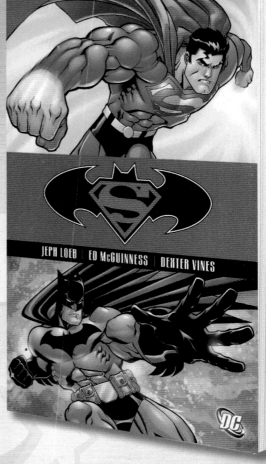